CW01338110

TOWARDS AN OPERATIONAL SOCIAL ANTHROPOLOGY

VOLUME 2

An Operational Social Anthropology

Michel Verdon

Grosvenor House Publishing Limited

This book is published by
Grosvenor House Publishing Ltd
Link House
140 The Broadway, Tolworth, Surrey, KT6 7HT.
www.grosvenorhousepublishing.co.uk

A CIP record for this book
is available from the British Library

ISBN 978-1-83615-115-9
eBook ISBN 978-1-83615-116-6

DEDICATION

To my brother Jean, who greatly helped my career,
I dedicate this last book

TABLE OF CONTENTS

PREFACE

This second volume cannot be understood on its own. It follows volume 1 (*An Epistemological History of Social Anthropology*), as a drastic cure follows a deadly diagnosis. In volume 1, I explained how these two volumes came out of a book I published in French in 1991, namely *Contre la culture*. In this translation, I have divided the initial book in two: in the first, I follow the epistemological history of social anthropology to understand why it failed in its original project, that is, the *rigorous* comparative analysis of social organization. I discovered that the traditional approach was fundamentally Aristotelian, yielding ontologically variable groups that made rigour and comparison impossible. The solution thus has to be a Galilean-type revolution, and this is what I develop in this second volume. I elaborate a radically new 'operational' conceptual framework, one defined in terms of social anthropology's original project, and not in terms of 'objects' intrinsic attributes (see Introduction, volume 1). In other words, anthropological 'objects' do not correspond to elements in reality that have 'anthropological attributes' but to a class of objects defined by the procedure of comparative analysis.

I then apply it to the three 'segmentary societies' that I reanalysed in *Contre la culture*, namely the Nuer from southern Sudan (studied by Evans-Pritchard), the Tallensi of northern Ghana (studied by Meyer Fortes), and the Tiv of central Nigeria (studied by Paul and Laura Bohannan). I have here added three more reanalyses, namely the Berbers from the Moroccan Rif (studied by Raymond Jamous), the Yao of Malawi (studied by Clyde Mitchell) and the Australian Aborigines (various authors, but especially Radcliffe-Brown). Apart from the text on Jamous, all the other studies have been published in prestigious journals (see bibliography), and the text on the Australian Aborigines was co-authored with Paul Jorion. I conclude this volume with general reflections on the new operationalized ethnographic landscape that this yields, and how it transforms social anthropology.

CHAPTER ONE

A cosmological break

Volume 1 traced the disappearance of groups from the anthropological discourse but groups do exist; ethnologists have described them and still observe them. They have emerged as legitimate objects of study but their analysis has failed for reasons I have already examined (see volume 1). The ethnologist who still wants to write about groups, but write about them rigorously, will have to repress the almost instinctive expression of his or her subjective experience of individuality and sociability to define the groups against the background of his or her project. He or she will have to rethink reality and its language in the light of his or her own aims, not his or her lived experience.

As early as 1965, Schneider realized what was wrong (see volume 1). He understood the aberration of the 'strength' of descent, the absurdity of the monolithic segments of descent and alliance theories. He saw the 'multifunctional' segment giving birth to this monolithic inflexibility because the segment must own its man globally. And Schneider concluded prophetically that we no longer needed typologies but an exhaustive list of elements that could be rigorously defined analytically and combined in different sizes, shapes and constellations (1965, p. 78).

An itinerary, sketched out with such clear-sightedness, nonetheless led its author into the impasse of a cultural transcendentalism so utterly relativistic as to stifle any aspiration for rigorous comparison. This was Schneider's challenge in 1965;

where others have tried to meet it with transactionalism, and Schneider himself with unremitting culturalism, I shall try to take it up with a new language, namely operationalism.

A cosmological malaise calls for a cosmological remedy. If interpersonal behaviour and the nagging question of its regulation have caused groups to break up into clouds of interactions, or to disappear in culture, then behaviour itself will have to vanish for groups to reappear.

What does removing interaction imply? One consequence of the old interactional view of groups in terms of interpersonal relationships is never explicitly mentioned: if groups are based on interactions, it necessarily follows that we consider them as *sums of relationships*. By removing relationships, the group is automatically transformed into a *sum of individuals*. Such groups can include very few or very many individuals. Demographers have long defined households as groups of individuals living in a dwelling-unit. But they soon realized that many households include only one person. They stoically accepted it and blithely declared that there are one-person households. Similarly, operational groups can also include only one individual. The smallest groups defined operationally, therefore, are one-individual groups! And many of them exist.

But, removing interactions is only one step because behaviours are not the only culprits, as Schneider once again clearly understood when he emphasized the multifunctional character of the structuralist monolithic segments. For a Durkheimian interactional logic weaves a very close interdependence between behaviour regulation and the segments' plurality of functions. Theories that feel the need to postulate monolithic segments or corporations also feel the need to completely assimilate the individual to its segment, and the segment will absorb or possess the individual all the more as the latter will experience almost no activities outside it. If the number of functions dictates the quotient of solidarity, the quantum of corporateness, it affects the very nature of the group; such groups cannot be ontologically indifferent to the number of functions they perform, and these 'interactional' groups vary ontologically according to the number of their functions[1].

In short, if we want groups to be ontologically indifferent to their principles of social organization, as I concluded in volume 1 by demonstrating the Aristotelian roots of our language, we will now have to apprehend them *outside the organization of behaviour and the multiplicity of functions*. This first means that we will have to take solidarity or sociability for granted. In an operational discourse on groups, the existence of society requires no explanation; it is bluntly stated that human beings are social, and their interaction governed and organized, but this interaction is no longer part of the group's definition. Furthermore, we will want these groups to be 'unifunctional'. For each type of activity (or 'function' in everyday language), we will henceforth associate a separate and distinct group in the analysis. When, empirically, the same set of individuals performs two or more functions, the analysis will dissociate as many groups as there are functions, while recognizing that these groups overlap, partially or completely. By superimposing all these one-dimensional groups, operational analysis gives back to groups as they are lived their ontological thickness, in an idiom that respects the nuances of each.

Let us take a classic example. Murdock wrote, and his statements were almost legally binding to the end of the 20th century if not beyond, that the family is a group that fulfils the functions of production, reproduction, socialization of children and residence (Murdock 1949). This is colloquial language, a language that all ethnologists understand and speak. Does it faithfully follow the contours of reality? Let us borrow the vocabulary of mathematicians and represent this family by a set of individuals: father, mother, adult married sons, teenage sons, adult married daughters, teenage

[1] Let me point out that the term 'function' has at least three different meanings in ethnology. First, what we might call a tautological definition, which consists in saying that 'reproduction is the function of the family'; this simply means that the family carries out reproductive activities. The function also reappears in a sociological definition, borrowed from Durkheim, where it defines only the creation of solidarity. It is also used more mathematically, or logically, when we assert that this or that institution 'is a function' of another.

daughters, and young children of both sexes. If the 'family' is defined around the mother's reproduction, let us think of it as a reproductive group. But is it a production group? Who actually produces? Husband and wife, perhaps, or father and teenage sons, or father and teenage and married sons; in short, only a 'subset' of the reproductive group is united in production. And, what's more, the production group may include individuals from outside the reproduction group, such as the father's brother living next door, or his son-in-law. Reproduction and production are groups that partially, but not completely overlap. And can we consider this same reproductive group as a residential group? Certainly not, because married children may have left from under the parental roof and, on the other hand, the house may be home to the father's younger brother, the father's mother or the wife's younger brother. Would it not be preferable and more accurate to rethink these multifunctional definitions by describing as many sets as there are activities: reproduction, production, residence and socialization of children in this particular case, and to conclude that these sets partially, but rarely completely, overlap? In an admirable analysis of the LoDagaa and LoWilii domestic groups, Jack Goody made a similar breakdown, delimiting a set for each type of activity. His ethnographic intuition sadly froze there, without ever spurring his theoretical imagination (Goody 1958).

Operational groups will assert themselves above all as those sets coupled to a single activity, but sets that overlap. If Schneider should have been able to reach this conclusion following his indictment of the structuralist segments' multiplicity of functions, an epistemological investigation now imposes it. But, long before these epistemological reflections, my own ethnography prescribed this same conclusion. If operationalism presents itself as the best way out of an epistemological impasse, it is above all because it appeared to me as the only way out of an ethnographic one.

Defining residence

My doctoral research bore on a group of three Ewe (pronounce Évhé, the 'vh' being a voiced bilabial fricative) villages, Kloe, Agove and

Teti, collectively known as the three Abutia villages. The Ewe, a linguistic group of some one million people occupying southern Ghana (Volta region) and Togo in the early 1970s, were divided into one hundred and twenty odd groups of collectively designated villages: the Abutia and their three villages, the Sokode and their three villages, the Adaklu and their seventeen villages, the Anlo (pronounce as if it was the French word 'anglon', where 'on' is a nasalized 'o', as in Verdon…) and their one hundred and some villages, and so on. The Abutia associated some practices that theory sought to dissociate. Not only did they exhibit Melanesian-style patrilineal descent groups (see volume 1 on Melanesian-type descent groups, pp. 111-113), but they also practiced almost preferential marriage within the lineage and clan. Weakly polygynous among ethnic groups that favour polygyny, they associated their patrilineal lineages and clans with a system of behaviour specific to so-called cognatic societies (as described by Gluckman, see volume 1), and their residential groups were strangely similar in composition to the neighbouring matrilineal Ashanti households. This motley assemblage defied all the 'typological' theories Schneider wrote about, forcing me either to alter the data to fit the corset of the theory, or to respect the facts and blow up the theories, as Schneider intimated. The latter path proved too seductive.

Of the many stumbling blocks that plagued the analysis of Abutia social organization, residential organization was not the least. Ethnologists insisted on seeing rational actors manipulating residence as part of their political and economic strategies (Buchler and Selby 1968; Stern 1973; Korn 1975), or domestic groups formed above all for the purpose of reproduction (Fortes 1949a, 1949b; Richards 1950; Bohannan 1963; Barnes 1960; Goody 1972a, 1972b). But maximizing actors and reproductively-oriented domestic groups did not help. The former presuppose a code behind the manipulations; the latter don't know what to make of reproductive groups that do not share the same roof, split between various domestic groups that are, for example, made up of duolocal couples. If duolocality severs the link between residence and reproduction, what then of a more generalized dissociation, when individuals occupying the same dwelling-unit take part in no other activity than that of occupying a bedroom in that dwelling-unit, and sleeping in it? This question is all the more pertinent given that the whole ethnology of domestic groups mistreats the home, even going so far as to deny it any reality, if not any social relevance (Fortes 1949a, 1949b; Goody 1972a, 1972b; Richards 1950; Bohannan 1963; Barnes 1960). Invoking 'principles' (affinity, maternity, agnatic or uterine descent) operating with differential power through individuals' life cycle and assembling them into various residential organizations throughout their existence, proponents of the so-called 'developmental cycle of domestic groups' saw in it only domesticity and reproduction. Residence? A simple corollary of the fact that a principle of affinity or consanguinity attracts spouses or agnates towards cohabitation.

The Abutia facts were deaf to these incantations. Many houses, for example, were home to just one man and one of his sisters, both married but not sharing their spouse's residence. The sister cooked in the house's purpose-built kitchen, but her dishes did not feed her brother; they went to garnish that of the husband living a few houses away. The wife, on the other hand, could not rely on her brother to provide the produce for her cooking, which came from her own ploughing and that of her husband. Brother and sister united in residence, but separated in all other respects: separated in sexual relations, in production, in the distribution of products, in consumption, in childcare. Without domestic or ancestral worship, the Abutia home did not even offer itself as a place of veneration. But, insofar as they occupy this house where a census finds them, brother and sister cannot be ignored. Their co-residence needs to be recognized, but how can we comprehend it? Are we to speak of a corporation because they own this patrimonial house undivided? But other individuals, their brothers and sisters, also belong to this corporation without living in the house. We can only represent the group formed by these two individuals by isolating the one and only activity that unites them: occupying this house to sleep in. I call this activity 'residence' because, come to think of it, it is what residence boils down to when dissociated from food preparation, consumption and other domus-related activities. Studying the Abutia residence meant defining a group around a single activity, highlighting the crucial role of activity in defining groups. The idea of activity is an old one, haunting anthropology since Spencer, if not before, and of all the ideas that have dominated anthropology, it is one that an operational epistemology preserves.

But activity is not interaction, and if an operational ethnology recovers activity, it nonetheless purges it of any idea of interaction, and of any desire to put more than one activity at the heart of the group. Ethnography in Abutia demanded, and epistemology exacts, that the group be apprehended by a single activity. All my operational terminology was built on the basis of these unifunctional groups.

Ethnological language must therefore be recreated at the intersection of activity and 'criteria'. From the outset, their combination yields four fundamental concepts. Wherever a certain type of activity is carried out (such as production, product distribution, consumption, legislation, arbitration or war, to mention but a few), the individuals taking part in it can welcome all comers, without any discrimination whatsoever. We then speak of a 'crowd'. If, on the other hand, they invoke certain criteria (such as sex, age, parentage, and so on) to distinguish between those who can join them and those who cannot, we are then dealing with a 'group' in the strict sense of the term. In short, the group emerges when membership criteria are added to an activity; without criteria, activities just define crowds. We are talking about *criteria* here, not membership rules. A rule governs, and we seek to void groups of all regulations; also, a rule can vary in its strength, be disobeyed. But a criterion does not regulate anything. As a tool for sorting out the eligible from the non-eligible, the criterion does not hint at any behaviour expected of group members, nor does it have any strength. Whether or not individuals choose to activate their group membership, whether or not they define a code of conduct for themselves, these are certainly questions worthy of analysis, but they do not enter into the group's definition. From an operational perspective, the group surfaces at the crossroads of one activity (and only one) and *one or more* membership criteria (I will come back to this plurality of criteria later). This definition banishes all notions of solidarity (or corporateness) and ownership. Insofar as corporateness denotes solidarity or collective action, I take it for granted; insofar as it reveals some notion of ownership, it calls again for more general considerations.

Defining ownership

People own resources which are both natural and man-made, and the man-made ones comprise both tangible and intangible entities. When lawyers form a legal corporation, for instance, the corporation owns their legal knowledge and skills. Even individual ideas can be owned, as patents and copyrights testify. An analysis of social organization depending upon a definitive formulation of ownership would be forever inhibited, because of the infinite nuances of rights of ownership. To overcome this difficulty, I adopt the most general definition of the phenomenon, by assuming that ownership implies a privileged access, some exclusivity in the disposition of resources which means that non-owners must seek permission before exploiting the resource. Different populations may define various types of collectivities around those rights. Hitherto, anthropologists have mostly contrasted individual to corporate ownership; I shall argue that resources can be owned in a manner which is neither individual nor corporate.

A corporation uses specific criteria of membership which give equal rights of ownership to all those who qualify; there are no possible gradients of rights varying from individual to individual. A corporation thus presupposes 'boundaries' in membership, and because of this also delineates its resources. If land is the resource to be owned by a corporation, we should expect this land to be bounded. I call such boundaries 'jural', and 'estate' the bounded resources owned by a corporation.

Let us now turn to some east-African cattle-herding societies where pasture land is owned neither individually nor corporately (Gulliver 1952). Although little or no restriction seems to be imposed upon membership, those using the land do feel that they have a special right in it, and may sometimes refuse newcomers permission to use it if it is over-grazed. Because permission must be sought from old-established occupiers and may be refused when resources dwindle, we can clearly speak of ownership of that land; but can we treat the herding group as a land-owning corporation?

Corporations are defined by exclusive criteria of membership, and not by their members' involvement in a common activity, two conditions not met by the east-African cattle-herders. There, membership is open, and only those who occupy and use that land (that is, are involved in a common activity) feel that they have a privileged access to it. Their rights do not stem from special qualifications, but from use and occupancy, from a given activity. According to my definitions they do not constitute either a group or a category but, as a set of individuals delineated through a common activity only, they form a 'crowd' – though the analytical distinction is here more important than the actual label. Analytically speaking, the 'crowd' of cattle-owners herding their cows together on this common land and easily accepting newcomers to join them does not form a land-owning corporation. We must consequently deal with this paradox: that the land, not owned by anybody in particular, is owned by everybody, yet not as a corporation.

Criteria of membership defining groups, categories and corporations confer equal rights upon those who meet the criteria. Where ownership is neither individual nor corporate, however, *rights actually vary in their intensity;* stemming, as they do, from occupancy and use, the rights are to be measured (subjectively) according to the time and intensity of occupancy and use. If a quarrel flares up in the use of the land, some individuals will certainly claim greater rights by virtue of their longer association with it, and will deny such rights to newcomers or mere visitors. All 'own' the land, but not corporately, and some own it more than others, Orwell would have said... Resources owned in this manner are not jurally bounded and cannot be considered an estate.

In brief, I distinguish rights of ownership stemming from membership of a land-owning category, a corporation in which individuals are all equal with respect to ownership (there are no gradients in the ownership itself), from rights of ownership springing from occupancy and use, where some individuals feel that they have more rights than others because of a longer association with the land, but where all have access to land (there is no restriction on membership). In the latter case, we cannot speak either of a land-owning corporation or of an estate. The land is owned neither individually nor corporately, but *collectively*.

In brief, collective land ownership introduces an element that I wished to eliminate: collective ownership introduces degrees of intensity of 'owning' according to occupancy and use, as some will feel that they own the land more than others. Activities are truly discontinuous, but this type of ownership is not, as it varies in intensity. This is admittedly a subjective appreciation. Those who have been linked longest with the land will have the strongest feelings of association to it, but how does it translate itself? This remains problematic. Let us keep this in mind when dealing with collective ownership while also considering that, objectively, land might be owned collectively by all equally while, subjectively, the various 'owners' might not feel so.

Land ownership raises further issues. First, there are at least two separate aspects to land: from our Western point of view, land is inert, so to speak. Crops obviously grow on it but we dissociate the two and consider the land separately. In many non-Western societies, however, land is above all a 'live' entity, considered precisely in its power to generate crops (see Yao analysis), or in its spiritual association with animal or plant species (see Australian Aborigines analysis). 'Land-owning' is radically different in the two cases. Again, I will limit myself to the 'inert' land. Let us add that when a group of individuals distinguishes itself from the rest of the world through its ownership of resources that are not legally circumscribed, we speak of a 'quasi-corporation' (see my re-analysis of Tiv ethnography below to appreciate this nuance). The notion of corporation involves nothing more than the property of an estate and membership criteria[2]. This is why corporations are not groups, and groups are not corporations, which in no way prevents them from overlapping, partially or completely, just as groups can overlap each other.

Cattle ownership raises different problems. Cattle can obviously be owned privately and, with cattle, we must rule out the 'collective' ownership that we find in land; it simply cannot be. The main issue is whether or not cattle can be owned corporately. Let us focus on the Old World pastoralists. Can people form corporations around cattle. I personally doubt it. I find it difficult because of the specificity of cattle. First, cattle breeds cattle. And, equally important, cattle can be decimated by epizootics or drought in a matter of days. Furthermore, many pastoralists are partly or wholly nomadic.

Let us leave nomadism aside and let us imagine a different scenario. Let us try to define a corporation around land if land begot land, but could also easily shrink. Let us imagine two more or less equal groups owning a similar amount of land corporately. But one's land could increase considerably while the other one's could shrink. This is impossible. It would be much easier to think of individual ownership of land coupled with all sorts of claims and debts to spread risks. In other words, if we think of land like cattle, it is impossible to imagine land-owning corporations. Thus, by

[2] To be more specific, we should add: if these criteria are defined in relation to the individuals taking part in the activity. On the other hand, when we use discriminating criteria whose point of reference is an individual or group of individuals outside the activity, I call the resulting association of individuals an exo-group. This seemingly far-fetched concept proves extremely useful in the study of residence, where it becomes necessary to dissociate residential groups whose composition is defined by reference to an owner who resides in the house itself, from groups defined in relation to an owner residing elsewhere (and where the right of residence does not derive from the payment of rent). If we call the former 'residential groups', we will call the latter 'exo-groups' (for the heuristic and analytical value of this distinction, see Verdon 1983, p. 141). Residential exo-groups perform an activity (residence) and are recruited on the basis of membership criteria defined in relation to an individual who is not himself engaged in the activity of residence (the homeowner does not reside in his house).

extension, I find impossible to think of cattle-owning corporations. Cattle are everywhere owned individually. And the same applies to horses and camels, although camels are less prone to epizootics because they are hardier, and because of their environment (desert).

II

Finally, in the absence of any activity or ownership, but where membership criteria nevertheless operate, we find that crucial notion that Schneider, Scheffler and Keesing bequeathed us, namely that of the 'social category'. If the crowd differs from the group in terms of criteria, the category differs from the group and the corporation in terms of activities and ownership. The social category is the assembly of individuals that recognizes itself without acting, the individuals that a single criterion matches without bringing them together in any one activity, or in ownership.

Common sense rebels, perhaps citing Schneider's latest theses (1984). Doesn't everyday experience teach us that codes of conduct, 'ways of doing things', are also membership criteria? Haven't we all heard of the heir expelled from his father's house and disinherited because of his lack of respect and obedience, his incurable laziness or his unfortunate choice of a spouse? It is only a short step to concluding that respect and obedience are membership criteria, on a par with patrifiliation and male gender (where sons inherit from their fathers), the same step Schneider takes in his last book (1984) (see volume 1, pp. 145–52).

Intuitively and spontaneously, every group manifests itself through criteria and a code of conduct. But is this the case from an analytical point of view? Isn't immediate subjective experience as deceptive as Murdock's multifunctional family? Could this *citimangen-fak* relationship, which Schneider describes as the basis of the Yap *tabinau*, really be defined by a cultural expectation (agreeing to provide for the *citimangen* in his old age) rather than by a bond of consanguinity or affinity (see volume 1)? Strangely enough, even ethnologists who place the organization of behaviour at the heart of the group's definition haven't gone as far as to include respect or obedience among membership criteria (for even in the case of the *fak*, this is ultimately what it is all about). As usual, Schneider pushes the idea of behavioural organization to its logical limit but, as far as I know, he is the only one to do so. Ethnologists before him have not hesitated to treat descent, kinship, affinity or locality as rules stipulating both membership and the rights and duties of status, but they have been careful to exclude respect and obedience from membership. Why? The answer is simple, even if Schneider refused to see it. If all structuralisms draw a boundary to the group – the discontinuity that our operational definition preserves – it goes without saying that they privilege certain elements, such as kinship, descent or affinity, whose discontinuity makes it easy to circumscribe. Kinship, affinity, age, are all attributes that an individual may or may not possess. One is either a consanguine or not; an agnate or not, but not both at the same time, or both optionally. Respect and obedience, on the other hand, do not follow the same logic. Where do respect and obedience begin and end? No one knows, and this imprecision renders them powerless to activate the discriminating mechanics of inclusion and exclusion, because respect and obedience are attributes that everyone can enjoy and play with at will. Kinship, age and even affinity are not characteristics we can manipulate at will, updating them today to deny them tomorrow; codes of conduct, on the other hand, lend themselves to every possible manipulation. Those who choose to obey today will disobey tomorrow, only to repent the day after and become obedient again. We learn a rule of behaviour and conform to it as we see fit (see Malinowski 1926, volume 1, p. 99), but we don't learn the 'fact' of being someone's physiological child, and we don't have to conform to it.

Each individual is characterized by a set of coordinates over which he or she has little or no control. These are precisely the coordinates that infiltrate to divide, to circumscribe the subsets that are groups, categories or corporations. If groups take shape against the backdrop of activity, of 'doing', their criteria must be thought of in terms of 'being', not 'doing', as Schneider would have it. One is potentially a member of a group because one 'is' this or that: an agnate, a son, a married man or woman, a friend, a man, an individual of this or that age. A group does not recruit according to 'ways of doing things': listening, respecting, obeying, providing for old age. On the other hand, a group *expels* in the name of a code of conduct. Can it be otherwise? In most groups, how can you reject an undesirable if the criteria are based on being? You cannot erase consanguinity or age, but you can invoke a code violation to eject an individual who is eligible in the name of the criteria, but unbearable in the name of interpersonal relationships. The Yap *fak* risks being disinherited if he neglects his *citimangen*, but it is not taking care of a *citimangen* that makes him a *fak*. It is, first and foremost, the fact of 'being' the child of the *citimangen*'s wife. If his behaviour can dislodge the *fak*, it cannot from the outset make him eligible for inheritance. Criteria define the class of eligible; rules of conduct drive out the undesirables.

On an operational level, groups behave like sets or subsets in mathematics, and the membership criteria like the axioms defining those sets. They are axiomatic, and therefore cannot vary in intensity. So a group can choose its criteria because of the value it attaches to its members, without this predilection undermining the group's ontological independence. A mathematician can select the axioms he or she believes are most likely to shed light on the problem he or she is trying to solve, without this selection ontologically degrading the sets the axioms define. The reasons that guide the choice of axioms, as well as the number of axioms, leave the ontological status of the set unchanged and unperturbed. Sets that are determined by different axioms contain different elements, and will certainly manifest different properties, but without being 'more or less' sets. A mathematical set may be fuzzy, may contain no elements at all, but it cannot vary in intensity.

In an operational framework, groups, corporations and categories evade all ontological variability. All types of activities (those notorious 'functions' of classical ethnology) are definitionally equivalent, as are the criteria. We will obviously find criteria only activated in special or extraordinary circumstances, we will see that membership of a group is often a membership criterion to another group, but none of this will generate 'degrees' of groupings, or an unequal importance of activities or criteria. No criterion will prevail by its superior strength, and no activity by its overriding importance. Different activities and criteria will obviously correspond to dissimilar groups, groups that vary in their size, their composition, the ways they grow and reproduce, by their demographic properties and the way they articulate to other groups, categories or corporations but they will never vary in their intensity, in their corporateness.

Ontologically invariable and equal groups are forever displacing those 'privileged reference groups' of classical social theory: the family and descent groups in structural functionalism, production groups in Marxist theory, or matrimonial exchange groups in alliance theory. They sweep away this Aristotelian social cosmos, hierarchized by the functions of its groups, as the Cosmos of antiquity was by the attributes of matter, to replace it with a Cartesian social space, neutral, homogeneous, isotropic, where individuals have no 'natural place' to move towards. The era of Social Theory and its hierarchical Cosmos, the Systems Era, stops at the threshold of comparative analysis and its isotropic, modular social space.

If we eradicate behaviour regulation from the definition of groups, it affects the notion of structure. What do I mean by structure? Once again, a very old and venerable idea, that of the division of labour. A group will appear 'structured' to me if and only if some related activities within one type of activity are performed, on a more or less permanent basis, by different individuals within the same group. This means that some groups have no division of labour at all (a group defined in terms of residence, for example). It thus follows that structure is extrinsic to the group's definition; it is added to it, superimposed on it.

Defining lineages

But social organization is not just a matter of groups, categories or corporations, as Abutia ethnography once again reminds us. If residence had proved a difficult piece to handle, the lineages gave even more trouble. Superficially, each Abutia village (Ewe: *du*) revealed itself to be a collection of sub-groups, known in the vernacular as *sâmewo*, each *sâme* (sing.) said to be composed of three and exactly three *agbanuwo* (sing. *agbanu*) descended from three wives of an unnamed, putative ancestor in the agnatic line, without ever specifying the genealogical link uniting the eponymous ancestors of the *agbanuwo* to the unnamed ancestor of the *sâme*. Each *agbanu* was in turn subdivided into several *fhomewo* (sing. *fhome*), each descended from an ancestor two or three generations beyond the oldest living generation, all the *fhomewo* of a single *agbanu* being linked agnatically to the *agbanu*'s eponymous ancestor. Within the *fhome*, and therefore within the *agbanu* whose eponymous ancestor was known and named, the genealogical links were explicit. This genealogical precision within the *fhome* and *agbanu,* and the simple presumption of common ancestry within the *sâme,* faithfully and happily repeated the classical distinction of British social anthropology between lineages and clans. I could declare *sâmewo* to be clans, *agbanuwo* lineages and the *fhomewo* to be lineage segments, these three levels articulated by patrilineal descent. Since there is no intermediate level between the *agbanu* and the *fhome*, I called the *agbanu* the maximal lineage, or simply lineage, and the *fhome* the minimal lineage.

Problems arise when we abandon macroscopic divisions for microscopic observation. Seen up close, *fhomewo* quickly shed their patrilineal appearance. Some of these minimal lineages had nearly half their members able to trace their membership through the mother, and no *fhome* counted fewer than 20 percent of such members. The minimal lineages revealed a strongly cognatic composition and, by extension, so did the lineages, despite the strictly agnatic arborescence of ancestral generations linking these minimal lineages and these lineages to each other. I thus encountered in Abutia the same problems and paradoxes faced by ethnologists in Melanesia (see volume 1), the ethnographic puzzle that led them to detach the 'composition' of groups from their 'articulation' by the language of descent, and which prompted Sahlins to separate the composition of local groups from their descent 'ideology' articulating them (Barnes 1962; Sahlins 1965). But beliefs or ideology had left the problem intact and the question was as urgent in 1975 to understand Abutia as it had been fifteen years earlier. The ethnography of lineage societies demanded then, as it still did, a different solution.

The irony of it all is that Maine's venerable notion of 'aggregation', so reviled by successors who never understood it, solves the riddle (see volume 1, pp. 16–20). Maine noted and understood that some communities are not made up of individuals, but of groups. Maine's idea is so simple, and yet so fertile, that it sweeps away all the pseudo-problems arising from corporatist cogitations. In the so-called pure sciences, the idea is commonplace, even trivial since Avogadro. We know that some physics speaks of atoms, and some chemistry of molecules. This physics asserts that the atom is made up of electrons and subatomic particles, and this chemistry declares that the molecule is made up of atoms, without the chemist thinking of considering the molecule as a compound of electrons and subatomic particles. A molecule, unless it consists of just one atom, is not made up of electrons and subatomic particles, but of atoms. On the basis of this analogy, we can say that groups are made up of individuals. However, some collectivities are not made up of individuals, but of groups, and it is totally mistaken to think of these groups of groups in terms of membership since, strictly speaking, their members are not individuals. Reducing these 'groups of groups' to a network of localities representing their relationships in terms of beliefs or descent ideology is just as fallacious. It repeats at the level of these mega-collectivities the mistake made at group level. Let me emphasize this once again. Until now, we have thought of groups in terms of the organization of interpersonal relationships, and we have also conceived of these composite communities in terms of the organization of relationships between groups. Both types of organization call for regulatory mental representations which, by definition, can only be exercised on the individual, with the pernicious consequences we know for the ontological status of groups, and of groups of groups (see volume 1). If the group is to be recognized as a reality in its own right, the requirement must be repeated for 'groups of groups'. This is exactly what Maine allows us to do.

Maine drew his inspiration from his own society to elucidate Roman society, and I will similarly look at our nation states to decipher descent groups. In the arbitration of certain disputes, a Canadian province manifests itself not as a group of individuals but as a collection of counties. On what basis do these counties merge into a province? On the fact that they are geographically adjacent, or geographically closest. Whether a county or province border crosses here or there is a matter of history and pure contingency, but it is the relative position of these groups that serves as the basis for the creation of supra-municipal, supra-county, and supra-provincial entities. Maine spoke of local contiguity, Morgan of territoriality. I will retain Morgan's usage and claim that, in the arbitration of some disputes (to mention just one activity), a Canadian province does not form a collection of individuals, but a collection of groups conglomerated into a province on the basis of territoriality. Territoriality is not a membership criterion; it is an element used to 'aggregate', in the context of specific activities, groups into larger communities. In our society, as in any other, I will define a 'territorial group' as a group aggregated on the basis of territoriality.

The idea of territoriality sheds light on descent. Like territoriality, descent is an element of aggregation. Unlike territoriality, however, descent ignores geographical contiguity, singling out genealogical links between ancestral generations, whether real or imagined. A 'descent group' – because it is really all about descent here, not unifiliation as many ethnologists, especially French ones, have believed – does not recruit. It is a mega-collectivity that takes shape when groups amalgamate through ancestral genealogy.

Descent as 'aggregation' dispels the Abutia and Melanesian enigmas and paradoxes. Between the *fhome* (minimal lineage) and the *agbanu* (maximal lineage), there is now a qualitative difference. As a minimal lineage, the *fhome* is a group; membership criteria determine which individuals are eligible. The *agbanu*, on the other hand, is not a group. It aggregates *fhomewo* through patrilineal descent. Between the two, between membership and aggregation, a certain indeterminacy becomes possible. While agnatic kinship defines membership of the *fhome*, it is not the only criterion at work; in some well-specified circumstances, matrifiliation also operates. It is even worth generalizing: nothing, absolutely nothing in the definition of the group, corporation or category requires them to have only one membership criterion. On the contrary, groups that recruit on the basis of a single criterion seem to be the exception rather than the rule. Everywhere and almost always, groups use more than one criteria, even if one of them operates in the most common circumstances and thus appears to be predominant. The multiplicity of membership criteria affects group composition, but does not hinder the aggregation of these groups on the basis of patrilineal, matrilineal or cognatic descent. The Abutia *fhomewo* can welcome some members through matrifiliation in some cases, while continuing to agglomerate into an *agbanu* through patrilineal descent without supposing contradictions or paradoxes, without declaring agnatic descent weak, or invoking a manipulation of agnatic kinship ideology. There is certainly a limit to this indeterminacy between membership and aggregation, and that limit is none other than contradiction; it is hard to imagine minimal groups recruiting exclusively on the basis of patrifiliation and aggregated on the basis of uterine descent! The element of aggregation and the criteria of membership must coincide to a certain extent, but an extent that often tolerates a surprising flexibility. As long as ethnologists thought of lineages in terms of individuals, descent and membership criteria had to harmonize perfectly. But when we loosen this unhealthy grip, we find that descent, even if unilineal, tolerates a certain range of criteria among the groups it aggregates.

More about kinship

This calls for more terminological refinements. With descent and territoriality now elements of aggregation, membership criteria also require a more sophisticated terminology. It is already there, scattered throughout our vocabulary: kinship and filiation (and their derivatives, agnatic, uterine and cognatic kinship, as well as undifferentiated filiation, matrifiliation and patrifiliation) have always been membership criteria and they remain so, with one major nuance. From now on, filiation will be dissociated from kinship like the singular from the plural. Let me explain. In some societies, an individual is entitled to claim membership of a given group because his or her father or mother belonged to it; he or she is eligible simply by virtue of filiation (implicitly, undifferentiated filiation) to his or her parents. If he or she can only hope to become a member of the groups to which his or her father belonged, then we speak of patrifiliation and, similarly, we separate patrifiliation from matrifiliation. Why separate filiation from kinship? Because in these societies it is specifically the fact of being the child of a parent that gives group eligibility. In Polynesia, some local groups will welcome their members' children. But if one of these children chooses to take up residence elsewhere, his or her children will no longer be able to reactivate their father's father local group eligibility (as in the Gilbertan *kainga,* see volume 1). Here, only patrifiliation makes one eligible; the fact that the father's father (not patrifiliation but agnatic kinship) belonged to the group is irrelevant, except in some circumstances. These very real situations differ radically from those in which Ego can claim membership to a group by virtue of the fact that his paternal grandfather belonged to it, whether or not his father was a member. In the latter case, it is no longer patrifiliation that determines eligibility, but agnatic kinship. By extension, I define uterine kinship and cognatic kinship in the same way. Kinship, the membership criterion, is now cut off from descent, and even detached from filiation. Filiation begins and ends with the generation of Ego's parents (let us call it G+1 in relation to Ego); kinship begins with the generation of Ego's parents' parents (so, G+2 in relation to Ego), but doesn't end there. Personally, I know of no society fussy enough to specify membership in relation to a kinship defined as

G+3 rather than G+2, or G+4 rather than G+3 and G+2, and so on. In the current state of our knowledge, I'm happy to speak of filiation, patrifiliation or matrifiliation when specifying membership by reference to G+1 vis-à-vis Ego – i.e. the singular of ascending generations with respect to Ego – and to speak of cognatic kinship, agnatic kinship or uterine kinship when determining membership by reference to $G \geq 2$ vis-à-vis Ego. This is the plural of the grammar of generations. Needless to say, these membership criteria divide categories and corporations as much as they do groups (see Table 1 at the end of this chapter).

III

After this detour about groups and their multiple criteria, descent also requires more distinctions. Descent may be an element of aggregation, but how will we recognize it? As ethnologists once did with so-called segmentary lineages, we see aggregation when minimal groups come together into a larger whole, acting as a single group under the tutelage of the new representative(s) of the aggregated group, in the context of a specific activity (political or religious), or of land tenure. But let us be explicit. First of all, this amalgamation of groups into more encompassing collectivities does not mean that a group of groups is ultimately just a group, and that we relapse into corporatism. The idea of a unique representation to the aggregated group and its unity in the execution of an activity does not negate the idea of aggregation any more than the idea of molecule negates that of atom, because nowhere does it imply that the components lose their identity. What is more, if aggregation necessarily leads to unique representation (by an individual or a group of individuals), the opposite proposition is false. A unique representation can be found without aggregation.

A short scenario will illustrate. Let us imagine autonomous trade unions, threatened by an unfavourable economic climate and anxious to present a united front to the government, sending a collective delegation to negotiate on their behalf. Under certain circumstances, it is not impossible to imagine this delegation being reduced to a single individual, or just a few, without supposing for a moment that the unions thus allied would transmute into a mega-union, a United Union within which the formerly sovereign unions would have lost their autonomy. Instead, we would speak of a coalition, a political alliance, as is commonly done in the case of NATO or the Common Market. To extract aggregation from alliance, or vice versa, we need to elucidate what this unity implies.

Abutia a chiefdom?

Let us return to Abutia for a better understanding. I have already described these elementary groups (the *fhomewo*) that agnatic descent amalgamated first into lineages (the *agbanuwo*), and then into clans (the *sâmewo*). These clans were descent groups, as I said, and their occupation of space made them *local* groups and *territoriality* brought them together in a village, a territorial group, the *du*, in the context of judicial activities (see similarities with the Tallensi *teng*, footnote 22). But beyond the individual village, this territorial group in the order of politics, what do we find? All ethnographers, missionaries and administrators of the Ewe country spoke of an ethnic group divided into groups of villages assembled under the supervision of a Paramount Chief (or *fiagâ* in the Ewe language). The documents agreed that this was a supra-village political organization, absorbing villages and hamlets into a centralized structure headed by the *fiagâ*. The same territoriality that aggregates clans into villages would have aggregated villages into a single political organization represented by the *fiagâ*. All three Abutia villages would form a territorial group in political terms. Was this right?

Each Abutia clan has its representative (some had an *ametsitsi* – an elder – other *sâmefiawo* had priests of deity, *fetish priests*, who are selected by the clan elders because of their personal physical and psychological qualities); each village also has its own representative (the *dufia*), who happens to be the chief of the clan that has always given that village its chief. The chain of automatisms does not stop there, however, since all of Abutia has always recognized the chief of the same village, namely Teti, as its 'chief' (*fiagâ*). It is as if the Canadian federal government always recruited the ten provincial premiers, and the premier of a given province always occupied, *ex officio*, the post of Canadian Prime Minister. Was I, like all previous writers, going to portray Abutia as a group of villages aggregated through territoriality (what these observers referred to as a 'chiefdom')? It was very tempting. So many elements converged: the unique and permanent representation, all the symbolism making Abutia an entity, a united and cohesive whole going beyond local identity to set itself, through the *fiagâ* its representative, at a supra-local level contrasting with neighbouring village groups: Sokode, Adaklu, Ho, Anlo. One fact would settle the question: was there a single activity in Abutia that required all the villages to be grouped together into a supra-local entity, and where the *fiagâ*, as representative of this supra-village group, had the power to carry out the activity alone, or at least to summon an assembly to carry it out? The witchcraft trials seemed to meet all these conditions, and they were the only cases (although very rare). They automatically brought together the three Abutia villages, and the *fiagâ* presided over them. But one fact stubbornly went against it. During these trials, the *fiagâ* had neither the power to arbitrate on his own, nor that of convening an assembly of notables to deliberate and pass sentence. Instead, the chief of the village where the crime was committed invited the notables of his village and of the other Abutia villages, politely calling on the *fiagâ* to preside over the proceedings. Invited as First Citizen, no doubt, and asked to preside in that same capacity, the *fiagâ* saw his prerogatives come to an end at that. A seemingly trivial fact, but that pointed in the right direction. The three Abutia villages were not aggregated into a supra-village entity, but formed a complex alliance.

The unity of an aggregated group thus presupposes more than just an activity; it also implies that the person(s) acting on behalf of the aggregated group is/are empowered to perform that activity, or to summon a subset of the group to do so. In turn, the unique representation that accompanies aggregation is also accompanied by: (1) specific criteria (coupled with a clearly specified procedure if there is selection, or election, or both) fixing eligibility for the role(s) of representative(s) of the aggregated group or corporation; (2) a power of execution on the part of the representative(s), with regard to the activity over which the aggregated group has jurisdiction (ritual, or arbitration, for example), or the power to convene an assembly for the same purpose. In the case of corporations, the representative(s) must be able to act with regard to the transfer of property. Finally, since the representative(s) of aggregated groups or corporations hold their position for some time (a new one is not chosen for each new occasion the group has to exercise its activity), aggregated groups and corporations usually work in the context of recurring activities, even if the interval between two activities (rituals, for example) may stretch over several years. In a word, representatives of aggregated groups are title-holders. But it goes further. Insofar as aggregation is not alliance, it can only amalgamate groups that are themselves headed by a title-holder or title-holders, and not leaders.

This definition of aggregation further inspired new reflections on political sovereignty and, consequently, on coalition or alliance. From my set of definitions it follows that the politically *sovereign* group is the political group where aggregation ends and alliances begin. The Abutia village, the last layer in the pyramid of aggregations and the first in that of alliances, therefore, knows only equals in the political order; the village is therefore sovereign, and Abutia was no territorial group, but a *village league*. Hence the sub-title of my monograph: *A Chiefdom that Never Was*!

The idea was most fruitful and helped explain the vast differences between Abutia and another ethnographically well-documented association of villages, namely the Anlo (Nukunya 1969). The Anlo populated the shores of the Gulf of Guinea, at the southern end of the Ewe country. Its ethnographer leaves no room for doubt: under the spiritual and political direction of a quasi-divine king, hamlets and villages were amalgamated into a supra-village entity to which the name kingdom could aptly be given. Abutia and Anlo, once conflated in the same ethnographic horizon where everything appeared as a centralized political organization, were now radically dissociated from each other, the Abutia as a league of only three sovereign villages and Anlo as a sovereign territorial entity, encompassing over one hundred villages that were not politically sovereign. This contrast suddenly explained a number of discrepancies that observers never mentioned: the complete localisation of clans among the Abutia and their dispersal among the Anlo; the growth and reproduction of descent groups and villages, infinitely slow and catastrophic among the Abutia, but gradual and continuous among the Anlo; polygyny, rare and repressed among the Abutia, sought-after and common among the Anlo; myths of origin, imbued with a static, quasi-geographical temporality among the Abutia, but narrating a genesis among the Anlo (Verdon 1981a, 1983). In addition to sovereignty, aggregation further told about alliances, their astonishing variety and the urgent problem it raises for ethnography[3].

Aggregation, alliance, membership – these are the perspectives called for by ethnography, demanded by epistemology, and dictated by our project. It will enable us to extricate ourselves from all that tuft of lived experience that weighs down and holds back the imagination, sinking our definitions in the immediacy of social life. And if science, and even mathematics, are only refined and transformed when they cut themselves off from all visual imagery, they actually teach us much more. They impose the familiarity of paradox, of an ontology of the multiple that accepts itself as a condition of knowledge. They tolerate the coexistence, even the complementarity, of opposites, reminding us of the artifice of our conceptualizations and dichotomies. Science and mathematics force us to live with the absurdities of our arbitrary languages. They tame the wave and the corpuscle, combining these ancient

[3] While aggregation does not vary, alliance does. Since the concept has so often been subsumed under that of lineage organization, as I shall demonstrate more fully with the Nuer and Tiv ethnographies, it goes without saying that everything remains to be done in this field. I confine myself here to separating alliance from aggregation, well aware that future research will inherit a gigantic task to accomplish in the study of political alliances.

enemies in an indissoluble marriage. Sometimes matter, sometimes energy, the reality of the new physics is composed of these different modes of being. It 'is' neither wave nor corpuscle; it is defined by the conditions of its intelligibility. Within the artificial and arbitrary net of an operationalist language, social reality will experience the distortions of a double ontology. If these one-dimensional groups, corporations or categories overlap and superimpose to recreate the thickness of lived groups, they also intersect with aggregated groups or corporations. Let me explain.

In some respects, and more precisely with reference to the arbitration of specific offences, the Abutia *fhome* belongs to those elementary groups that agglomerate into an *agbanu*, or lineage, when offences pit members of different *fhomewo* but of the same *agbanu* against each other. In terms of judicial activities, the *agbanu* appears as a descent group, an aggregated group whose minimal components are minimal lineages (*fhomewo*). In terms of land ownership, the *agbanu* is radically different: it is a corporation. The same group of individuals (*agbanu*) is here an aggregated group, there a corporation. Its various manifestations only become intelligible through the mutually exclusive concepts of corporation and descent group.

Agbanu, like the notion of family in our own language, is in itself nothing more than a nebulous and deliberately vague notion conceived for and by social action, a 'cognitive shortcut', so to speak, that allows much to be said without having to explain, and which an explanation would contradict. From the point of view of analysis, the Abutia *agbanu* is multiple, not 'a group with multiple functions'; it is disarticulated into two superimposed surfaces that overlap, but not completely. Seen in terms of arbitration, it is a group of groups, a compound of *fhomewo* in which some affines are included; seen in terms of land ownership, it is an agnatic corporation excluding affines. But for the social agents who live and act, a single concept suffices. They say '*agbanu*' like we say 'family', and they get along just fine. The context says what the word doesn't and what analysis reveals. For the dislocation of groups and their simultaneity to stop surprising us, we need to make this shift, this Gestalt shift, so that we can measure our concepts, not by the yardstick of a subjectivity that seeks to objectify itself, but within the very artifice of a language that recognizes its power of invention.

IV

Methodological implications

Before ending those conceptual considerations, more needs to be said about our starting point: activities. By activity I mean 'type of activity', what ethnologists have always described as 'function'. But how do we decide where to stop in the classificatory movement that separates and contrasts the various types of activities, in this taxonomic arborescence where each function should find its place? Here, judgment and ethnographic experience dictate. In one society, a single notion of production group will suffice; in another, it will prove analytically useful to separate the agricultural production group from the animal production one and, within each of these, other groups perhaps. There is no rule other than that of all operationalism: if the distinction pays off analytically, if it illuminates and simplifies, let us impose it on the analysis; if not, let us dispense with it.

This is not all; if we exclude societies with economic corporations and restrict ourselves to societies traditionally studied by ethnologists, aggregation takes place in three contexts only: 1) in political activities (judicial, legislative, executive and military), 2) in religious activities (mostly related to some types of ancestral cults, as with the Tallensi – see below) and (3) in land tenure (where land is corporately owned; see Tallensi again). This is not supposing a differential importance. In terms of survival, tilling the land is certainly more important than worshipping the gods! But it, together with most activities, does not lead to aggregation. Methodologically, however, we must focus on these two types of activities first, to assess whether or not we find aggregation. And we should start with political activities, since religious aggregation is rarer. These are important methodological considerations.

The ethnographic sense nonetheless has its limits, which are those of our conceptual requirements. We do not stipulate at will. We invent. We distil, we refine, we seek to enrich terminology, but within the constraints imposed by our epistemological requirements. Residence, for example, appears to me as an activity, whereas it was before always presented as a membership criterion or a principle of social organization. Similar considerations force me to see 'locality', which has also always been considered as a membership criterion and a principle of social organization, as another activity. The locality is the occupation of a geographical area intended primarily for habitation, and the local group is the group that carries out this activity and is recruited according to membership criteria: marriage, filiation, kinship, or even membership of a group or corporation. Locality and territoriality, which so many texts have confused, break apart. As for reproduction, it raises theoretical problems of such magnitude that I defer its analysis to the appendix (see Appendix). All we need to know at this point is that marriage arises operationally as a membership criterion to a group, the conjugal group, and that the family encompasses this conjugal group and all the individuals issued from its reproduction, whether real or fictitious.

This operational framework has some other important methodological implications. By definition, as I separate every activity, I initially define the minimal group that performs that activity. I thus invert the traditional social anthropological manner of starting the analysis from the maximal groups to move down to the minimal ones. Quite the contrary, I initially identify the minimal group in a given activity, and then move up to more encompassing ones in the case of political and religious activities (see above). I analyse from bottom to top, the only way to ascertain if there is aggregation or not.

Another innovation follows. As I start from the minimal group and work my way up through aggregation or alliance, it became important to define genealogical reckoning more rigorously. The standard anthropological tradition knows only one way of calculating the number of generations when genealogies are involved. Whether moving from the top or looking at the edifice through Ego, they all include all the generations from the youngest to the oldest one. I keep the generational calculus of looking at generations from Ego's point of view for some cases, Ego's generation being the youngest one. But I define a radically different one, namely a 'group calculus', so to speak. For this group calculus I identify the most important generation, namely G°. G° is the oldest living generation and may easily have two to three generations beneath it (depending on the age of the oldest living person in the group studied). G+1, therefore, is the first *ancestral* generation, the first generation of dead people. This distinction is crucial, in that it easily subtracts two to three generations to the numbers mentioned by ethnographers. Thus, a group allegedly having seven generations will end up with only four or five. When I refer to ascending generations in what follows I am always referring to generations defined in relation to the group, unless otherwise stated.

At the end of this conceptual journey, what have we achieved? I have removed the organization of behaviour from groups, made structure (as division of labour) extrinsic, conceptually postulated a different group for each type of activity (a single function per group), separated activities (doing) not only from codes of conduct or rules of behaviour (ways of doing) but also from ownership (having), and kept only the criteria (which can be multiple) for defining groups, categories and corporations. I have also separated (elementary) groups from groups of groups, discovering that groups of groups can be aggregated either by descent or territoriality. I have emphasized the overlap between groups, corporations and categories, and between any of these and aggregated groups or corporations, specifying that while groups, corporation or categories call for membership criteria, composite groups or corporations call for elements of aggregation. Finally, I consider residence and locality as activities, marriage as a membership criterion, and separate kinship from filiation (see Table 1). All that remains is to demonstrate how this new language recomposes our ethnographic vision. Since most of the concepts we deal with have developed around the ethnography of so-called segmentary lineages, I turn to this ethnography to re-examine its three greatest classics: the Nuer, the Tallensi and the Tiv. To those I will also add a reanalysis of the Yao of Malawi, the Moroccan Berbers and the Australian Aborigines.

Table 1. An operationalized conceptual framework

<table>
<tr><td colspan="3"></td><td colspan="2">Individually-based criteria</td></tr>
<tr><td colspan="2"></td><td>No membership criteria</td><td>Individual participates in activity</td><td>Does not participate in activity</td></tr>
<tr><td>Activity</td><td>Present
Absent</td><td>Crowd
—</td><td>Group
Category</td><td>Exo-Group
?</td></tr>
<tr><td rowspan="2">Ownership</td><td>Legally demarcated estate</td><td>—</td><td>Corporation</td><td>?</td></tr>
<tr><td>Non-legally demarcated estate</td><td>Collective ownership (non-corporate)</td><td>Quasi-Corporation</td><td>?</td></tr>
<tr><td colspan="2">GROUPS, CORPORATIONS AND CATEGORIES</td><td colspan="3">MEMBERSHIP CRITERIA</td></tr>
<tr><td colspan="2">Individual membership</td><td>a) In relation to G+1 vis-à-vis Ego:</td><td colspan="2">Undifferentiated, patrifiliation, matrifiliation</td></tr>
<tr><td colspan="2" rowspan="2">Individual membership</td><td>a) In relation to G≥2 vis-à-vis Ego:</td><td colspan="2">Cognatic kinship, agnatic kinship, uterine kinship</td></tr>
<tr><td>b) Other criteria</td><td colspan="2">Sex, age, matrimonial status, group or corporation membership, etc.</td></tr>
<tr><td colspan="2">COMPOSITE GROUPS</td><td colspan="3">ELEMENTS OF AGGREGATION OR ALLIANCE</td></tr>
<tr><td colspan="2">1. Group aggregation</td><td colspan="3">Descent, territoriality, generational level of ancestors.</td></tr>
<tr><td colspan="2">2. Group alliance</td><td colspan="3">Ritual collaboration, economic collaboration, military collaboration.</td></tr>
<tr><td colspan="5">COMPOSITE CORPORATIONS</td></tr>
<tr><td colspan="2">Aggregation:</td><td colspan="3">Descent</td></tr>
</table>

CHAPTER TWO

Translating the Nuer ethnography[4]

British social anthropology reached its apogee in the analysis of segmentary lineage societies. Through their study it refined its concepts and built its cosmology. An operational translation of these great classics, and above all of the sacred trinity of the ethnography of segmentation – the Nuer, Tallensi and Tiv ethnographies – will help unmask this ethnology that has wanted to be, and has believed itself to be, so transparent in its empiricism. I begin where theory and ethnography have been most closely wedded, among the Nuer, whose social organization I briefly described in volume 1 (pp. 39–42).

Evans-Pritchard's segmentary model

Evans-Pritchard's ethnography belongs to a social anthropological tradition that strove to extricate groups from interpersonal relationships (see volume 1). Evans-Pritchard wrote two eminent monographs about Nuer social organization, namely *The Nuer* (1940) and *Kinship and Marriage among the Nuer* (1951), that reproduce these two analytical axes respectively, namely the political and the domestic. In *The Nuer*, Evans-Pritchard studied political groups, examining the relationships between territorial and lineage segments. Within these groups, within the village, the household and the various networks that the fortunes of marriage

[4] Originally Verdon 1982a.

and consanguinity create between individuals, we are dealing with the domestic universe, the world of interpersonal relationships that the 1951 monograph explores.

Other contrasts follow. The first volume discusses ecology, territory and lineage relationships in the indigenous language of the *thok dwiel* and *buth*. The second monograph deals with herds and bridewealth, in the indigenous language of the *mar.* According to Evans-Pritchard, the *mar* is to the *thok dwiel* and the *buth* what kinship and interpersonal relationships are to descent and relationships between lineage segments. The indigenous distinction between *thok dwiel* and *mar* would correspond to this series of oppositions between political and domestic, relations between groups and relations between individuals, descent and kinship, territory and herd.

The Nuer opens with cattle and their economic and sentimental importance to the Nuer, although their beloved cattle leaves the stage as soon as Evans-Pritchard moves on to the study of politics, anxious to define what he means by 'tribe'. He gave the Nuer tribe a distinct name, a specific sentiment, a common and delimited territory, and a moral obligation on the part of its members to unite in war and to settle feuds and other disputes between themselves (1940, p. 122; the following references are to this book only, unless otherwise mentioned). Evans-Pritchard found political unity only within the tribe, and made it the sovereign political entity.

Unity, perhaps, but in and through plurality, since the tribe is also a structure fragmented into opposing sections to which correspond lineage segments of a dominant clan, segments also in opposition but which also fit together right up to the social boundaries of the tribe (p. 122). The tribe is a territorial organization supported by a lineage organization, but a segmentary territorial organization in which the elements share the characteristics of the whole: each tribal section also has a name, special feelings, and a territory. Each also stands in opposition to sections of the same order and grafts itself onto a lineage segment of the dominant clan of the tribe. We are told that this opposition is real, fuelled by endemic armed conflicts that arbitration nevertheless manages to quell.

Both substance and relationship, real and virtual identity, the Nuer territorial section lives uncomfortably with the duality of its being:

> "There must always, therefore, be something arbitrary about our formal definition of the tribe by the characters we have earlier listed [...] for opposition between segments of the smallest section seems to us to be of the same structural character as the opposition between a tribe and its Dinka neighbours [a neighbouring ethnic group, which the Nuer constantly raid]" (p. 148).

It is pointless to look for diacritical marks that would mechanically and precisely determine where a section of any order begins and ends. Everything is a matter of context (p. 149), as shown by the feuds. Through the feud, never ended, always revived, the sections would assert their distinct identity. But the feud had to be controlled, submitted to arbitration to curb civil war and stem tribal schisms. The feud calls for arbitration, and arbitration would delimit the boundaries of the tribal space. To Evans-Pritchard, through the language of force, the feud reveals the basis of Nuer law: the use of physical violence. The Nuer will only find justice if they know how to impose it, if they know that it is ultimately up to them to ensure that their rights are respected.

Faced with this fierce individualism, where the individual acts as his own judge and arbiter, where violence breeds the latent violence of these feuds that explode sporadically, how can one talk about a political society? How can anarchy be organized? – Through the lineage system. The description is now classic: "A clan is a system of lineages and a lineage is a genealogical segment of a clan [... and] the commonest Nuer word for a lineage is *thok dwiel*" (p. 192). Moreover, "agnatic kinship between lineages is called *buth*. *Buth* is always an agnatic relationship between groups of persons [...]" (p. 193) and *buth*, as agnatic relationships 'between collateral segments' is opposed to *mar* as cognatic relationships 'between people' (p. 193).

We find in the lineage system the segmentation of the territorial system. However, precise genealogical knowledge is not to be found at all lineage levels; it stops at the minimal and sometimes minor lineage, without going any further. Beyond that, the Nuer speak the language of settlements, of the relative geographical position of groups, rather than the more permanent idiom of precise genealogical positions. Moreover, "in normal everyday usage Nuer employ the word *cieng* [where we would expect to hear them speak of the *thok dwiel*] (p. 195)", this *cieng* which in fact designates a hamlet, a village; which denotes, in a word, the local group and not lineage segments. As Evans-Pritchard confesses, the Nuer see these so-called relationships between lineage segments as relationships between groups of relatives associated with local communities (p. 202), to the extent that,"outside certain ritual situations, [the Nuer] evaluate clans and lineages in terms of their local relations" (p. 203).

The boundary between lineages and local groups gets increasingly blurred as the analysis progresses. The Nuer lineages slowly lose any corporate character, even becoming detached from any local attachment. Evans-Pritchard does isolate a core of agnates with whom the village is identified and who form the minimal lineage segment, adding that,

> "In social life generally they [lineages] function within local communities of all sizes, from village to tribe, and as part of them. A Nuer rarely talks about his lineage as distinct from his community, and in contrast to other lineages which form part of it, outside a ceremonial context [...]" (p. 203).

Slowly, the Nuer lineage loses all the insignia of its identity, even if relative, losing all relevance except ceremonial, leaving 'community values' to dictate behaviour in most situations, including political ones. In the final analysis, 'lineage values' would dominate the field of religion, and local values, that of politics. Despite all these detours, snags and denials, Evans-Pritchard did not abandon his original thesis: it was the lineage system that formed the framework on which political relations were grafted (p. 240), even if a lineage, "had [with other lineages of its clan] *only a vague ceremonial relationship*, and this relationship may never be expressed in corporate action" (p. 245, emphasis added). This briefly outlines the backdrop against which the Nuer segmentary model develops, together with its contradictions and its theoretical straightjacket.

An operational translation

The Nuer have often been reanalysed and all but one of these reinterpretations have preserved the segmentary lineages. In 1979, however, Holy moved the Nuer lineages into 'representational models' (see volume 1), while nonetheless retaining the idea of segmentary lineages. But did the Nuer really have lineages?

Evans-Pritchard describes a nesting structure of territorial units (*cieng*) ranging from the local group (hamlet) to the tribe, and a corresponding set of lineages (*thok dwiel*) ranging from the minimal lineage to the clan. To answer our question, let us first ask whether the hamlets are aggregated into villages, the villages into tertiary sections, the tertiary sections into secondary sections, and so on up to the tribe and, secondly, whether the *thok dwiel* and its *buth* (Evans-Pritchard defines the *buth* as a collateral lineage of Ego's lineage – p. 194; 1950a, pp. 366–67) are aggregated into progressively more inclusive segments (also called *thok dwiel*), all the way up to the clan. In short, do the territorial sections, on the one hand, and their lineage counterparts, on the other, form aggregated groups?

Let us first look at the territorial organization. In the rainy season the Nuer live in permanent settlements which they leave during the dry season to congregate in cattle camps near waterholes. These permanent settlements, or localities (Nuer: *cieng*) vary in size according to ecological conditions (1950a, p. 362). Some are small and homogeneous (not internally divided into hamlets), while others are much larger, strung along a ridge above the water and divided into hamlets. These hamlets, Holy has shown, are the real foci of Nuer political life, and their composition is far from agnatic (Holy 1979b). On the contrary, agnates of the dominant clan often compete for political leadership and the ambitious ones, if wealthy, charismatic and generous, secede to found their own settlement by attracting a following of cognates and affines (Evans-Pritchard 1950a, p. 379; 1950b, p. 40; 1951, p. 143; 1933, pp. 48–49; Holy 1979a). These leaders, or 'bulls' (*tut*) achieve their social prominence by giving cattle away to poorer kith or kin, or by foregoing their rights over part (or all) of their daughters' bridewealth in return for the sons-in-law's political allegiance (1933, p. 49; 1947, p. 185; 1950a, p. 376). Many Dinka are absorbed in Nuer settlements through this process, thereby swelling the following of Nuer leaders. The hamlets thus recruit on the basis of cognatic kinship and affinity and, as soon as a newcomer has built a cattle byre, he or she enjoys full membership of that hamlet as a cattle-herding, land-utilizing, and political group (p. 218; 1945, p. 62).

The Nuer appear to lack any legislative, executive, and administrative groups; their only political groups emerge in judiciary and military activities. In the wake of earlier missionaries and traders, Evans-Pritchard unfortunately perpetuated what a recent historian regards as the myth of the aggressive and truculent Nuer (Johnson 1981) whose only judicial recourse, according to the famous English ethnographer, was self-help (pp. 151, 162). The truth is less romantic, however, in that disputes could be, and were, settled, although the specific composition of these judicial groups was never spelled out. The evidence presented by Evans-Pritchard suggests that the wet-season hamlets or villages and dry-season cattle camps were the main groups of reference in judiciary activities; should a dispute flare up within those settlements or camps, its elders would assemble to settle the conflict (1933, p. 16; 1934, pp. 38, 40–42; 1935, pp. 38–59; 1940, p. 178). Within these judiciary groups, however, none of the 'bulls' (whether there was only one, or many) ever acted as a representative of a hamlet. Disputes between neighbouring settlements might lead to small skirmishes but the elders would soon convene, with or without the mediation of leopard-skin chiefs, to settle the issue (1953, p. 16)[5]. Specific mechanisms, namely eldership

[5] Interestingly enough, it is the weakest who are interested in appealing to leopard-skin chiefs (1935, p. 59). Haight developed this theme (1972, p. 1316).

within the framework of an age-set system and leopard-skin chiefs, or ritual expertise, thus operated to ensure the maintenance of law and order, as Evans-Pritchard himself emphasized in his early writings (1934, pp. 38–40; 1937, p. 210), but nowhere is there any evidence of aggregation. This is not surprising since no one could act as a representative of a hamlet or village and certainly not of a larger association of settlements. The pattern of groupings in military activities, however, does convey a strong impression of aggregation; I will examine this below.

In short, can we be surprised at the absence of territorial aggregation if, according to Evans-Pritchard, the *cieng* amalgamate into progressively more inclusive communities on the basis of a segmentary opposition rooted in the segmentation of the agnatic lineages (*thok dwiel*) of the dominant clan of a tribe (i.e. the clan whose ancestors were the first to settle in the tribal territory)? This superimposition of territorial and lineage organizations implies that, if there is aggregation, it should take place in the lineage system and not the tribal organization. However, everything belies this lineage-based interpretation of Nuer political organization. Evans-Pritchard repeatedly states that Nuer political organization links localities, that the Nuer themselves perceive this organization in geographical terms and that they even express their descent relationships in the language of the locality (pp. 195, 203, 204, 235, 238, 242–244; 1950a, p. 364). Moreover, the lineages would only have ritual relevance (pp. 193, 203, 211, 228, 210, 227, 245), and even then only 'vaguely' so. In order to assess the interpretation of the *thok dwiel* as a lineage or lineage segment and, by extension, the entire Nuer lineage edifice encompassing the *thok dwiel* and their collateral *buth*, we must therefore look at ritual activities.

Among the Nuer, most ritual activities of any importance involve sacrifices, which fall in two broad types: (1) personal ones, concerning an individual's relationship to ancestral ghosts or the Divinity, or (2) 'collective' ones, concerning the relationship between two individuals and their respective groups (1956, p. 198). Collective rituals always involve a 'master of ceremonies', the *gwan buthni,* who starts the ceremonial invocations by shouting the spear-name of his clan (1956, pp. 287–288). As his title suggests, *gwan* (master) *buthni* (of the *buth*) the 'master of ceremonies' represents the *buth* and cannot in any circumstances be *mar* to those organizing the sacrifice (more about *mar* later; let us temporarily follow Evans-Pritchard in defining it as cognatic kin up to G+5 (in his genealogical calculus; it could be only G+3 in mine) but must nevertheless belong to the same clan (i.e. belong to the same exogamous group, identified by an exclusive spear-name). These facts lead Evans-Pritchard to define the *buth* as a *collateral lineage.* Collective sacrifices would therefore involve a 'lineage' *(thok dwiel)* responsible for the sacrifice and a 'collateral lineage' *(buth)* represented by the *gwan buthni* who acts as 'ritual attorney' for those organizing the sacrifice. The lineage and its collateral lineage were thus depicted as merged into a more inclusive segment. Collateral lineage segments thus appeared to be aggregated into more inclusive segments, and this all the way up to the clan.

If the association of a *thok dwiel* and its *buth* represented a true case of aggregation, we would expect one person to officiate on behalf of the whole group. Moreover, if a lineage X divided into A and B, and if A sundered further into C and D while B also subdivided into E and F, we would assume that a ritual representative would officiate for A when C and D sacrificed together, that a different one would perform for B when E and F collaborated in rituals, and that one of these two (or another one altogether) would act on behalf of the whole of X when the descendants of A and B assembled ritually. But none of this occurs in Nuerland. The *gwan buthni* does not officiate as representative of a larger segment including a *thok dwiel* and its *buth*, but as representative of a category (see below). Evans-Pritchard further specifies that the *gwan buthni* does not act as a priest but as a layman (1956, p. 289). Also, different families of the same clan have different *gwan buthni* while one family sometimes has many different ones (1950a, p. 368; 1956, p. 288)[6].

[6] Evans-Pritchard does not mention how some individuals come to be selected as a family's *gwan buthni*. However, we know that they officiate in rituals in which

There is thus no aggregation whatsoever of *thok dwiel* and *buth* in ritual activities, and none in political activities either (excepting military action for the moment). One does find judiciary and ritual groups, the composition of which are never specified clearly but which lack permanent representatives and are not aggregated. Since lineages are aggregated groups, I thus conclude that the Nuer do not have any lineages and, even more strongly, do not have any 'segmentary' lineages. How, then, should we represent their social organization? As Burton (1981) has already pointed out, the answer is to be found in their cattle. As Evans-Pritchard exclaimed in *The Nuer*, '*cherchez la vache!*'

Let us *chercher la vache* where Evans-Pritchard exiled it, in the *mar*, the *mar* that he contrasts with the *buth* as cognatic to agnatic kinship, or as kinship to descent, or interpersonal relations to relations between groups (pp. 193–194; 1950a, pp. 365–366; 1951, p. 6; 1956, p. 288). The facts, once again, belie this interpretation. Is *mar* cognatic kinship? – No, since spouses become *mar* to one another's *mar* relatives after they have had two or more children (1951, pp. 6, 12, 96, 100, 101, 104). I find this fact disturbing but it does not worry Evans-Pritchard. He sees it as additional proof of the operation of a 'unilineal descent principle' since matrimonial relationships are transformed into kinship ones by the couple's common offspring, since filiation transmutes affinity into consanguinity!

We also know that the Nuer describe the *mar* in terms of rights over the bridewealth's livestock. Are Ego's *mar* all those who claim rights over the livestock transmitted at the marriage of his sisters and daughters, as well as those who recognize the rights of Ego over the livestock transmitted at the marriage of their sisters

individuals have to be separated in order to foster or restore unity (such as marriage, severing the *mar* to allow marriage, building of a new byre, end of initiation, and so on - 1934, p. 14; 1956, pp. 199, 217, 288). A person who simultaneously stands outside the *mar* but inside the clan and formerly the *mar* is eminently qualified to perform these rituals which complete insiders or outsiders could not perform.

and daughters (1934, p. 29; 1950a, p. 366)? These ties to cattle explain the extension of the rules of incest and exogamy, and even matrimonial prohibitions in general (1933, p. 40; 1934, pp. 7, 8–13; 1937, p. 211; 1951, pp. 32–33, 40). Against Evans-Pritchard, I hold that spouses become *mar* of their affines because they mutually inherit their rights to livestock through their children. A husband can claim his deceased wife's cattle dues if she has left two children, especially sons, and wives enjoy the reciprocal prerogative (1951, p. 33; Howell 1954, p. 123). It is no doubt possible that the *mar* concept came to refer to a vague category of 'consanguineous relatives' but, as Evans-Pritchard repeatedly asserts, the original meaning of the term derived from rights over bridewealth cattle.

The distribution of rights over bridewealth cattle (for details see 1945, pp. 24–26; 1951, pp. 74–86) thus delineates an Ego-centred set of cognates descended from forebears in G+4/G+5 (1950a, pp. 365–366) or even G+6/G+7 (Howell 1954, p. 110; again, we might have to correct with a group calculus), together with their spouses: these peoples are *mar* to one another. Over time, however, *mar* lapses as the claims over cattle cease, and the relationship is transformed into one of *buth* (1950a, pp. 365–366). Since *buth* relatives all share the same spear-name, allegedly transmitted through men only, how can *mar* (a cognatic set) become *buth* (an agnatic set)? To answer, let us look more closely at the *buth.*

Since women become *buth* to their husbands and affines through the cattle paid for them at marriage (1934, p. 15), it is a mistake to equate *buth* with agnatic kinship[7]. It is equally unwarranted to define it in terms of rights in the sacrificial meat (1950, p. 366; 1956, p. 288) since all the participants at a sacrifice,

[7] In fact, no one can claim that *buth* relationships are truly agnatic since it is impossible to verify that spear-names are transmitted agnatically. Since *buth* relationships are too distant to be traced genealogically with any precision, it could well be that people related to the sacrificers through their FFFM have nevertheless adopted their spear-names and are treated as *buth.* Since individuals are named after the kin with whom they associate in herding, spear-names may eventually be passed on to people whose forebears were *gaat nyet* (children of women) to their hosts.

be they *buth* or not, enjoy this privilege. The participants in collective sacrifices can therefore be divided in at least three subsets: (1) those who can share in the sacrificial meat and can also claim live (bridewealth) cattle from those organizing the sacrifice, that is, their *mar* relatives; (2) those who have a right to the sacrificial meat but none over the live (bridewealth) cattle. This latter subset is *buth* only to those sacrificing, together with (3) the wives of those who sacrifice, who are both *buth* and indirectly *mar* through their children (by proxy, so to speak). Wives are only residually *mar* because they have no direct right over the live cattle of the sacrificers.

What, then, entitles the *buth* to a share of the sacrificial meat? It is not their ancestors' *mar* relation to the ancestors of those sacrificing, since they represent only a small (agnatic) fraction of that category. The non-agnatic fraction would have been victim of genealogical amnesia. A great proportion of *mar* relationships would fade with the passage of generations and a small fragment, those of specifically agnatic relationships, would metamorphose into *buth*; let us however remember that the *buth* also includes living spouses. The key to the enigma is not to be found in ritual; instead of looking for it in the cattle sacrificed, I will look for in the rights to cattle in general.

I will take my clue from another piece of evidence. Elsewhere, Evans-Pritchard reports that a woman "comes under the protection of (her husband's) lineage spirits and ancestral ghosts" (1951, p. 104) when she has been married with cattle, and I believe this fact entitles such women to their share of the sacrificial meat, and consecrates them as *buth.* If this is true, are *buth* those who come under the protection of the sacrificers' ancestral ghosts, but have no claim over their live cattle, and are excluded from the *mar* network? Since the protection of ancestral ghosts is transmitted from men to their children and wives (whereas women can only transmit it to their husband's children) it delineates within the *mar* an agnatic line plus their wives. When *mar*ship lapses, this underlying agnatic link could be remembered as *buth.*

However, if the sacrificers' *mar* relatives can also share in the sacrificial meat (and there is no evidence to the contrary), this right cannot be transmitted through men only. The available ethnographic evidence does not enable us to solve the problem satisfactorily. I would nevertheless assume that ancestral protection follows the cattle, which moves in two directions: (1) agnatically through devolution after death; and (2) to cognates and affines, through bridewealth. Therefore, both *mar* relatives and those whose *mar* connection is discontinued but are related agnatically to the sacrificers' ancestors through a common spear-name, together with the wives of those responsible for the sacrifice (the only ones to be both *buth* and *mar*) enjoy a right to a share in the sacrificial meat.

It is thus clear that the *buth* do not form collateral *lineages,* but represent an Ego-centred *category* comprising those who share Ego's spear-name, are outside his or her *mar* but whose fathers or forebears were *mar* to Ego's father or forebears. The *gwan buthni,* therefore, is the representative of that category. If the *buth* is no collateral lineage, what then is the *thok dwiel?* To answer this question, we must turn to the devolution of cattle after death which, according to Evans-Pritchard, is essentially lineal and excludes women (1945, p. 28; 1951, p. 85; Howell 1954, p. 190).

Claims over cattle, be they 'owned' by men or women, are inherited by sons, if there are any (1950b, p. 38; 1951, pp. 77, 85, 128) and by brothers otherwise (1951, p. 88), although brothers can only act as trustees if they inherited from a brother since they must use the cattle to marry a wife to their brother's ghost (see below). Since women cannot sacrifice (1956, p. 236), and can only own cattle in their own name if they have earned it (and mostly through divining: 1960b, pp. 23-24; 1954, p. 31; 1951, p. 128), there is a privileged relationship, both economic and spiritual, between men and cattle to the extent that Nuer perceive a

> "[...] unity of a lineage and its cattle, the cattle which sustain the lineage by their milk (the cow suckled the ancestor) and by constant calving provide them with bridewealth for marriages whereby sons are born and the lineage continued, and with a means of maintaining communication with Spirit and ghosts" (1956, p. 259).

This agnatic consciousness could perhaps account for the existence of the *thok dwiel.*

Evans-Pritchard regarded *thok dwiel* and *buth* as complementary concepts, implying that the sacrificers in collective sacrifices formed a *thok dwiel.* We have seen that both the sacrificers' *mar* and *buth* could participate at collective sacrifices and claim their portion of the sacrificial meat. Among the *mar*, the devolution of cattle and ancestral protection (as well as spear-names) delineate an agnatic subset which may be responsible for special phases of the rites and this subset, in fact a patrifiliative ritual group, could constitute the *thok dwiel.* But the ethnography is silent on the ritual division of labour and this interpretation, plausible as it is, raises one major problem. Indeed, Evans-Pritchard claims that the Nuer do not use this concept for agnates related through an ancestor placed earlier than G+4/G+5 (1933, pp. 28, 32; 1940a, p. 192; 1951, pp. 6–7). I find it difficult to imagine that any man responsible for organizing a collective sacrifice would try to assemble agnates with whom he is related in G+4, or G+5, when in fact precise genealogical recollection may not always reach that far (1940a, pp. 201–202). I would therefore prefer to look elsewhere for an answer to this problem.

In *The Nuer,* Evans-Pritchard noted that "it may be supposed that a lineage [therefore a *thok dwiel*] only persists as a distinct line of descent *when it is significant politically*" (emphasis mine, p. 246). On the preceding page, we also learn that lineages are more likely to be remembered in larger tribes than smaller ones, knowing that larger tribes are almost exclusively confined to Eastern Nuerland (1953, p. 7). The Nuer infiltration of Eastern Nuerland has given this region the features of a frontier zone of pioneer settlers. This situation, in my opinion, has exaggerated the importance of personal leadership. If we compare the eastern village of Konye (1950, pp. 370–371) to the western one of Nuyeny (1945, pp. 31–38, 55–61) we gain the firm impression that the first one, more recently settled, completely orbits around its 'bull', whereas the second lacks any outstanding personality acting as its dominant 'bull'. Ecological variations between Eastern and

Western Nuerland also reinforce this pattern (1940a, pp. 118–119; 1940b, pp. 275–276; Glickman 1972b). Western villages are more autonomous and stable because of the greater availability of water, whereas the eastern ones are much less so. Land is also more abundant in the east, and the strong leadership of individual 'bulls' presupposes vacant land into which dissatisfied *diel* (descendants of original settlers) can move with their supporters. Indeed, the very status of *diel* is much more pronounced in the east (1940a, p. 215).

It is tempting to associate the *thok dwiel* with the existence of a strong leadership and to suppose that they are more in evidence in the east than in the west of the Nuer country. Howell, administrator and ethnographer of Nuerland, compares the *thok dwiel* to the Hamitic or Semitic 'house' which brings together the descendants and political clients of an important sheikh (such as the 'house of David', of biblical notoriety – Howell 1954, p. 21). Why not see the first leaders or 'bulls' who establish themselves in a new region as the founders of a 'House', anxious to pass on their political pre-eminence to their sons (1934, p. 41)? After a few generations of reproductive and political success, this 'House' would be named after its founder, especially if the latter had had the good fortune to perpetuate his leadership through an agnatic line of male descendants. This House would include *gaat nyiet* (children of sisters) and, in short, be referred to as *cieng* So-and-So (*cieng* followed by the name of the *tut*, or founding 'bull') because the *tut* had first and foremost founded a local community. But it is also possible that in localities where political power has been kept in the agnatic line of the eponymous founder, the agnatic descendants of the original leader are aware of their distinct identity and see themselves as the founder's *thok dwiel*, although the line separating *cieng* from *thok dwiel* is very tenuous:

> "By minor lineage I mean the ancestor to whom the Nuer refer when they answer the question 'who is your *thok dwiel*?', i.e. the first forefather in their common genealogy to whom a large number of families refer as their common

> ancestor and whose name is used to name their village or district. Thus a large number of families from the Lou tribe will tell you, if you ask them the name of their *thok dwiel*, that they are members of the *cieng* PUAL [...]" (1933, p. 32).

When asked about the *thok dwiel* they belong to, the Nuer named their *cieng*. It may be, but the ethnographer does not tell us, that these families of the Lou tribe are scattered over the Lou territory and call their *thok dwiel* a *cieng* where they do not even live. Some of the agnatic descendants of the eponymous founder will have left his local group but will nevertheless consider themselves members of his House, which would explain how the Nuer can so easily substitute one for the other *cieng* and *thok dwiel*. The *thok dwiel* would only include the agnatic line of a House, even if dispersed over several localities, whereas the House would normally be represented as *cieng*. As to whether this agnatic subset within a House performs certain specific rites during sacrificial ceremonies, it is impossible to know since the ethnography is once again silent on the topic. If the *thok dwiel* plays such a role, it would be the only occasion on which it appears as a group; otherwise, it is simply an agnatic category, whose existence is so vague that we can understand why Evans-Pritchard mistook it for a lineage and ended up talking about its "vague relevance in ritual matters".

Mar, *buth* and *thok dwiel* are therefore not groups aggregated on the basis of descent, but various categories (with the possible exception of *thok dwiel*, which may represent a ritual group) delineated through the transmission of cattle, either through bridewealth (*mar*), or devolution after death (*buth* and *thok dwiel*). The evidence regarding adjudication, rituals and the transmission of cattle (as well as land, see footnote 3) warrant such conclusions but it could be argued that Evans-Pritchard perceived a segmentary organization in military activities only. Indeed, the segmentary opposition and fusion of *cieng* operated in defence and raiding, according to Evans-Pritchard, thanks to an underlying system of 'dominant lineages' aggregated into various levels up to a 'dominant clan'. But if lineages did not exist in Nuerland, they could not have provided the skeleton of this segmentary organization. Admittedly, villages or settlements of a 'tertiary section' did unite to fight another tertiary section, tertiary sections of a 'secondary section' could also associate to fight another secondary section, and so on to the level of the tribe. In those military activities, however, as in any political ones, the hamlets, villages, sections or tribes did not have any leadership which was, to use Evans-Pritchard's own terminology, "institutionalized and permanent" (1940, p. 294). Although Nuer villages could emerge as military groups, we could never speak of their *aggregation* into sections – but of their military *alliances.* To clarify this point, let us use an imaginary scenario.

Let us suppose that NATO does not exist and that a civil war rages in Italy. If Spain chose this moment to attack Italy, the opposing factions might unite to defend the country. If France used this opportunity to invade the two warring countries, the two might possibly unite against their common enemy, but they might also ally with France if all three were threatened by an alliance between England and Germany. This admittedly is a historically improbable but theoretically possible permutation. If it occurred, it would describe a neat pattern of 'segmentary *alliances* (or coalitions) and oppositions' between nation states without assuming aggregation of the allied groups. Evans-Pritchard recognized a similar distinction in his exchange with Coriat, who accused him of arbitrarily singling out the tribe as the largest political unit when Nuer tribes had been known to unite for offense and defence. Evans-Pritchard replied:

> "I was aware of these combinations, and *I preferred to regard them as alliances between two political units.* In the same way in Europe, nations, the largest political units of our culture, combine together for purposes of warfare, but they do not lose their political autonomy by doing so" (1933, p. 12, emphasis added).

The mistake, however, was to assume Nuer tribes to be aggregated when in fact they are not, whereas European nation states are. If we distinguish aggregation from alliance, we thus obtain a different picture of Nuer segmentation.

The minimal Nuer settlement, be it the hamlet of a large village or a small homogeneous village, is essentially a cattle-herding group within which economic cooperation is vital for survival, either in the care of cattle (1937, p. 211) or even cultivation (1940b, p. 273; Jackson 1923, p. 136). Within those minimal settlements, conflicts are peacefully settled. We could therefore represent them as the politically sovereign groups (groups above which there is no aggregation). These groups vary in size, and to uphold their sovereignty they must be able, if threatened by a given force, *to oppose an equal force.* They can only achieve this by weaving a complex network of alliances. Alliances, however, vary in degrees, so that some are more binding than others[8]. Contiguous hamlets or villages, or hamlets that convene in the same cattle camps share a common interest in suppressing serious conflicts to preserve their close collaboration. Their alliances are the strongest, and this strength makes them look like sovereign political groups themselves. Conflicts do erupt between these strong allies because of their intense interaction, but these conflicts are normally settled. The weaker the economic collaboration and interdependence, on the other hand (which, Evans-Pritchard writes (1937, p. 211) is the very essence of kinship in Nuerland) the fewer the kinship and affinal connections, the greater the geographical distance and ecological barriers, the fewer the conflicts but the more difficult their settlement. The 'segmentary organization' of the Nuer does exist, but it is nothing else than a pattern of military alliances woven in such a way that the parties opposed in a conflict can muster a force equal to that opposing them. The celebrated

[8] Military coalitions do vary in their organization as the existence of NATO intimates, and there are also instances where they do threaten the sovereignty of their participating groups. The Delian League, for instance, started as a military alliance between sovereign Greek city states, but the coalition was implemented in such a way as to favour one city, Athens, and to incite eventual aggregation. Since partners in military alliances are not always equal in strength (witness the Warsaw Pact, or NATO), the more powerful often use the alliance to their own benefits.

'equilibrium' is therefore not one of lineage segments or aliquot parts, but a *balance of numbers*. It is a demographic equilibrium, without which hamlet or village sovereignty would be a utopia. Indeed, despite Evans-Pritchard's steadfast attempt to present the segmentary organization in genealogical terms, the relevance of the factor of size could not wholly elude him (1935, pp. 39, 73, 79; 1940, p. 145).

Admittedly, these alliances are not created from nothing and are somewhat preordained by existing genealogical connections. The *diel* who move out to create new hamlets, like other migrants, will remember their former links with the settlement they left, and the recollection of *buth* serves this purpose admirably since it perpetuates the memory of a close association without imposing a tedious genealogical knowledge. The genealogical connections thus provide a natural basis upon which to build coalitions, but the network of friendship that individuals develop over a lifetime also engenders alliances; both types of associations, however, are translated into the language of agnatic kinship both because it is convenient and because devolution of cattle, as well as political leadership (whenever possible) goes from father to son. This 'agnatic grid'[9] thus serves as a convenient mnemonic to support a network of segmentary military alliances between local groups, but the dynamics of local group reproduction is not genealogical; it is ecological. Indeed, villages split because of changing relationships of cattle to land (1937, p. 210)[10] and the pattern of association from

[9] Since many links are in fact remembered through women, the grid is only predominantly agnatic.

[10] Among the Dinka, this relationship is even more conspicuous. Lienhardt has indeed shown how the various levels of territorial alliances among the Dinka directly spring from ecological adaptation to the environment (1958). The wet-season camps form subtribes, while the dry-season camps delineate a tribe. There is no reason to expect the Nuer to act differently. Indeed, the larger Nuer villages correspond to tertiary sections and neighbouring villages congregate in cattle camps, thereby delineating secondary sections. The maps presented in *The Nuer* reveal a further pattern: the wet-season settlements are all clustered and this somewhat nucleated conglomeration of hamlets and villages, surrounded by their dry-land pastures, forms the largest territorial assembly, the 'tribe'. However, the

hamlets to tribes is not rooted in genealogical segmentation, but in the ecological exigencies of herding cattle in the particular Nuer environment.

Overall, then, the Nuer have no descent groups. *Thok dwiel* and *buth* are not collateral lineages merging into more inclusive lineage segments up to the level of the clan so that Nuer clans themselves are not aggregated groups. They are exogamous categories, membership of which is acquired through fathers and husbands. When looked at through the exigencies of herding cattle and transmitting it among the living and after death, the paradigm of lineage segmentation modelled on the contrast between byre and huts within the polygynous homestead now appears as a folk model without analytical validity.

Holy did away with the agnatic interpretation of the Nuer village but retained the segmentary lineage at the level of representational models. By doing away with the lineages altogether, we obtain an interpretation that is more in keeping with the political and local dynamics that he describes, and that also adheres more closely to the residential dynamics that he unfortunately neglected. If the 'agnatic nucleus' at the heart of the Nuer locality is a myth, so is the so-called 'agnatic extended family' that would have been theirs. Let us take a close look at the residence at Nuyeny (1945, pp. 29–39); of the 26 concessions, 11 are headed by women without husbands or lovers, and of the 15 residential groups headed by a man, only one is made up of a father and his married son (agnatic extended family). A few

---

territory is also traversed by natural boundaries, such as rivers, which delineate primary sections (see 1940a, p. 112). As Glickman has demonstrated, the ecological necessity of using such large areas of land for herding cattle (in Eastern Nuerland) jeopardizes the autonomy of Nuer settlements and renders necessary large-scale alliances from villages to tribes, via tertiary, secondary, and primary sections (1972b). In Dinkaland, the greater availability of water gives villages a greater autonomy and therefore reduces the need for large-scale alliances, and the use of an extended grid to encompass the various local groups. Since conditions in Western Nuerland approximate those of Dinkaland, we would expect those paradigmatic features of Nuer society to be most conspicuous in the east.

unmarried brothers lived together on the same concession, but no married brothers; moreover, married brothers did not even try to live on neighbouring concessions. We find them scattered across different hamlets and villages, while brothers and sisters are often neighbours. And residence also brings us back to livestock.

The composition of Nuer residential groups, like that of Nuer hamlets and villages, is influenced by the great mobility of Nuer men and women, which is made possible by the abundance of land and the wide range of criteria of membership to local groups. Members of local groups welcome any of their cognates and affines (if they are not troublesome, that is) because they increase the group's manpower and bring more cattle to their herds. These conditions favour migrations, but why do individual Nuer decide to emigrate from one locality to another? Once more, because of considerations related to cattle: soil exhaustion due to overgrazing (or overcultivation (1938, p. 44; Howell 1954, p. 14)), declining herds (1938, p. 44; 1940a, p. 210), strained relations between neighbours, normally due to cattle debts (1940a, p. 210; 1945, p. 47), or a number of features peculiar to the marriage system, such as the freedom of widows (1951, p. 113), local exogamy (1951, p. 35) and the division of loyalties between one's genitor and one's pater, generated by the practices of ghost-marriage, women-marriage, leviratic marriage, and concubinage (1945, pp. 43–44, 49, 60). In other words, when they are not quarrelling over cattle or looking for better pastures, Nuer men change settlements because their own mother moved (left her husband's settlement). Women, on the other hand, are mobile because divorce is virtually impossible if they have borne their husband two children (1951, p. 92), and because of the high incidence of widowhood and the freedom of widows to refuse a levir (1951, pp. 112, 115). However, the bonds of cattle and the high incidence of widowhood would not produce these conditions if they did not promote conjugal separation (from a husband or levir) and conjugal separation is rife among the Nuer because Nuer women have a strong bargaining power. Indeed, Nuer women are needed everywhere because they alone can milk cows. They also cultivate and, since land is abundant and not owned either privately or corporately, women have free access to it and are always assured to find an eager companion. All this facilitates 'concubinage' (to use Evans-Pritchard's terminology). In sum, then, the mobility of Nuer men and women and, as a result, the composition of Nuer residential and local groups, spring directly or indirectly from considerations related to cattle, as do also most of their matrimonial practices[11].

Let us take the levirate, for instance. To the Nuer, an adult man or woman is worth a certain number of heads of cattle which can never be paid twice for any man or woman (without the return of the cattle previously paid). A woman who wants to divorce and remarry must therefore convince her father to return the cattle of her bridewealth (if she has not borne two children) and an equivalent amount will be repaid to him by the new suitor. The death of a husband does not free the wife from the bonds of marriage because cattle has been paid for her once, and normally from a paternal herd to which her husband's siblings had equal rights. To marry their late brother's wife, these brothers would first have to divorce her. This, however, is nonsensical, since they would have to claim the cattle back from the very people to which they would pay it back as new bridewealth. Consequently, a man's brother or first cousin can never 'marry' his wife (1945, p. 15) but can only become her levir and raise children in the dead man's name.

Ghost- and woman-marriage evolved from different necessities. The distribution of bridewealth claims, in fact, is premised on polygyny (or at least bigamy), in that the cattle given

---

[11] In Nuyeny, 15 of 33 women were widows, 9 of whom did not have any lover. Moreover, about one-third (10 of 33) of the Nuyeny women were living as concubines (1945, p. 38). All these concubines, either widows or simply separated from their husbands, as well as many of the women married to other women (9 percent in Nuyeny) and to ghosts (15 percent in Nuyeny, but Burton mentions 30 percent of marriage to ghosts in any generation among the Atuot, Burton, 1978, p. 403) give birth to children whose genitor is not their social father and who will want to go back to their social father's hamlet upon maturity if they believe there is more cattle to be had there. This is one of the main factors to this immense Nuer geographical mobility.

to the mother of the bride will be used for the marriages of her own sons whereas the cattle given to the father is channelled to his sons from *another* wife (not the mother of the bride) (1951, p. 79). Many factors, however, seem to inhibit the practice of polygyny, such as the formidable size of marriage payments (see Turton 1980)[12], the prohibition against sororal polygyny and the fact that all brothers must get married (from the paternal herd) before any of them can marry a second wife. In other words, very few men achieve this ideal of polygyny (1951, p. 140) and men sometimes marry wives to their late fathers in order for him to have married at least twice, to create a collateral branch (Howell 1954, pp. 76, 78). A more common reason for ghost-marriage, however, is to create a line of male heirs for a dead man (1945, p. 11; 1956, p. 163).

Indeed, if Nuer men marry late (Burton 1978, p. 44), rarely succeed in marrying more than one wife, and die relatively young (Howell 1954, p. 75), an inordinately large number of them will die without male heirs[13]. As we know, women cannot inherit cattle in their own name (1950b, p. 24); if a daughter survives an heirless father, it will be her duty to marry a wife in her father's or brother's name (Burton 1978, p. 402) and this accounts for the existence of woman-marriage. If devolution of cattle is lineal, cattle and cattle claims should not devolve to siblings (1951, p. 85). If a man dies childless, it is therefore the duty of his trustees (i.e. his siblings or first cousins) to marry a wife to his ghost (1945, p. 10)[14], a view

[12] The Masai, who own on average forty times more cattle per inhabitant, only pay between one-fifth and one-eighth the bridewealth that the Nuer pay (Turton, 1960, p. 76).

[13] With lower mortality rates and an earlier age at marriage for men, Wrigley has calculated that 40 percent of the married men in preindustrial Europe were likely not to be survived by a male heir (1978). With higher mortality rates, later age at marriage for men and a low incidence of polygyny, we should not be surprised if 50 percent and even more of the Nuer men were not survived by a male heir.

[14] Admittedly, the compulsion to marry a wife to a ghost varies with the number of cattle and claims inherited and the personality of the trustees. If they can get away with it without any penalty, I would surmise that most Nuer men would keep their late brothers' cattle and marry wives for themselves, but the living fear the ghosts' vengeance. As soon as misfortune strikes, diviners are bound to remind the

that finds further support from the fact that ghost-marriage is only practiced for initiated males or, as the Nuer say, for lads who "have known cattle" (1945, p. 6). It is only after initiation that a man gains full rights over the cattle of his *mar* and, if he dies, these claims and whatever cattle he owned must be transmitted. Wives are thus married to ghosts to keep intact lineal transmission. The very practice of ghost-marriage, in turn, decreases the incidence of real polygyny among the living. Many men who marry wives for their dead kinsmen die before having married a wife for themselves so that the practice tends to perpetuate itself to the extent that, in Nuyeny, only 3 of 33 women were married in "simple legal marriage" (1945, p. 38).

Instead of interpreting the levirate, woman- and ghost-marriage in terms of an 'equivalence of siblings' emanating from the operation of an alleged 'principle of agnatic descent' which seems to be flouted in every other sphere of Nuer social life (Holy 1979a), it thus seems less paradoxical and more coherent with Evans-Pritchard's own advice of *chercher la vache* to derive these practices, like most other features of Nuer social organization, from the transmission of cattle and cattle claims.

Translated in an operational language, the Nuer ethnography is transformed. They lose their descent groups and their corporations, since cattle is owned individually and land belongs to all. Cattle, relegated by Evans-Pritchard to the level of interpersonal relationships, replaces the territory and completely shifts the centre of gravity in an operational analysis. The segmentary mechanics, now a case of alliances rather than aggregation, moves to the periphery. Old questions disappear, but new ones come up: why, for example, this lineal transmission of livestock, why such astronomical marriage payments, why this ideal of polygyny, and these segmentary alliances? Some questions can be answered immediately from the Nuer ethnography, while others will have to away further research and comparative analysis in the future.

renegade of their failure to fulfil their brotherly duties, thus precipitating the ghost-marriage (1945, p. 11).

Among the questions that ethnographic analysis can answer, three stand out from the outset: why this lineal transmission of livestock, why such a high bride price, and why this implicit bigamy in matrimonial payments?

Why does the bridewealth's distribution presuppose polygyny when polygyny is rare? To answer, let us imagine the opposite scenario, i.e. Nuer monogamy. Monogamy would eliminate the need to distinguish between the bride's mother's livestock and her father's (since the two are only separated in order to pass on the livestock to children of the same father but of different mothers). The father would receive the bridewealth in full, and women would become superfluous in the transmission of property. Since the uterine uncle only claims a fraction of the cattle of his uterine niece because he inherited this right from his own mother (i.e. the uterine niece's maternal grandmother), how could cattle be passed on to matrilateral relatives if women lost their role as intermediaries in the transmission of rights to livestock? In short, the circulation of livestock by women at marriage, the distribution of the bridewealth to matrilateral relatives and the polygynous ideal are all interconnected strategies. Denying one is tantamount to denying them all, and calls for new strategies.

Of these three strategies, two seem to follow from the third, namely the distribution of bridewealth cattle to the maternal parents. Why recognize the maternal parents' right to the cattle? The answer, or certainly an important part it, lies in the ecological and economic factors elucidated by Glickman and Turton (Glickman 1971; Turton 1980). First, Nuer cattle are often prey to epizootics which can decimate an entire herd in a matter of weeks. To reduce these risks, it is preferable for an owner to spread his animals over as large a territory as possible by means of a complicated system of rights and debts between cognates and affines (Glickman 1971). In addition, maternal relatives can only receive a share of the cattle if the payment is high enough. And why would the Nuer, who are relatively poor in livestock, pay such an astronomical price? Turton gives a very plausible answer. Despite their image of pastoralists, the Nuer live mainly from agriculture but rarely manage to produce enough to avoid deadly shortages, so that cattle protects them from famine. Since they have relatively few animals, they cannot allow them to accumulate in the hands of a minority of individuals or families, or to be concentrated in a few localities, and must therefore spread them as evenly as possible over as large an area as possible, which is made possible by excessive bridewealth payments when it is distributed through a complex maze of claims from cognates and affines. When epizootic diseases have reduced the size of the herds, the number of heads of cattle to be paid at the wedding is reduced without changing anything in the distribution network. The bride's father and mother were the first to relinquish their share, while the more distant relatives, and especially the matrilateral ones, never did so (Evans-Pritchard 1947, pp. 181, 184, 186; 1951, pp. 83, 84, 89; Howell 1954, p. 110).

In short, high marriage payments made it possible to widely disperse rights over livestock in order to counter ecological threats, a scattering that was achieved by favouring polygyny and circulating these rights between men, but through women, thus separating groups of paternal half-brothers from one another and exciting a certain amount of competition between them, since the Nuer saw them as 'bulls' fighting to possess the same resources (1951, pp. 156–157). This rivalry between paternal half-brothers inhibits the collateral transmission of livestock at death, a collateral circulation that could only create unbearable insecurity and exacerbate these fraternal jealousies, because the low frequency of polygyny, the late marriage of men and their high mortality rate leave many without children, or at least without male heirs. If the Nuer knew that their livestock would drift towards their half-brothers or agnatic cousins, a very frequent case if they transmitted collaterally under such demographic conditions, they would desperately try to marry several women during their lifetime to increase their reproductive success, which they could only achieve by drastically reducing the marriage payments. In so doing, they would be aggravating an already serious ecological threat. A colossal bridewealth and a high incidence of polygyny cannot coexist in Nuer country. Since collateral transmission of livestock would stimulate polygyny, it makes more sense to maintain lineal transmission.

Finally, only sons inherit men's livestock (we know nothing about women's), with women receiving them only as trustees. If women were entitled to inherit the men's livestock, the very organization of bridewealth would be disrupted since, once in possession of the cattle the women could divorce as they wished by returning the bride price to their father. Some women owned livestock (the majority of them diviners, it seems) and, as might be expected, these women chose celibacy, a secular celibacy that had nothing to do with their religious vocation and everything to do with their economic condition.

These are some of the immediate questions that Nuer ethnography can answer. But at the end of the day, how can we explain the sovereignty of the Nuer localities, or those segmentary alliances unknown to their Dinka neighbours? Only patient and in-depth comparison will reveal this, and while this is the ultimate goal, it is not the purpose of this epistemological work. Before comparing, we must first translate ethnographies into an operational language to identify and isolate societies that share similar practices, in order to reconstruct the categories of our discourse. This is what I will do here, by extending my operational translations to the second classic ethnography of segmentary lineages, that of Fortes on the Tallensi.

CHAPTER THREE

Translating the Tallensi ethnography[15]

Fortes' segmentary model[16]

From a theoretical point of view, Fortes' ethnography repeats the dichotomies of Evans-Pritchard's. Two main monographs, *The Dynamics of Clanship among the Tallensi* (1945) and *The Web of Kinship among the Tallensi* (1945), reiterate the classical oppositions: the former is to the latter what relations between groups are to relations between individuals, what politics is to domestic, descent to kinship, agnatic to cognatic kinship, filiation to marriage, and so on (see Verdon 1984). For the analysis of Tallensi segmentary organization, the first ethnography is the only really relevant one.

A so-called acephalous society, hemmed in by the great Mossi, Dagomba and Mamprusi kingdoms of northern Ghana, the Tallensi occupy a kind of no-man's land in the interstices of these great states. A savannah country, Taleland is inhabited by farmers who settled on the summits and slopes of the Tong Hills in northern Ghana. The Tallensi are culturally and politically indistinguishable

[15] Originally Verdon 1982b.

[16] The classic presentation of the Tallensi segmentary organization is taken solely from *Dynamics of Clanship among the Tallensi*, so that where page numbers only are mentioned, they refer to that work (1945).

from their Kusaasi, Namnam and Gorunsi neighbours, with no linguistic, cultural, political or structural boundaries separating them. Only a 'segmentary principle' would define 'segmentary relations' whereby "social groups are identified in relation to one another by a technique of contraposition" (1945, p. 17). Fortes thus begins his analysis of segmentary organization from above, so to speak, through the hardly discernible totality that is Tallensi society.

From the outside, for a Gorunsi for example, the Tallensi form an entity. A deceptive unity, however, since it conceals a profound division: only the hills people call themselves the 'true Tali'. The others, those who live on the plains around the hills, with their capital Tongo, which the British administration had chosen as capital of Tallensi country, are not true Tali. They are immigrants, the Namoo.

A powerful cultural segmentation distinguishes Namoo from Tali, dividing the Tallensi country in terms of clothing, funeral ceremonies and other rituals. The Tali are the people of the land, they are its ritual custodians; the Namoo are those of the chiefship, the immigrants of Mamprusi origin who brought with them the insignia of a political power without contact with the land. Myths tell of a great pact between the first priest of the land and Mosuor, the first Namoo immigrant to settle in Tali country. Irreducible cultural duality, coupled with sporadic hostilities, which are nevertheless transcended through politico-ritual collaboration.

Despite this cultural polarization the Tallensi (the social unit made up of Tali and Namoo) emphasize the stability and continuity of their society, based on their lineage organization and its religious counterpart, an elaborate ancestor cult (p. 26). Fortes then elaborates his classical paradigm of this lineage system, the backbone of the entire Tallensi social organization. These lineages vary in depth, according to the ancestor of reference. The smallest, or minimal lineage (a group, not an aggregated group), brings together the children of the same father, while the largest, or maximal lineage, encompasses all those who trace a common, linear ancestry to the most distant ancestor in the genealogy, the eponymous ancestor – Mosuor among the Namoo.

The Tallensi would identify the minimal lineage as the source of lineage segmentation, where each adult male potentially stands out as the founder of a new lineage segment, but where each is linked to the father by common descent. This indigenous conception explains why lineage ties are referred to as *sunzop* ties, or sibling bonds. As a result the Tallensi family, patrilocal and polygynous, appears to them as the matrix of all lineage differentiation since a woman's sons are distinguished from the children of her co-wife, while recognizing that they are the children of the same father. By extension, a maximal lineage is a segment that traces no *sunzop* links with other segments. Strictly speaking, it is no longer a lineage segment, but the global, or maximal, lineage.

Very early on in the analysis, Fortes' paradigm of segmentary lineage is actually belied by the organization of Namoo clans. All claiming to be children of Mosuor, the Namoo have dispersed to form four different localities, which Fortes refers to as 'sub-clans'. Within each of these, 'accessory' lineages (descended from a sister of one of the ancestors) and assimilated ones (descended, it is believed, from slaves) are grafted onto the 'authentic', i.e. strictly patrilineal ones. Marriage is forbidden between the authentic lineages of the four Namoo sub-clans, as well as between authentic and assimilated lineages. United in their opposition to non-Namoo, the four Namoo sub-clans have peaceful reciprocal relations.

In reality, these four divisions of Mosuor's posterity make up a dispersed maximal lineage, the only one of its kind in Tallensi country. Mosuor settled in Tongo, died and was buried there, and some of his descendants settled there. Each of the four Namoo localities has its own ancestral altar (the *boxhar*), the burial place of its own founding ancestor (himself a descendant of Mosuor), to which each sub-clan sacrifices separately. Although Mosuor is the common ancestor of all four sub-clans, responsibility for his worship rests exclusively with those of his descendants who have remained in Tongo, although occasional sacrifices are made in the name of all Mosuor's descendants.

The Namoo are also the only ones to possess what, for want of a better term, we will call the 'chiefship' (*na'am*), with each

Namoo sub-clan represented by its own 'chief' (*na'ab*). Each recognizes a certain pre-eminence to the *Na'ab* of Tongo, but this does not introduce any hierarchy whatsoever between the four chiefships. The four Namoo sub-clans are 'structurally' equal, each behaving as a major segment of a maximal lineage. In any situation that brings them together, they act according to the principle of equilibrium of aliquot parts.

With the Namoo clan, we find something of the dilemma Evans-Pritchard had encountered; like the Nuer, Mosuor's descendants have no term to designate this reality that Fortes identifies as a clan. They simply call themselves the 'children of Mosuor' when the context demands it. But the problem does not stop at the terminology; contrary to the very idea of descent groups, Namoo clans are not exclusive. According to the classical model, a lineage segment is bounded and can only belong to a single segment of an immediately superior level. By extension, if a clan amalgamates lineages in the language of patrilineal descent, a lineage can only be descended from a single eponymous ancestor, and can only belong to one clan. However, a Namoo lineage can be spread over various clans, depending on whether it acknowledges (a) a proven patrilineal ancestry, (b) a putative patrilineal ancestry or (c) a cognatic link (through sisters) with other lineages. The Namoo clan is not a closed entity; its boundaries are permeable, so much so that "all social ties between corporate units in Taleland, whether they are based on actual or putative genealogical links, on local contiguity, on ritual collaboration or interdependence, or on political connexions, tend to be assimilated to clanship" (p. 59)!

The Namoo clan then defines itself as "a local unit, occupying a specified locality from which it takes its name" (p. 62). Despite the variability and contradictions of the Namoo clan, Fortes does not waver: he still claims the core of the clan to be a maximal lineage (p. 62). He sees any anomalies as minor deviations caused by the vagaries of demography, migration and settlement.

If the inextricable maze of clan networks surprises, it would simply be because the Namoo social organization is flexible in the extension of its principles! It translates ritual ties, or simply neighbourhood ties, into *sunzop* ones, the sibling ties that defined the lineage and now define the clan. It injects kinship (or an ideology of siblingship) wherever social relations are such that they can be likened to relations of consanguinity. But is what is true of the Namoo also true of the Tali? More or less, says Fortes.

Zubiung, a Tali locality on the plains (and not in the hills, it should be noted), also appears as a clan made up of three maximal lineages. This time, however, the top lineages have neither sibling nor kinship ties with any other group, and openly tell their diverse origins. Each jealously defends its autonomy from the other two, each proudly represented by a *tendaana* (Master or Guardian of the Land) who is also the lineage elder (*kpeem*). The Tali, it should be remembered, have exclusive responsibility for the altars of the earth (the *tongbana*). Their spiritual life is thus more complex than the Namoo's: they worship the *boxhar* – altar of the lineage ancestor – and the *tongbana* – altar of the earth – although each lineage also has an altar to its lineage ancestor (the *dugni boxhar*) as well as its particular altar of the earth, and these altars are only particular manifestations of a transcendent reality. In fact, these *dugni boxhar*, ancestral altars specific to each maximal Tali lineage, are part of the great Outer *Boxhar*, altar of the 'ancestral collectivity', just as each altar of the earth attached to a particular lineage is linked to the Great altar of the Earth, where the locality first settled. And the *tendaana*, priest of the land, also sacrifices to the collective ancestors. In the ancestor and the land, the Tali find their lineage and clan identities. Their clans are also as permeable as the Namoo's, with one major qualitative difference: their clans interpenetrated and overlapped to such an extent that Fortes preferred to refer to them as 'clan fields' that look like coats of mail (p. 87, see Figure 1)!

The reality of clan ties finds its most immediate expression in sacrificial rituals. Among the Namoo, sacrifices to the founding ancestor separate authentic lineages from accessory ones. When the Namoo sacrifice to the founding ancestor of a sub-clan, all heads of its authentic lineages must be present. The Namoo know nothing of the Tali Outer *boxhar*. Each *boxhar* of a Namoo sub-clan is a *dugni*

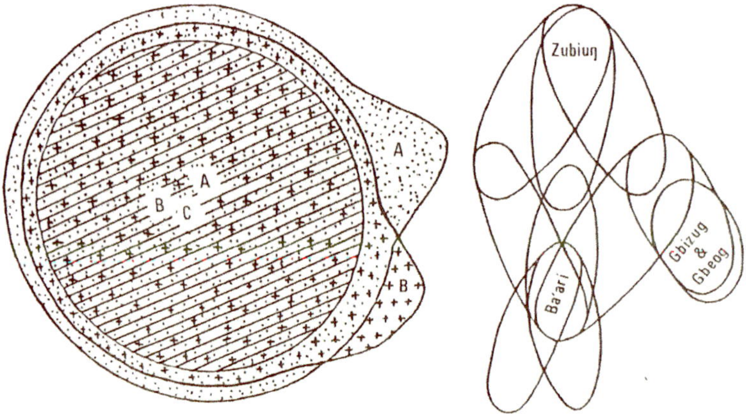

Clan overlapping in a Namoo locality

Clan overlaps among the Plains Tali

Figure 1. Closed Namoo and open Tali localities (Fortes 1945, pp. 63, 86)

boxhar, an inner *boxhar*, so to speak, like that of a Tali maximal lineage. It is 'inner' because it is kept in the homestead of the elder of the lineage segment responsible for its cult.

Let us re-examine the case of Zubiung (Plains Tali), whose clan unity stems from the collective worship of the Outer *Boxhar*. This *boxhar* is external because it is located outside any of Zubiung's homesteads and because it is not linked to any of the founding ancestors of Zubiung's three maximal lineages. Each maximal lineage also has its *dugni boxhar*, the domestic and inner counterpart of the Outer one. This inner *boxhar* represents the ancestors exclusive to the maximal lineage, whose altar sits in the homestead of the lineage elder.

Between clans, no ties operate; ritual collaboration replaces them and, in rituals, Namoo and Tali manage to forget their internal divisions as well as their ethnic rivalry. Divided by their particular cults to ancestors and the land, the Tali are united in their veneration of the Great Outer *Boxhar* and the Earth. The interweaving of Tali ritual ties mirrors their clan ties. One witnesses the same proliferation, the same confused, tangled overlap. Through this luxuriance of clan and ritual ties, clan ties that are said to be ritual and ritual ties that are said to be clan ties, the Namoo and Tali, segmented from within and opposed to each other, nonetheless form a single political unit. A segmentary, acephalous unity, according to Fortes, but a unity, nonetheless.

When we infiltrate this segmentary hierarchy to examine the lineage mechanics within the clan, it is in space that locality and the lineage system meet and intermingle, supporting each other, bracing together to build the segmentary architecture of Tallensi society. Although stable and permanent, the locality (*teng*) has no physical boundaries, and its intelligibility is impenetrable to those who fail to decipher the lineage grammar and syntax that articulate it. Continuous in their occupation of space, localities physically merge into one another. Their boundaries are social, not geographical, but these social demarcations themselves are uncertain. In the final analysis, *teng* reveals itself as a dense configuration of ties based on geographical proximity, lineage ties, and mystical ties to the land, distinct customs and specific politico-ritual offices (p. 166).

Despite this rather hazy reality of the clan, Fortes persists in describing the lineage as the true skeleton of the tallensi *teng*, concluding his analysis of politics with that of the lineage. He had already presented his paradigm at the start of the book, and he concludes his study with a detailed examination of one particular lineage (*Lebhtiis yidem* – pp. 191–220). In terms of action, the minimal lineage Fortes described in his paradigm would only have a morphological reality. The first corporate group in economic and ritual matters would be the 'effective minimal lineage', which groups together the descendants of an ancestor in G+1 (in my group calculus). Fortes concludes: "We thus have a hierarchy of lineage segments: the effective minimal lineage or segment, the nuclear lineage or segment, the inner lineage or segment, the medial lineage or segment, the section or major segment, the maximal lineage" (p. 205). Localities would wrap themselves around these lineages and their lineage segments, which were supposed to organize their relationships. Lineage segmentation is said to drive the whole mechanism of fission and fusion, division and union, which unites Tallensi society in its infinite diversity.

The Tallensi: an operational reading

The language of segmentation, of the equilibrium of aliquot parts within an encompassing totality, prompted Fortes to emphasize the unity of Tallensi society, giving a description of what is essentially the Namoo lineage organization as the paradigm of Tallensi society. By dissociating the Namoo from the Tali, I will test this assertion.

1. The Namoo social organization

The first monograph (1945) repeatedly demonstrates that minimal groups, in ritual and judicial matters, agglomerate into higher segments or groups through agnatic descent. These minimal groups, like the amalgamated groups that encompass them, have their representative, the *kpeem*, whose position satisfies all the conditions of aggregation. The Namoo thus have agnatic descent groups, lineages in other words, and I will not overload the analysis by repeating the obvious. It is rather the details of this lineage organization that I will examine.

Fortes depicts this lineage aggregation in terms of segmentation, a segmentation that goes from the effective minimum lineage to the maximal one[17], going through several intermediate levels, as we have just seen. Several ethnologists have already cast doubts on this particular hierarchy (Firth 1951b, p. 158; Worsley 1956, p. 67; Barnes 1971, pp. 226–237; Calhoun 1975, pp. 26–63) but without really questioning Fortes because, like him, they considered lineages to be multifunctional units. To go further it will be necessary to separate land ownership from ritual activities (and more specifically, from the transmission of ancestral altars), and to isolate these two activities from judicial ones. It should be stressed,

[17] By definition, a maximal lineage is a lineage. In the case of levels below the maximal lineage, I specify: minimal lineage, intermediate lineage, etc.

however, that the tallensi ethnography, while very rich in some respects, suffers from an inexplicable paucity of information on these subjects, and I will have to make do with snippets of information to build hypothetical scenarios.

Fortes portrays the 'effective minimal lineage' as the 'agnatic core' of a residential group, the homestead (1949a, pp. 64–65). However, no activity uniquely and exclusively brings together this set of agnates who, for this reason, do not form a group (see definitions in Chapter 1). Moreover, the 'nuclear' lineages (or segments) into which the effective minimal lineages are supposed to aggregate seem to play an important role in land ownership and transmission. In my opinion, the effective minimal lineage is a fiction of Fortesian ethnography, and some agnates of the same homestead, those that Fortes identified as the 'nuclear lineage', form a corporation in matters of land ownership. Since only men are entitled to inherit land, and receive it from their male agnates, these corporations recruit through agnatic kinship and male sex.

Beyond the nuclear lineage, Fortes sees internal and medial segments. Since he has elsewhere confused these two levels, his commentators have concluded that only one level exists (Firth 1951, p. 158; Calhoun 1975, pp. 44–52). If the nuclear lineage is in fact a corporation in matters of land ownership, as I claim it is, it seems appropriate to follow the hypothetical transmission of land over a few generations (this scenario is based on the rather sparse information Fortes gives about land ownership; I had to omit ownership of livestock, of which Fortes says nothing)[18].

Let us start with an imaginary plot of land and its imaginary owner (see Figure 2). The first ancestor, 1, takes possession of land A, which he passes on undivided to his eldest son, 2. The latter divides the land equally between himself and his brothers but, on his

[18] The reality would be even more complicated if the Namoo formed corporations in the ownership of their altars, but the ethnography does not allow us to decide. Some altars, the *boxha* (sing. *boxhar*) lineage altars, are the exclusive property of some groups who appoint their guardian, or priest, thus constituting a corporation, but there are several other types of altars about which we know almost nothing.

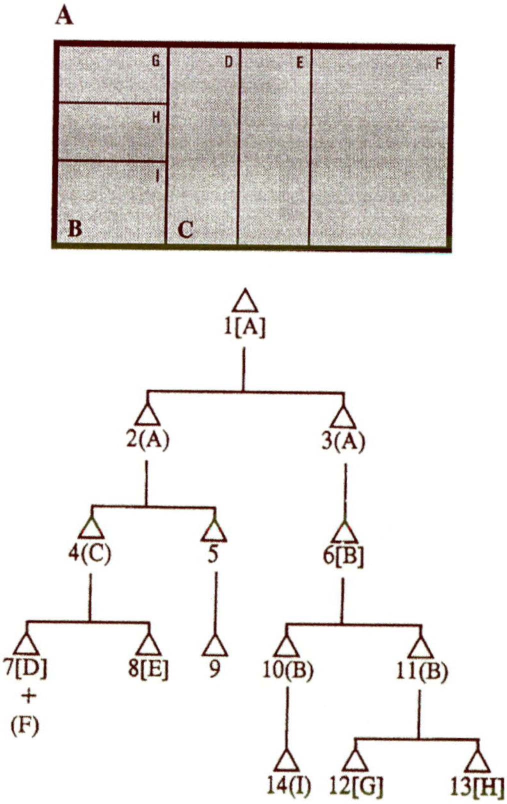

Legend: ( ) inherited land. [ ] ceded land

Figure 2. Hypothetical scenario of land transmission among the Namoo

death, these different shares are reunited and bequeathed to number 3 (all this is inferred from the rules of inheritance; Fortes 1949, pp. 158, 259). As the last survivor of his generation, 3 carves out a fragment of this patrimonial land and gives it to his son, for whom it becomes personal property (such plots are called *senseyar* – 1949, p. 205; on these carvings and donations, see 1949a, p. 158). A generation later this allotment, which I shall call B, becomes the patrimonial property of the agnatic descendants of number 6. The remainder (fraction C) goes to number 4. If numbers 5 and 6 die before him, 4 will have the right to amputate two more *senseyar* plots from the patrimonial land under his jurisdiction (the new plots D and E) for his sons 7 and 8. When 4 dies, the original patrimonial land, now reduced to portion F, passes to number 7, his eldest son.

Let us now turn to the fate of the new landholding B. Number 10 will inherit it undivided and pass it on to his brother, number 11. The last of his generation, 11 will snatch up two new plots (G and H), which he will give to his children, numbers 12 and 13, and this land will become the property of a corporation formed by the agnatic descendants of 12 and 13 a generation later. A different corporation will assemble the agnatic descendants of number 6 around what remains of the original patrimony (initially B, now I) and another corporation will congregate the agnatic descendants of number 1 (hence a group of greater genealogical depth and collateral extension) around what remains of the original patrimonial land (initially A, now F). The heirs to these parcels of land will *ipso facto* represent these corporations.

The demography and ecology are obviously imaginary. In reality, whole groups disappear and their lands are absorbed by collateral branches; some leave many sons behind, others take over new lands by clearing, while still others settle on the edge of Tallensi country while waiting to inherit, or die long before. However imaginary, this scenario highlights an important dimension of Namoo social organization since it illustrates how corporations of ever-increasing genealogical depth take shape around the ownership of these various patrimonial land parcels. The initial conditions of ownership and demography will of course vary for each corporation, and their genealogical depth and reciprocal articulation will vary accordingly, but we can nevertheless expect that this depth will rarely exceed G+5[19]. In short, everything suggests that we are dealing with minimal agnatic corporations (from which women are excluded) aggregated into more inclusive ones through agnatic descent. For example, individuals 12, 13 and 14 belong to a corporation I by virtue of their agnatic kinship with individual

[19] All genealogical references will be by 'group calculus', unless otherwise stated.

number 6 (located in G+2), while belonging to a more inclusive corporation owning plot F, by virtue of their agnatic connection with ancestor 1 (in G+4). In this scenario, minimal corporations (Fortes' nuclear lineage, defined in G+1) merge into what we might call 'aggregated corporations' on the basis of agnatic descent. Some demographic conditions could give rise to an intermediate level of aggregation between the minimal and maximal corporations, but I doubt that such circumstances are frequent.

This idea of an 'aggregated corporation' gets more complicated as soon as we take the type of property into account. In the case of land, it seems likely that the corporation's representative also had some judicial powers in the case of disputes, and was responsible for the allocation and management of allotments, although Fortes says nothing about this (he remains silent on the whole arbitration process). Among the Namoo, whoever inherits the plot of land may also inherit the altar of the ancestor associated with that plot, a religious responsibility that perhaps sanctions his judicial powers in matters of land ownership. Fortes is equally silent on this point, and also provides no details on the transmission of ancestral altars down the generations. It is therefore impossible for me to consider the link between the transmission of land (and hence the formation of corporations in matters of land ownership) and the arbitration of land disputes, on the one hand, and the transmission of altars (and hence the formation of corporations in matters of religious ownership, as well as the formation of cult groups), on the other.

The ethnography's omissions on these topics seriously hinders any operationalization, but the mere distinction between land ownership and religious ownership, on the one hand, and between religious ownership and cult activities, on the other, allows me to rethink this intermediate hierarchy of lineage segments that has dumbfounded Fortes' commentators, and with good reason. For, above the nuclear lineage Fortes detached an internal lineage from a medial one, only to add that "a lineage which functions as an internal lineage in one situation may be treated as a medial lineage in another" (1949a, p. 10). Firth concluded without hesitation that if by their functions and forms the different levels of lineage segments tend to blur, it would be better to abandon such terminology (Firth 1951b, p. 158). Calhoun expressed the same unease (1975, pp. 44-45), noting that the critical zone where genealogical amnesia and the telescoping of generations reorganize segments (1945, pp. 32, 35; 1944, p. 367) is located precisely at this segment's level, both internal and medial (Calhoun 1975, p. 367). Would it not be simpler, wrote Calhoun, to abolish this distinction between internal and medial segments (or lineages) and replace it with a more vague and general category of 'intermediate segment'?

If only the problem boiled down to a question of language! The problem is that of all ethnography, stemming from this fundamental inability to extract, disentangle and disengage the various types of interlocking groups, so deeply linked that they give the illusion of a multifunctional segment. To see through the fog of internal and medial segments, let us go back to the ethnography itself. The internal lineage is what Fortes called the 'narrow *dug*' in the first monograph (p. 203) and simply *dug* in the second (1949). What is this *dug*? When speaking of the homestead, *dug* refers to the wife's quarters. In terms of lineage, moreover, the *dug* manifests itself as the first level of grouping associated with what Fortes calls a 'lineage *boxhar*' (1949, p. 111). If we can elucidate the events that precipitate the creation of a new *boxhar*, and thus trigger the foundation of a new *dug*, we will be in a better position to grasp the dynamics of its formation.

Since *dug* is linked to ancestral altars, Yin altars suggest an analogy that will help my examination of *boxhar* (on Yin altars, see 1949a, pp. 154, 227–230; 1959, pp. 36, 41–52). Every male Tallensi is born under the spiritual protection of a Good Destiny (Yin), who must ensure that his protégé will reach maturity and even survive into old age, making him an elder. The young boy learns early on the identity of his Good Destiny, but does not erect an altar to her until she has shown her benevolence. He builds his first altar to her in his wife's apartments (her *dug*) and later removes it to another location, still within his homestead (*yir*). It is only after his death that his son moves this altar outside his father's homestead, at the entrance to be precise. These various locations reflect the man's progress through his life cycle, from childless married son to father and, finally, grandfather with grandchildren. In other words, the itinerary followed by the Yin in the homestead describes the demographic itinerary of the individual in his quest for physical and social reproduction. The Tallensi's Yin, for the lay observer, is nothing other than his Good Demographic Destiny (or Reproductive Success).

What applies to the living also applies to the dead. Every Namoo aspires to become not just a grandfather, but an ancestor – in other words, a true spiritual personality that generations of prolific descendants will recognize, guaranteeing his immortality in return. There is thus a 'death cycle'... from the deceased to the ancestor, culminating in his near-immortality (only 'near' since, demographically speaking, immortality is never an accomplished fact!). I believe that when a deceased man has proved his Demographic Good Fortune by climbing the ladder of generations, always followed by numerous offspring, his descendants hasten his accession to ancestor status, claiming the right to erect a *boxhar* altar for him – the lineage equivalent of the living individual's Yin altar. Based on Fortes' texts, four to six generations of reproductive success would appear to be necessary for an ancestor to pass the test of near-immortality that guarantees his right to a *boxhar*[20], his right to become a full ancestor. The more numerous his descendants, the more they will make their weight felt in lineage affairs, and the greater the urgency with which others will have to recognize this growing political influence (1949a, p. 329). But demographic factors are not the only ones at work; economic and ecological ones also operate, bringing us directly back to the question of land ownership.

As land ownership moves down the generations, it sometimes divides and subdivides to such an extent that nothing, or almost

[20] Although Fortes asserts that internal lineages only reproduce every three or four generations (1949, p. 330), his own genealogies rather support my thesis, since all the internal lineages described are descended from an eponymous ancestor placed at G+5 or G+6 (1945, p. 206; 1949, p. 152). What is not clear from his genealogies, however, is whether these generations include the living ones. If they do, we are probably talking about G+4 at the maximum.

nothing, remains of the original patrimonial land around which the most inclusive corporations were defined (those built around ancestors located at G+5). This is the inescapable fate of owners who proliferate and leave behind many generations of heirs. The corporation that increases in number over the generations sees its patrimonial land shrink proportionately; at this point of convergence between ecology and demography, at this crossroads where the multitude of survivors heralds the disappearance of the original patrimony, the 'maximal corporation', so to speak, loses its raison d'être. It is at this point, I believe, that a corporation losing the support of ownership reasserts its identity in another way, through the creation of a *boxhar* that makes it live on and proclaims its distinct identity through ritual ownership.

However, the events culminating in the decision to found a *boxhar* cannot be explained simply in terms of land ownership. It is likely to occur after there is little or no patrimonial land left to own and therefore to pass on; it is also a demographic and political event (the great number of members supporting their influence and claims) and it is also an event intimately intertwined with ritual activities and altar ownership. Once again, Fortes' silence confines me to generalities.

Namoo forefathers protect and help all their cognatic descendants, who in turn worship them through 'domestic' cults. Although their altars are passed down from father to son, any cognatic descendant can join the congregation present at the sacrifices during these domestic rituals. Yet it is these same ancestors, whose spiritual influence extends and branches out through all the cognatic lines of their posterity, who also serve to aggregate agnatic ritual groups through the action of agnatic descent when they are 'ancestralized', so to speak, that is, when the ordinary altar dedicated to their cult is promoted to the status of *boxhar*. From that moment on, they become spiritually split, and their altar, always the site of domestic cults open to all their cognatic posterity, suddenly becomes the site of esoteric rites restricted to their agnatic descendants (Fortes uses no specific terminology to designate these exclusive cults; if they are not domestic, I will take my cue from Fortes himself, and call them 'political') (1949a, pp. 302, 321).

This interweaving of domestic and political cults creates a highly complex organization of agnatic ritual groups and agnatic religious property-owning corporations, both aggregated on the basis of agnatic descent in esoteric cults. In the case of domestic cults, on the other hand, cognatic 'spiritual categories' (delimited by the ancestor's field of spiritual influence) and cognatic 'ritual groups' (those who gather around domestic sacrifices to the ancestor) are paradoxically aggregated on the basis of agnatic descent. Let us take a closer look at this apparent anomaly.

Let us imagine an ancestor in G+2 important enough to rally cognatic cult groups around his domestic altar. Now, let us look at an ancestor in G+4: he will gather around his domestic altar cult groups that are also cognatic, but more inclusive this time, since they are spread over a greater number of generations, and by definition embrace a greater posterity. But note that we are not talking about just any ancestor in G+4; we are here speaking precisely about the agnatic grandfather of the ancestor in G+2. We therefore find ourselves in the presence of *cognatic* cult groups, but aggregated through *agnatic* descent – a paradox that Keesing was unable to identify, and which led him to see cognatic descent among the Tallensi because he mixed up groups' 'composition' and 'aggregation' (Keesing 1971). In reality, the only descent at work among the Tallensi is agnatic descent; it operates on agnatic cult groups in the context of sacrifices to the *boxhar*, but also aggregates cognatic cult groups during domestic sacrifices.

The way I see it, the transformation of a simple domestic altar into a *boxhar* can be interpreted as a claim to reproductive (and therefore social and political) success; yet the *dug* (which, it should be remembered, appears in Fortes' later texts as the first level of grouping that clusters around a *boxhar*) represents precisely the level of grouping that claims control over its own reproduction:

> "The *kpeem*'s [the *dug*'s representative] functions are most visible in relation to the wives and children of the lineage, for they stand for the greatest common interest of the lineage. It is

the *reproductive powers* of the wives and the existence of the children that secure the perpetuation of the lineage and the immortality of the ancestors" (1945, p. 229, italics added).

By themselves, as a distinct unit owing its existence to the ancestor's Good Demographic Destiny, the individuals whose ritual groups aggregate into a single *dug* claim control over their demographic destiny, control over their members' entry and exit. The Tallensi even claim that "one does not reproduce beyond the border of the [intermediate] lineage" (1949a, p. 147), a clear way of declaring that the *dug* (we will henceforth refer to it as the 'intermediate lineage', to use Calhoun's expression) is the largest autonomous group in terms of reproduction. It is within this intermediate lineage that sexual intercourse with 'sisters' is incestuous (beyond that, it escapes this prohibition), that adultery with agnates' wives is a heinous crime, and that remarriage of widows is practically compulsory if the widow is still fertile (1949a, pp. 111, 116, 123, 124, 153, 275–276). The same intermediate lineage is responsible for its members' marriage and funeral (1945, pp. 229–230; 1949a, pp. 208–220[21]). If the *dug* is an intermediate lineage associated with ancestral cults, at least four organizations intertwine: the first, strictly lineage-based, evolves around cult groups. A second, hitherto nameless, brings together cognatic cult groups through agnatic descent. Finally, the other two, organizations of minimal and aggregated corporations, are grafted onto land ownership and religious property.

With land and ancestors echoing each other, it is not surprising to find such an overlap between land ownership, altar ownership and ritual groups. The same individuals found in minimal and aggregated corporations in land matters are likely to be members of

[21] If the internal lineage (*dug*) claims control over its own reproduction, why does the *dug*'s elder play a purely nominal role (a ritual one) in matrimonial transactions? Quite simply because the Tallensi marry with their livestock, which is also individually owned. So it is the individual responsible for bride price payments who takes the most initiative in matrimonial transactions and related decisions. The eldest pays nothing, and is content with ritual intervention. As elsewhere, speaks who pays!...

the corporations formed around religious property, and will also be found in the intermediate lineages formed around the *boxhar*. What's more, the same elder who represents the minimal and aggregated corporations in land or religious ownership will possibly represent the minimal or aggregated ritual group (the lineage proper) which, once again, explains the confusion of an ethnography for which groups are multifunctional.

But the sources of confusion do not stop here. The same title-holder may be a proxy in all four organizations (representative of corporations in matters of land and religious property, and priest of an ancestral altar), but he may be so in relation to different ancestors. Let me explain. I believe that only after a 'maximal' corporation can no longer exist as a corporation (having no more patrimonial land to own), and would therefore be on the verge of fragmenting, that the corporations that compose it gather around a *boxhar* which they dedicate to their common ancestor, thus creating a political cult group. Under certain demographic conditions, the person who inherited the altar from the father of individual number 1 in our previous diagram (see Figure 2) and who would *ipso facto* become the priest of his *boxhar*, could also find himself at the head of a corporation formed around land originally acquired by the son of individual 1. In conclusion, one and the same elder could act on behalf of a corporation aggregated in relation to an ancestor in G+3, and also officiate at rituals on behalf of an agnatic descent group aggregated in G+4 or G+5, and provoke precisely the kind of situation that confused Fortes and worried his commentators when he asserted that "a lineage which functions as an inner lineage in one situation may be treated as a medial lineage in another" (1949a, p. 10). The many confusions and contradictions of Fortesian ethnography vanish as soon as we analytically disentangle the many facets of Namoo practice (ownership and transmission of land, ownership and transmission of altars, as well as ritual activities relating to altars).

This operational translation also accounts for the fact that new intermediate lineages (the *duget*, sing. *dug)* are not created from below, so to speak, as if new segments were bifurcating ceaselessly over the generations, as Fortes (pp. 198, 206) would have it, but rather from above, as Calhoun suggested, because the consecration of a new *boxhar* cannot be a spontaneous, automatic event. I rather perceive it as a long, slow process in which individuals and communities presumably reassess their relationships to collateral branches and possibly reinterpret their genealogical connections in the higher generations where manipulations and deformations are easiest to achieve. It cannot be any other way, as the individuals who aim to transform their forefather's altar into a *boxhar* are already within a descent group aggregated around an existing *boxhar.* They must therefore reinterpret the genealogical position of the forefather they wish to consecrate in relation to the ancestor whose *boxhar* they have hitherto worshipped. This reinterpretation calls for manipulations and genealogical distortions that may explain why an intermediate zone of confusion lies between the minimal groups and the maximal lineage. Confusion that is not confined to the intermediate lineage, unfortunately, since in addition to the four organizations already identified, and that wrap so intimately around each other, there is a fifth one that cuts across the first two and asserts itself in the context of some judicial activities that the ethnography has failed to describe in detail.

Again, this neglect is excusable when one considers (1) that some disputes relating to land probably fell under the jurisdiction of representatives of land-owning corporations, (2) that some disputes called for ritual arbitration and, (3) that still other quarrels were likely to require neither land nor ritual justice. When we consider that these conflicts, which we might call residual, and their arbitration give rise to a fifth organization; when we think that the same *kpeem* at the head of the minimal or aggregated corporations and the minimal or aggregated ritual groups, also head these judicial groups, and that most of the individuals who had to appeal to their 'residual' justice also fell under their power in matters of ritual and land ownership, confusion was inevitable. Of this confusion and fifth organization we find irrefutable proof when Fortes discusses the upper echelons of what he calls the Namoo lineage hierarchy (pp. 192, 98) and more specifically when he refers to *Lebhtiis yidem* as a medial lineage, i.e. a Puhug *dug*.

Puhug is a district, or section of Tongo (the *yizug* mentioned above); this Tongo which, in Fortes' time was the most populous market town, the administrative capital of Tallensi country and the seat of the pre-eminent Namoo chiefdom. Fortes describes Puhug as a *dug* of Tongo (p. 203), which leads him to proclaim that medial lineages (such as *Lebhtiis yidem*) merge into sections (such as Puhug; p. 205) and that sections amalgamate into a maximal lineage (all Mosuor descendants domiciled in Tongo). Here, Fortes ignored his own definitions. Tongo's sections are clearly neighbourhoods that bring together affines (wives and consanguines of wives), cognates and individuals who are neither cognates nor affines; they are not groups that recruit on the basis of agnatic descent (Fortesian definition of lineage), so they cannot, in Fortes' own conceptual framework, be lineages. What exactly are these sections (*yizuget*, sing. *yizug*)? Fortes confesses that in a 'compound clan' males from the same maximum lineage would tend to reside in the same neighbourhood, or section (*yizug*) of a locality (*teng*) (pp. 166, 205). These sections propel us into a different type of organization, one that we must at all costs separate from the land and ritual organizations we have just outlined.

It is neither property nor ritual that brings together the groups of this fifth organization (the *yizuget* and *tes* sing. *teng*, i.e. neighbourhoods and localities), and descent is not what aggregates them. They emerge in the context of specifically judicial activities and, in the exercise of this justice, the homestead (*yir*) appears as the minimal group since its head, the homestead's representative, seems to have the power to arbitrate disputes considered internal. Rattray says this explicitly about the Gurunsi, ethnic neighbours so close to the Tallensi that they are easily confused, even according to Fortes, and who have a political organization almost identical to that of the Tallensi (Rattray 1932, p. 261). As minimal judicial groups, it is the homesteads, and not the lineage segments, that are aggregated into sections under the leadership of a representative, the *yizug kpeem* (p. 212), in the exercise of this residual justice. Like the homestead representative, the *yizug kpeem* accedes to his position according to specific criteria of eligibility (these criteria are the same that dictate accession to the title of representative of aggregated groups and corporations) and can arbitrate on behalf of the group he represents.

The Namoo sections are further aggregated into a higher level, the *teng*[22], represented by its chief, the *Na'ab*, also appointed according to specific criteria and endowed with the power of judicial intervention. We are talking here about the 'aggregation' of homesteads into sections, and of sections into a *teng*, no longer through agnatic descent but through *territoriality*. We clearly discern among the Namoo what I call a territorial organization, i.e. a set of minimal groups aggregated into more inclusive ones through territoriality, an organization that only partially overlaps with lineage and corporations since it includes affines, consanguines who are neither affines nor agnates, as well as individuals who, linked neither by blood nor marriage, are simply domiciled in a homestead. What is more, although the lineage elders *(kpeem)* and corporation representatives are simultaneously heads of homesteads and sections, there is one major exception: the 'chief' (*na'ab*), representative of the territorial group encompassing localities in this judicial framework, stands outside any lineage organization, genealogical reference or land ownership. He owes his title to his political talents; the *na'ab* is the most politically astute individual, the one who manages to convince others to choose him as leader and who receives the ultimate sanction of his title from the Supreme Chief of Mampurugu, capital of the Mamprusi kingdom located to the south of Tallensi country. Unable to detect any aggregation beyond the Namoo *teng*, I conclude that it is the sovereign political group.

By dissociating land ownership from some activities (here, ritual and arbitration), we see Namoo social organization in a radically different light (see Table 2). Where Fortes discovered a long hierarchy of lineage segments organizing relations between local groups, I perceive at least five different organizations wrapped up together, four using agnatic descent to aggregate either groups

[22] From the point of view of the occupation of space, *teng* is a local group, but from the point of view of its judicial activities, it is a territorial group.

or corporations, and the fifth using territoriality as an element of aggregation. And where he sees segmentation, I do not.

Evans-Pritchard's lineage interpretation of the Nuer was a late development, and Fortes' representation of a long hierarchy of lineage segments cannot be found in his earliest publications either. His earliest writings do not mention this multiple nesting of lineage segments, but only 'clans' (which he later called 'clan settlements', or 'clan localities' – 1970, p. 147), lineages (*yir*; these lineages would become the maximal lineages of his later ethnography – incidentally there is no Tale word to designate lineages but only *yir* – house)) and 'sub-lineages' (the famous *duget*, sing. *dug*) (1936, pp. 239–240). In 1936, *dug* and *yir* stood as the only two tiers of what would later become the famous lineage 'segmentation'[23].

Finally, Fortes spent most of his fieldwork in Tongo itself, and his ethnographic testimony narrates the social organization of this Namoo capital. Was it representative of the Namoo country? Despite the peculiarities of this large town, I believe Fortes when

[23] In a text on the Nankansi (Gurunsi), close neighbours of the Tallensi in terms of geography and social organization, Rattray also read three levels in the organization of localities: the *yizuo* (*yizug* in the Talne language), the *deo* (*dug* in the Talne language) and So-and-so' *bisi* (*biis* in the Talne language) (Rattray 1932, pp. 243–246).

Moreover, it is no coincidence that we find different terms at each level of aggregation. Minimum lineages aggregate into intermediate ones (*dug*), intermediate ones into maximal lineages (*yir*) among the Namoo. In another context, concessions (*yir*) aggregate into sections (*yizug*) and sections into a *teng*. Fortes notes that no indigenous concept corresponds to what he calls the clan. The Tallensi speak of the clan in terms of sibling ties between maximal lineages, or ritual collaboration, or simple ties emanating from geographical proximity, but the resulting entity is never identified by a specific concept. In itself, this fact seems worthy of note since, in my opinion, there is no aggregation into a clan among the Namoo or the Tali.

Another fact is worth mentioning, although it is more a matter of research than demonstration. It turns out that where we do find real aggregation, it doesn't take place over several levels, as ethnographers of segmentary lineages would have us believe. The Namoo's complex lineages only have three levels. Analysis may reveal that groups cannot aggregate by descent on several levels, and that a tripartite aggregation (minimal, intermediate and maximal lineage) is among the most complex.

Table 2. Fortes' and operational sequences compared

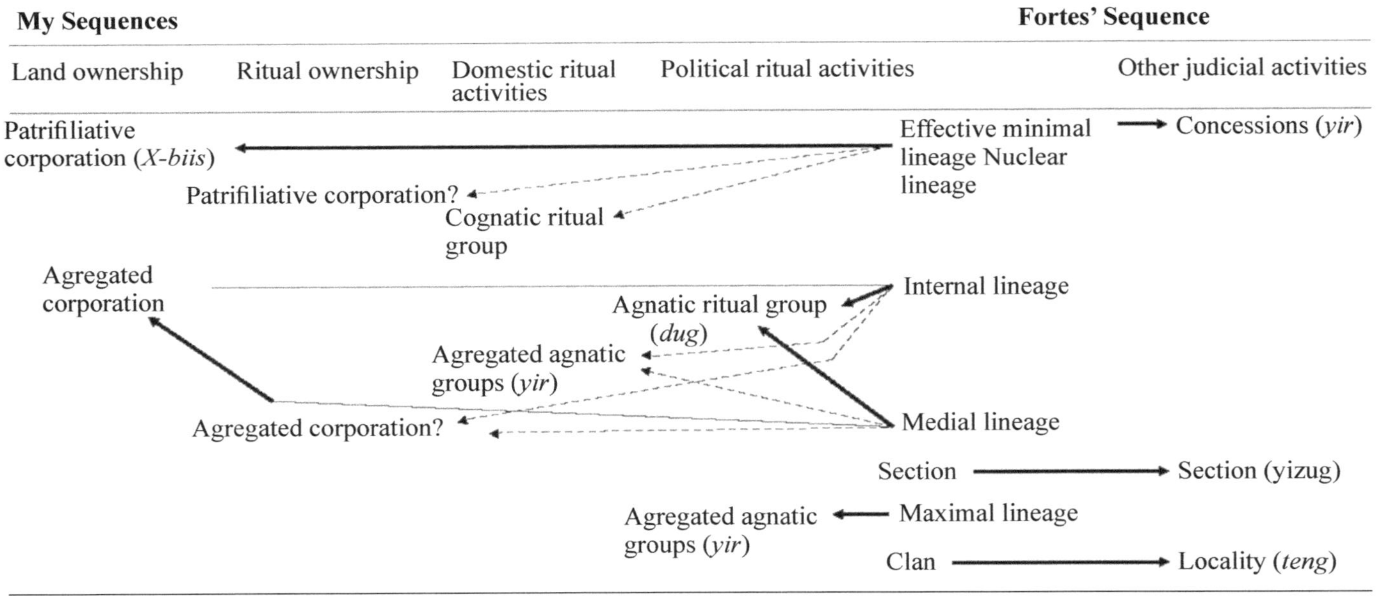
My Sequences
Fortes' Sequence
Land ownership
Ritual ownership
Domestic ritual activities
Political ritual activities
Other judicial activities
Patrifiliative corporation (*X-biis*)
Effective minimal lineage Nuclear lineage
Concessions (*yir*)
Patrifiliative corporation?
Cognatic ritual group
Agregated corporation
Internal lineage
Agnatic ritual group (*dug*)
Agregated agnatic groups (*yir*)
Agregated corporation?
Medial lineage
Section
Section (yizug)
Agregated agnatic groups (*yir*)
Maximal lineage
Clan
Locality (*teng*)

Legend: The groups followed by a question mark are those that the ethnography does not allow us to clearly detect but that, in all logic, could exist.

The solid lines represent the 'translations' that I am relatively sure of and the dotted lines those translations that the ethnography does not enable us to establish with certainty.

he affirms this, but I protest vehemently when he uses the Namoo social organization as a paradigm for the Tali one.

2. Tali social organization

The Namoo lineages that provide the framework for ritual activities unfold over three 'levels', or tiers, and presuppose a linear genealogical memory spanning a few generations. A particular ancestor cult underpins this memory. The Namoo bury their dead near their homesteads, build altars to remind them of the exact location of the graves, and remember the names of their agnatic forebears and ancestors over several generations (p. 184). Namoo lineages and their three levels of nesting are based on the worship of individual, named ancestors[24]. The Tali, on the other hand, bury their dead in collective cemeteries and do not remember their ancestors' names over so many generations (p. 184). If lineages stretch with genealogical memory, they contract in its absence. Logically, if the Tali can hardly remember the names of their great-grandfathers, their lineages should not be spread over several levels. Supposing this, I deny that the Namoo lineage organization can be used to understand the Tali one. Unfortunately, Fortes' ethnography does little to help us in this task, since it postulates a fundamental similarity between Namoo and Tali, so that I will have to accumulate indirect evidence in support of my thesis, all of which nevertheless points in the same direction.

In short, if there is an intermediate level between the Namoo minimal lineage and the maximal one, thus creating this tripartite nesting (or double aggregation), and since I doubt this is the case with the Tali, we should find lineages without an intermediate level among the latter. Their minimal groups should be aggregated into a more inclusive one, the aggregation not going any further. In short, Tali lineages should have only two levels (minimal lineages

[24] The Namoo also worship collective ancestors, but they form the residual category of forebears who have failed their 'death cycle' and never made it to ancestor (pp. 208–209, 215).

aggregated directly into maximal ones), so that a maximal Tali lineage should correspond to an intermediate Namoo one (*dug*). How can I demonstrate this? Let us look at a few facts that support this thesis.

1) Among the Namoo, it sometimes happens that the intermediate lineage (the *dug*) owns a residue of patrimonial land, either because collateral branches within the *dug* have disappeared, or because the original land has not been completely wiped out by progressive subdivisions (p. 178). Translated in my language, this means that *boxhar* priests would also act on behalf of a corporation in matters of land ownership, a corporation encompassing the male agnatic posterity of the *boxhar*-titled ancestor. As for the maximal Namoo lineage, it never owns land. Among the Tali, on the other hand, some plots of land are quite often attached to the title of *tendaana*, priest of the land and elder of the maximal lineage (1949a, p. 159), a fact which strongly suggests that a Tali maximal lineage is the equivalent of a Namoo intermediate one. Other elements point in the same direction.

2) Among the Namoo, the elder of the intermediate lineage is the one who receives the placatory gifts that initiate matrimonial transactions (1949a, pp. 208–209). Speaking of the special ties between Gundaat and Tambok, two Tali localities, Fortes further observes: "When the placation gift is sent for a bride from one of these units, the live cock which forms part of it is always presented to the head of the other. *This reciprocal privilege is usually confined to the component lineages of a single clan*" (p. 96, italics added). However, according to Fortes himself, lineages that make up the same clan are by definition maximal lineages, so that the head of a maximal Tali lineage receives the gifts that are addressed to the head of an intermediate Namoo one. Maximal Tali lineages therefore act like Namoo *duget* (intermediate lineages) in matters of land ownership and marriage.

3) The size of Tali lineage segments reinforces this impression. In Gundaat, Fortes relates that “the maximal lineage [...] is not subdivided into ritually and jurally differentiated major segments” (p. 202), an absurd statement if one assumes this Gundaat maximal lineage (hence Tali) superior to a Namoo ‘nuclear lineage’, since there is nothing comparable in Namoo ethnography. In Soog (another Tali *teng*), “one of the component maximal lineages of the clan comprises two major segments which function as medial lineages in corporate affairs […] When Sebeg, the head of one of these segments, died, the most senior eldest remaining member of this unit was his eighteen-year-old son [...]” (1949a, p. 150). If this segment were an intermediate lineage, as Fortes claims, it would have very few children whereas among the Namoo “numerically *Nodegher yir* [an intermediate lineage] is exceptionally small, for it has only eleven male members. The other segments have between twenty and thirty male members each, counting infants as well” (p. 197). If on the other hand we consider this segment of Soog a nuclear lineage, its small size is not exceptional. In general, there is no mention of very small groups among the Namoo, to whom both monographs are dedicated. By contrast, amid the rare, scattered and patchy fragments about the Tali, two mention extremely small maximal lineages or lineage segments. Could it be due to sampling hazard? I doubt it. I find it more plausible to see this smaller size as proof that Tali maximal lineages do not span three levels. While Namoo lineages appear complex (multi-level), Tali lineages are simple (a single level of aggregation). I consider that minimal Tali lineages are aggregated directly into a maximal lineage without any intermediate level. Hence their small size, which is reflected in the size of the localities. The smallest of Tongo’s four sections has no fewer than 400 inhabitants. Fortes does not mention the size of the Tali settlements but from the map he shows (p. 109 – where Tenzugu alone has no fewer than six settlements – pp. 166-167), there are at least ten settlements for a population of 2,000

(1949, p. 185), thus averaging 200 inhabitants per settlement, equivalent to half the size of the *smallest* Namoo settlement.

The network of so-called clan ties also supports my hypothesis. To Fortes, the Namoo clan organization forms an 'open system' (p. 44) but, if by clan we understand 'a level of aggregation above the maximal lineage based on real or putative descent' following my distinction between aggregation and alliance, then the Namoo have no clan since no descent amalgamates their maximal lineages in a more inclusive level of grouping. The Namoo maximal lineages may have appeared aggregated because of their partial localization in the section and of the *territorial* aggregation of sections in a single *teng*. This is the illusion of an ethnography that does not dissociate the lineage organization from the territorial one and Fortes, going back a thousand times over his definitions, confesses that "the clan [...] is a local unit occupying a specified locality, from which it gets its name" (p. 62). Looking at it more closely, the so-called Namoo clans are nothing but networks of alliances between maximal lineages (alliances described in terms of *sunzop*, or siblingship ties – p. 84) and the sharp differences between Namoo and Tali networks confirm my hypothesis.

4) Namoo localities are made up of authentic maximal lineages, to which accessory lineages are attached. The male members of the minimal groups merged into authentic lineages reside for the most part in a section (*yizug*) aggregated into a *teng* through territoriality and represented by the *na'ab*. Leaving aside accessory lineages and bonds between the four branches of Mosuor's children, authentic Namoo lineages have almost no *sunzop* links outside their *teng*. Whatever Fortes may say, the Namoo *tes* (sing. *teng*) are strongly inward-looking, and their authentic lineages have formed very few alliances other than those linking them to accessory lineages. The Hill Tali localities, on the other hand (those we have so far called simply Tali) are completely open. Fortes did not sketch the tangled knot of alliances that bind the Hill Tali, but he did leave us an outline of

this translocal entanglement among the Plains Tali (see Figure 1). This tangle is even greater among their hill neighbours and reveals a powerful contrast between the almost closed Namoo localities and the almost completely open Hill Tali ones.

This difference in local groups' openness between the two ethnic groups shows a deeper divergence between the two types of localities. I have no reason to believe that Tali sections are aggregated into a *teng* through territoriality, and there is no evidence that homesteads are aggregated into a section either. It could be that there was no territorial organization whatsoever among the Tali; if so, the maximal lineages would then emerge as sovereign groups. Beyond the Tali maximal lineages aggregation ceases and alliances begin, ritual alliances so dense, luxuriant and complex that they embrace the hills, the plains and their surroundings.

5) Also remarkable is the fact that accessory lineages are numerous among the Namoo and virtually absent among the Hill Tali (not to be confused with the Plains Tali, among whom accessory lineages are also many), a dissimilarity that may be explained by ancestor worship. If complex Namoo lineages rely on the cult of individual ancestors whose names are remembered for several generations, and if Tali lineages have no such cult, it affects the assimilation of immigrants. An immigrant to Tale country receives land. The descendants of these immigrants, if they decide to settle where their parents or forebears lived, will face three possible situations: either their numbers or a favourable political situation will enable them to aggregate into an independent maximal lineage. Or one of the autochthonous maximal lineages will absorb them completely. Or they will remain clients of one of the native lineages, as an accessory lineage, to use Fortes' terminology.

However, it seems that the type of genealogical memory, as well as its social use, will largely determine the most likely scenario. If individual ancestors are worshipped and remembered as distinct personalities over many generations, it will be very difficult to assimilate the descendants of an immigrant, who will retain an accessory status. If, on the other hand, all genealogical memory is lost after two or three generations, and the ancestors are then merged into an anonymous collectivity, as the Hill Tali do, the immigrants' descendants will quickly lose their accessory status and will either be assimilated, or recognized as an independent lineage, depending on demographic, ecological and political circumstances; hence the scarcity of accessory lineages on the hills.

For the same reasons, Namoo immigrants would remember their genealogical links much longer, to safeguard their connection with the Mamprusi kingdom and preserve their cultural identity vis-à-vis the Tali (Fortes, personal communication), as the existence of *Mosuor biis*, this mega-lineage of 'Mosuor's children' testifies. Don't the four Namoo localities all identify themselves as descendants from Mosuor, which I place in G+8 in an Ego calculus? The great-grandchildren of a Tali immigrant, on the other hand, would have completely lost the memory of the genealogical relationships linking his forebears to the locality where he settled, and they would compensate for this genealogical amnesia by multiplying ritual alliances, *sunzot* links to the original locality. The Namoo thus express their alliances through genealogy, through the addition of immigrants in accessory relationships, and through the memory of a common ancestry between authentic lineages and even localities, while the Tali, unconcerned with a deep genealogical memory, translate their alliances through rituals.

In short, the type of genealogy and the way it is used seem to shape alliances because, in the final analysis, they modify the way lineages organize and reproduce themselves. Long Namoo genealogies and their political and ritual relevance hinder the splitting and reproduction of maximal lineages, which consequently have to 'segment' from within (i.e. they have to reshuffle their internal relationships and create new intermediate lineages, or *duget*, as I analysed earlier), thus giving rise to multi-level lineages, with an intermediate level of aggregation. These multi-level lineages can easily graft immigrant groups as accessory lineages, but they only manage to absorb them with the greatest reluctance, and find it extremely difficult to recognize them as authentic maximal lineages. If immigrant groups in Namoo country are ultimately assimilated or promoted to the rank of authentic lineages – if this is possible at all – it can only be after several generations. In the final analysis, authentic Namoo lineages are complex and very large, like their localities, which are much more self-sufficient and inward-looking than Tali ones, in that the only alliances they form are genealogical ones.

Within maximal Tali lineages, on the other hand, there is no intermediate level (*dug*). I believe that maximal Tali lineages are unable to segment from within; when one of their minimal lineages reproduces much faster than its collateral ones, I believe it breaks away. The breakup would not be instantaneous, of course; it would be relatively slow but would take place at a considerably faster rate than the splitting of Namoo maximal lineages, if the latter is even possible[25]. Without an intermediate level of aggregation, the Tali simpler lineages are considerably smaller than Namoo ones, and their localities remarkably less populous. Finally, this dynamic of lineage reproduction would explain why Tali lineages do not easily

---

[25] The following quotation indirectly alludes to the process of maximum lineage formation among the Mountain Tali: "At Soog, one of the component maximum lineages of the clan comprises two segments which function as medial lineages in corporate affairs. Each of these segments is represented by its head at ceremonies at the External *Boxhar* of Soog" (1949, p. 150).

I have already suggested that these so-called major segments are presumably only minimal ritual groups and possibly mere corporations (although it is absolutely impossible to disentangle the question of religious ownership from land ownership among the Hill Tali from the known facts). If this assumption is true, we should expect that minimal lineages that grow faster will start asserting their distinct identity, not by creating a new intermediate lineage (*dug*) within the maximal one, but by almost breaking off from the maximal lineage in which they are aggregated to participate directly in the most important initiation cults as quasi-autonomous groups represented by their own head. Logically, the next stage should have been the creation of a new *tendaana* title and a separate *dugni boxhar*. Unfortunately, Professor Fortes was unable to observe this phenomenon due to the length of his fieldwork.

link immigrant groups as accessory branches; they either absorb them or rapidly give them their independence.

There are too many dissimilarities between the Namoo and Tali social organizations (see Table 3) to accept Fortes' conclusions. Namoo social organization cannot serve as a paradigm to understand the Tali one. We are dealing with different societies, as an ethnologist who has worked among the Tallensi since Fortes already noted:

> "The division between the Namoo (with their *large, expanding, unitary descent groups*) and the 'true' Tallensi [Hill Tali] (with their *small, maximal lineages of shortened generational depth)* almost never enters the analysis [...] It should be remembered, however, that the bulk of Fortes' ethnography relates to the colonial period and to the Tongo Namoo, among whom he did almost all his fieldwork" (Hart 1974, pp. 12–13, italics added).

In reality, things are even more complex, since between the Namoo and the Hill Tali lie the Plains Tali who, geographically halfway between the two, represent a mid-way organizational formula. They share the funeral customs of their Tali cousins, but bury their dead near their homesteads like the Namoo (p. 220). They have accessory lineages that nevertheless function as independent maximal ones (for Zubiung, see pp. 84–85; for Baari, see pp. 88–89). Most do not worship the Outer *Boxhar* (1970, p. 157) but Ba'at Da'a, a most powerful altar of the land. More importantly, they are the real natives! All but one of the most antiquated land-related titles are associated with Plains Tali localities (pp. 22–23), and the Hill Tali call themselves immigrants!

Why are there are so many differences between the Namoo and the Hill Tali? Almost all the elements of an answer elude us, but Fortes nevertheless provides a major clue:

> "In clans that have the chiefship (*naditib*), the natives explain, the most important thing is for every man to be able to show exactly how he is connected by descent with

Table 3. Differences between Namoo and Hill Tali social organizations

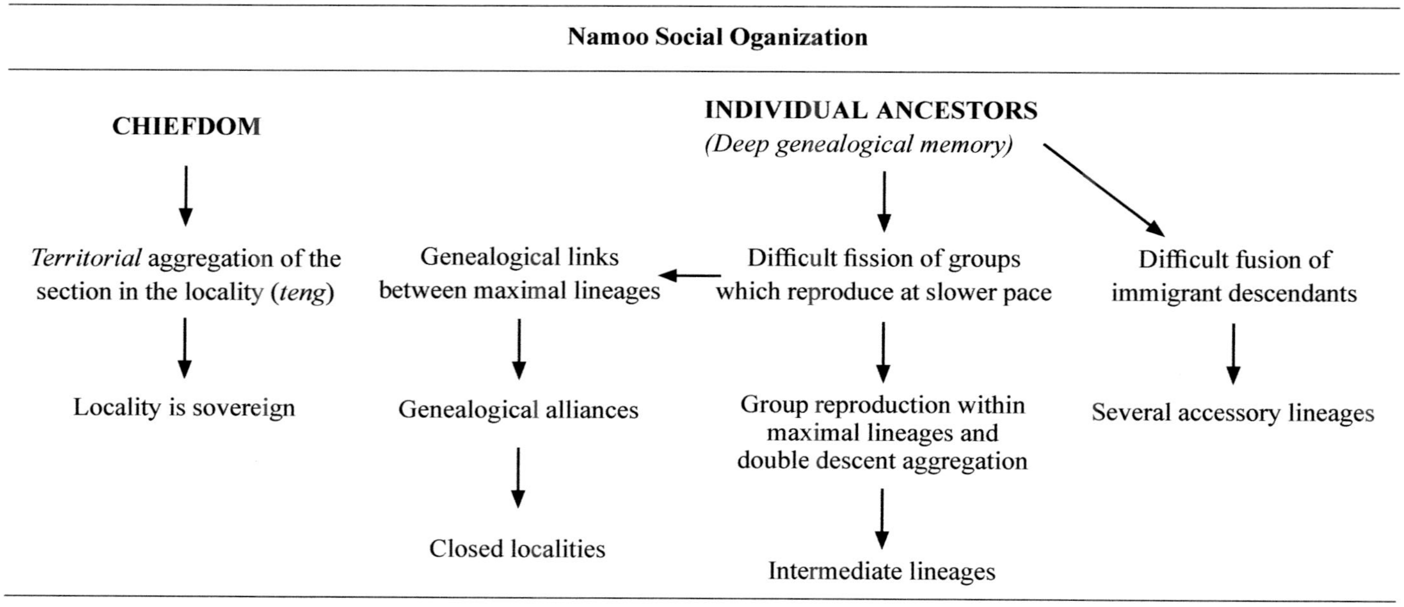

Hill Tali Social Organization

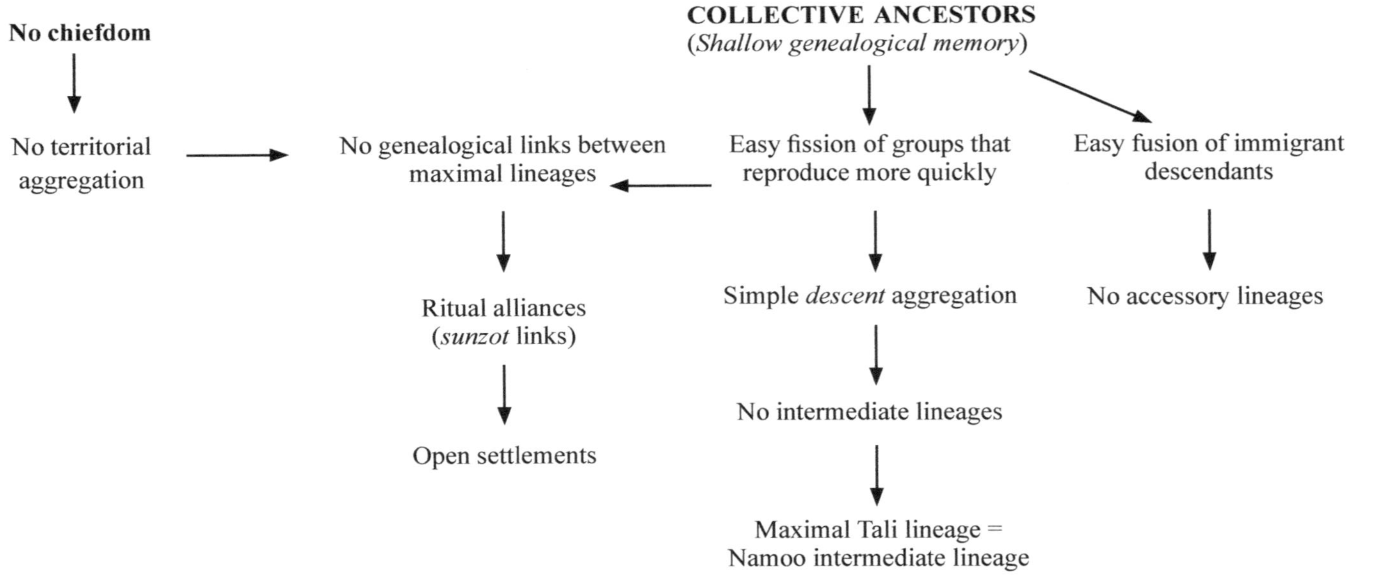

No chiefdom
No territorial aggregation
No genealogical links between maximal lineages
Ritual alliances (*sunzot* links)
Open settlements
COLLECTIVE ANCESTORS
(*Shallow genealogical memory*)
Easy fission of groups that reproduce more quickly
Simple *descent* aggregation
No intermediate lineages
Maximal Tali lineage = Namoo intermediate lineage
Easy fusion of immigrant descendants
No accessory lineages

> previous holders of the chiefship; whereas in the *tendaanatib* clans [*tendaana* localities], this is unimportant as all the members of the clan have the same ritual bonds with the Earth" (p. 184).

Chiefship, and the Namoo desire to preserve links with the Mamprusi kingdom, would therefore explain this elaborate cult of individual and named ancestors, and the complex lineages associated with it. Without a chiefdom, the Hill Tali are happy with fewer ancestors, and collective ones at that. As mountain refugees, the Hill Tali must remain open to immigration and the easy absorption of new refugees, but closed enough to form a common front against their enemies, the Namoo (and presumably the populations involved in the slave trade). They remained open to refugees and united in defence through a tangled network of ritual alliances, and through their collective ancestor cult, the Outer *Boxhar*, which admirably facilitated the integration of new immigrants while defining a Tali identity through its initiation rites.

CHAPTER FOUR

Translating the Tiv ethnography[26]

The Bohannan segmentary model[27]

Settled in the central provinces of Nigeria, the Tiv claimed to be descended from Tiv, the eponymous ancestor whose name they proudly bear. Almost all were farmers when studied, fiercely independent and egalitarian like the Nuer and, like them, constantly expanding their territory in this savannah country whose southern part was still quite wooded in the late 40s, and whose population numbered around 800,000. A politically acephalous society, supposedly balanced according to the same Nuer or Tallensi segmentary plan.

Like the Tallensi, the Tiv live in homesteads (*ya*, plural *uya*), domestic compounds where residence after marriage was ideally patrivirilocal; this made them 'extended families', grouping together in the same dwelling a man, his wives, all his unmarried children, as well as his married sons with their wives and children. In reality, approximately 80% of a concession's members were agnates.

The compound's eldest member, the *or u ya*, heads and manages it. Master of the spiritual powers governing the universe, he combines ritual, judicial and economic responsibilities within the homestead. He is also responsible for the debts and bride price of his juniors, and enjoys certain economic and judicial privileges which he cannot abuse, since any male adult can leave a homestead

[26] Originally Verdon 1983a.

[27] This presentation is taken from Paul and Laura Bohannan's book only (Bohannan 1953).

he or she does not like, and join a concession of his or her choice. In practice, emigration channels are nonetheless restricted by the emigrant's ties of consanguinity, affinity and friendship. As a result, the composition of homesteads changes quite often, although the disgruntled ones still seek to get physically close to their agnates. The homestead head generally belongs to the patrilineal lineage on whose land the homestead was built, but a homestead is known by the name of its head, not that of the founding ancestors.

The Tiv social landscape reminds one of the Tallensi country. Scattered here and there, in no apparent order, dwellings are distributed over the land in a relatively uniform fashion. There is nothing in their layout that suggests the territorial divisions and supralocal groupings that speak the language of agnatic kinship and fit the Nuer or Tallensi segmentary model. As with the Nuer, however, generational distance measures social one, and households united by the same ancestor in G+1 and G+2 are geographically the closest, welded into a more or less compact and exclusive geographical block within which the lands of different compounds intertwine, although they also intermingle with those of neighbouring blocks. Moving up the genealogical ladder, at G+4 or G+5 we reach an ancestor whose entire agnatic posterity occupies a well-circumscribed geographical area, whose homesteads and lands are not intermingled with those of neighbouring ones. These distinct and discrete territorial units are the *utar* (sing. *tar*), a term that designates each level of territorial nesting, from the first distinct and discontinuous geographical block that the Bohannans call the minimal *tar*, to the confines of the Tiv country (*tar Tiv*).

The smallest agnatic group that can be treated as a segment (*ipaven*, plural *uipaven*) corresponds to the minimal *tar*, and the same name designates both the minimal *tar* and the *ipaven* that corresponds to it. Both are *Mba*-X, 'those of X', 'X' denoting an eponymous ancestor placed in G+4 or G+5. The Tiv assert that the minimal territorial segment (*tar*) and the minimal lineage segment (*ipaven*) are one and the same thing, although the situation is quite different below this minimal level. The minimal *tar* is subdivided into concessions, while the minimal *ipaven* is segmented into genealogical sub-units, the 'segments-within-the-house', which are not strictly speaking lineage segments. Intimately conjugated, *tar* and *ipaven* thus emerge as two sides of the same segmentary system, with neighbouring *utar* aggregating into a superior *tar* and genealogically representing their fusion in terms of lineage segments derived from the same ancestor. As with the Tallensi, the lineage architecture underpins the territorial organization, with relative position in space expressed in terms of *utar* (territorial segments) whose social distance is expressed in the language of genealogical distance, a lineage organization that dictates the grammar and syntax of territorial relationships.

The Bohannans repeat the classical social anthropological distinction. On the one hand, lineage and territory frame corporate groups within which the individual must define the space of his social relationships. The socio-centric dimension of *tar* and *ipaven* is matched by the ego-centric dimension of different groupings, the *nongo* and *ityo*. To discover the social identity of a stranger, the Tiv will ask him what his *nongo* is, to which the stranger will reply by mentioning the salient political figures in his entourage, or in his territorial segment. *Nongo* would thus designate the lineage span, since it locates the individual among the lineage's living representatives, and not their forebears, since its frame of reference is horizontal, so to speak. The *nongo* would reveal the laterality of relationships; the *ityo*, on the other hand, would tell the linearity traced by common descent. *Ityo* also defines itself in relation to Ego, which it usually situates in an agnatic lineage whose depth varies according to the situation. In other contexts, *ityo* contrasts with *igba*, one serving to define the other. The *igba* is the *ityo* of a grandmother, a collateral and matrilateral branch that defends one against one's own *ityo*.

The context determines *ityo*'s genealogical reference. When spoken of as an entity in itself and not in contrast, *ityo* designates any agnatic set to which one's *pater* belongs; when contrasted with *igba*, on the other hand, its genealogical extension is limited by one's parents' marriage. Whatever the context, *igba* must always exclude one's father, and its genealogical depth stops one generation before the ancestor who links one's parents (a single genealogy, remember, links all the Tiv), delimiting by ricochet the extension of *ityo* perceived in a relational sense. If one's parents share a common ancestor in G+6, one's *ityo*, conceived in opposition to one's *igba*, cannot extend beyond the paternal segment derived from a son of this ancestor in G+5, and one's *igba* cannot extend beyond the collateral segment.

In the course of one's life, one's *igba* and *ityo* intervene in different ways. One's *ityo* gives one a wife, access to land and allies in war, and also gives one an inalienable right to live in the *tar*. A primary security, the same *ityo* is also the ultimate threat, for sorcery kills only within its borders. The *ityo* distributes rights and duties; the *igba* weaves emotional and moral relationships. The *igba* is an unconditional refuge, always open, to which we rush when we feel threatened by the dark powers of *ityo*. The *ityo* threatens, the *igba* protects, and the bigger the *igba*, the better the rescue. This is why Ego seeks to marry those who are socially distant from him, in order to enlarge proportionally the size of his children's *igba*.

Genealogical proximity reflects the social distance between territorial segments. Two neighbouring *utar* who perceive themselves as lineage segments descended from the same ancestor will assert their friendship, joining forces in defence as well as in attack, whereas two contiguous *utar* who see themselves as more distant cousins will provoke each other more easily. War can break out between segments eight to ten generations apart, but the segmentary system, whereby only units of the same level can oppose each other, will tend to stifle a general conflagration. As with the Nuer, two opposing segments will unite to fight a collateral superior segment that is attacking them.

The Tiv were also known for their pre-colonial practice of marriage by exchange. The children of the same father, or sometimes a group that could include all the agnates from the same great-great-grandfather, depending on the demography, constituted a 'marriage exchange group' (*ingol*); they were the guardians of their sisters and daughters, the matrimonial wards they exchanged to obtain their wives. In their religious practice, the Tiv worshipped certain ritual emblems and fetishes (the *akombo*) whose cults brought together initiates attached to various segments; these cult groups (*akombo biam*) exercised a judicial power over some religious cases. In more secular disputes the elders – the *mbatsav*, i.e. those with *tsav*, or supernatural power over life and death – intervened, without such gatherings ever mobilizing more than the elders of a minimal lineage segment (minimal *ipaven*).

In short, the Tiv revel in the relative. Relative is the composition of the *akombo biam* group, the *ityo*, the *igba*, the exogamous groups, the matrimonial exchange groups, although within this relativity operates a constant which, depending on the context, determines the lateral extent and generational depth of lineage segments. This constant is the segmentary principle, the principle of the opposition of equivalent segments. There is a Tiv order, and it is the one imposed, however vaguely, by segmentary classification, claim the Bohannans.

Through this labyrinth of segmentary lineages, one also finds a leadership system, relative like the rest. It can't be attached to this rather than that segment, and it annoys the professional ethnographer because it goes against the egalitarian ideology that infuses Tiv culture and society. To rise above others is to rise at the expense of others. And since the segmentary principle postulates that a segment can only distinguish itself in opposition to a segment of the same order, leadership implies that a segment cannot have any internal unity. Leadership is not simply relative; it must also be contextual, depending on the groups involved. The leader must constantly take care not to tickle egalitarian and segmentarian sensibilities too much.

Leaders are either elders, or rich and prestigious men, or those who combine the two and become politically important. To be an elder, on the other hand, is not simply to reach a respectable age. An elder is more than just an old man; he is someone who has mastered the rituals of several *akombo* used to maintain the *tar*'s peace and prosperity, someone whose oratorical skills give prestige and authority in councils, to whom genealogical knowledge gives superiority in argumentation. Last but not least, an elder must have *tsav*, a supernatural power that enables him to bewitch and thwart bewitchment. Although only the better-off will be able to afford several *akombo* initiation rites, elders derive their social and political pre-eminence from the mystical powers associated with *tsav* and *akombo*. In short, the Tiv leader must combine poise and charisma, wealth, prestige and eldership.

The Tiv: an operational reading

Among the Tiv, we find the same descriptions that dominate Nuer and Tallensi ethnographies: territorial segments merging into higher ones, the latter in turn merging into more encompassing segments, a vast segmentary symphony driven by a lineage organization. But, once again, are we really talking about lineages?

The Tiv concession breaks the monotony of the savannah landscape. The *or u ya*, the concession head, rules over this domestic universe, as domestic administrator and judge of internal disputes (Bohannan, P. and L. 1953, p. 18; Bohannan, P. 1953, pp. 3–4). The Tiv lacked any executive or legislative groups. The concession thus emerged as the minimal judicial group, or even the minimal political one. But were these homesteads aggregated in judicial matters? It seems not; Paul Bohannan tells that concession heads were the highest traditional political bodies (Bohannan, P. 1957, p. 8). Some *or u ya* certainly enjoyed greater prestige and influence. They might have been invited to come and deliberate in councils mediating between quarrelling concessions, but these influential men had no authority to convene a council beyond their own residential group. An *or u ya* will only meddle in the affairs of neighbouring concessions if asked to do so and, even if invited, he can only try to convince the council. He does not dictate, and we will often see the plaintiff rallying behind his *igba* to impose a fair settlement, whatever the political personalities present. With the exception of military activities, to which I shall return later, there is no mechanism for aggregating political concessions. The Tiv concession is the Tiv state, and it would be wrong to see them aggregated into a single minimal *tar*. Moreover, if the *tar* is the territorial projection of the *ipaven* (Bohannan, P. and L. 1953, p. 20), and if the minimal *tar* is not an aggregated group, what about the minimal *uipaven*? Did they form a real lineage hierarchy?

According to the Bohannans, minimal *uipaven* emerge in the context of land ownership. Tiv law recognizes everyone's axiomatic right to cultivate the land of the minimal *tar* to which their minimal *ipaven* claims exclusive access, and every Tiv belongs to a minimal *ipaven* by virtue of agnatic kinship. As a group of agnates ostensibly claiming exclusive ownership of a parcel of land, the minimal *ipaven* would seem to have all the attributes of a corporation in terms of land ownership. This is an illusion, however, because rights to land do not derive from membership of the minimal *ipaven*, and are only indirectly attached to concessions (Bohannan, P. 1954, pp. 34–36). In reality, every adult Tiv is entitled to all the land necessary to satisfy his subsistence needs and those of his dependents and, consequently, any concession head can claim as much land as he needs for himself and his dependents. He has no permission to ask before clearing new land, as long as he respects the rights of others to the land they have ploughed and takes into account the existence of neighbouring *uipaven*.

A woman's labour gives her son or husband rights over the land she has cultivated. The Tiv clearly delimit the perimeter of farms and plots of land bearing the testimony of previous ploughings, parcels of land over which only a son or husband has usufruct rights by virtue of a mother's or wife's work. These rights vanish when a plot is left fallow long enough for nature to erase all traces of cultivation. In conclusion, a concession head will only appropriate land which no longer has a known owner and will avoid clashing with members of the same minimal *ipaven* in his quest for available land, or land he is thinking of cultivating. If his minimal *tar* is short of land he will instead encroach on the lands of contiguous but genealogically more distant *utar* (in a segment-by-segment genealogical calculation and not in terms of true genealogical distance; to understand the difference, see Bohannan, L. 1958). Despite what the Bohannans suggest in some places, neighbouring minimal *utar* farms intermingle to some extent, and the territory occupied by a minimal *ipaven* is not circumscribed either in fact or in law (Bohannan, P. 1954, pp. 34–36). The Tiv are eminently aware of this fact, a state of affairs they try to perpetuate despite government attempts to impose legal boundaries on their lands (or *utar*). If there are no formally demarcated landholdings that are explicitly the possession of the minimal *ipaven*, if rights to land are in fact individual, and if no elder represents the *ipaven* in matters of ownership, the minimal *ipaven* cannot be a corporation in matters of land ownership. Tiv ethnography then raises an interesting but thorny question: how can we reconcile the fact that the minimal *ipaven* is a group that recognizes a privileged relationship with a given geographical area, while denying itself the real status of a corporation?

I believe I can answer this question on the basis of what I consider to be the basic axiom of the Tiv constitution, namely the homestead's political sovereignty. On the one hand, we might expect a sovereign concession to surround itself with a circumscribed territory and interpret as seditious any attempt by its members to leave it to create a new concession, i.e. to found a new sovereign political group (see Verdon 1980c). The fact that this separatism does not provoke more protests is, in my view, evidence of a paradox in the very idea of the homestead's political sovereignty, i.e. the sovereignty of a residential group. To create a new residential group one has to be married, have dependents and probably be an elder or in the process of becoming one, but with no hope of fully achieving this within an existing political group. A concession head who thwarts these separatist aspirations will incite rebellion or simply desertion. To safeguard the political integrity of his state he must therefore know how to concede a certain measure of autonomy to his dependents, how to keep them in his concession by recognizing their privilege to leave. On the other hand, this Tiv sovereign must also know how to assert his group's autonomy 'against the rest of the universe'. Small in size, Tiv concessions are extremely sensitive to variations in fertility and gender composition, so that some of these residential communities, advantaged by favourable demographic circumstances, will grow much faster, threatening by their numbers their numerically weaker neighbours. Economically responsible for his dependents, the *or u ya* must know how to meet their land needs while protecting himself against sometimes more powerful neighbours seeking to satisfy the same needs. In my view, this dual requirement prescribes a solution that the Tiv have found, on the one hand in their segmentary organization and, on the other, by defining minimal *uipaven* that exhibit almost all the features of a corporation but escape its rigid frameworks. Indeed, the *or u ya* will only protect the autonomy of his group through political coalition, and the most natural alliance, in a sense, is that which, born of patrifiliation, mobilizes agnates. This agnatic *confederation* is, in a word, what I consider to be the minimal *ipaven*.

The Tiv live their early years in their father's homestead, with their brothers and very often their agnatic cousins. When, in middle age or on the threshold of old age, they take over the management of a concession, their brothers and older cousins who are still alive will likely administer neighbouring concessions and, together they will form a category of individuals who know, rather than believe, they have common genealogical links. These genealogical ties are known, or 'real', insofar as they derive from direct, immediate experience. The individual holds this knowledge to be real because he knows with all humanly possible certainty who his father was, and presumably who his father's brothers were, because he will have intimately known close relatives who personally knew his father's father, as well as the brothers of this paternal grandfather. From the point of view of an elder located at G°, descendants of agnatic forebears from G+2 to G+4 will *know* they are genealogically related, whatever the ontological status of this knowledge. Beyond that, they will simply assume the existence of genealogical links. However, the minimal *ipaven* does not extend its ancestral roots beyond G+2/G+3 (Bohannan, P. 1954, pp. 8–14).

We can thus identify a social category Tiv, none other than the minimal *ipaven*, a sociocentric category recruited through agnatic kinship, genealogically capped at G+2/G+3 and seeking to ensure its members access to land as well as sovereignty over their concessions, something it cannot achieve if its members intermingle their lands with those of other *uipaven*. From the outside, *uipaven* give the impression of occupying a well-defined geographical area, carving out a compact territory but, in reality, those living on the outskirts of the minimal *tar* intermingle their lands with those of neighbouring minimal *uipaven*, and the *tar*'s apparent boundaries change from year to year. As an agnatic category attached to property without precise boundaries, the minimal *ipaven* is what we might call a 'quasi-corporation'. As for the minimal *tar*, it designates both the area that the lands of the minimal *ipaven* enclose without precision – the 'country' they enclose, as it were – and the people who inhabit this country. As a social category, the minimal *tar* includes affines or uterine relatives (wives or uterine nephews living in the *tar*) that the *ipaven* excludes. Members of the same minimal *ipaven*, of the same political coalition with the appearance of a quasi-corporation, concession heads domiciled in the same minimal *tar* clearly seek to discourage any belligerence, working skilfully to maintain internal peace.

In short, sovereign homesteads could not tolerate minimal *uipaven* being true corporations in matters of land ownership because, in this case, the homestead heads of the same minimal *ipaven* united in a single corporation possessing a land with exact boundaries (the minimal *tar*) could not stop them aggregating within this *tar*. The corporation would soon appoint a representative who would ultimately act as land administrator, occasionally judging disputes over land. Authorized to arbitrate or convene an assembly responsible for some judicial decisions, the *tar* representative would soon extend his influence to the judicial level, and the concessions thus aggregated would automatically lose their sovereignty. On the other hand, if the concessions were to claim to be corporations in matters of land ownership, they would only reproduce with extreme difficulty, and their coalition would be undermined by the tug-of-war this land tenure system would cause. A quasi-corporation such as the minimal *ipaven* seems the best solution for a firm, stable political association between the heads of sovereign concessions.

The institution of the *mbatsav* illustrates this intrinsic paradox of the sovereignty of domestic local groups. When attacked by supernatural agents, concession heads convene a deliberative assembly of the elders of their minimal *tar* who are *mbatsav*, i.e. 'those with *tsav*'. *Tsav* is a mystical substance that grows inside the human organism and gives its possessor the power to give or take away life; it is the supernatural source of all power (Bohannan, P. and L. 1953, pp. 84–85; Downes 1933, pp. 39–43; East 1939, p. 238; Abraham 1940, pp. 14, 40) but, because of the evil uses to which it can be put, the *tsav* is an ambivalent attribute that no one wishes to claim for himself. *Tsav* is analogous to charisma, albeit in a negative way; it doesn't exist because I claim to have it, but because others recognize it in me. Those who presume to be the victims of someone else's *tsav* impute possession of *tsav* to them, thus contributing to their reputation as *mbatsav*.

Ethnographers write of *mbatsav* as a group, but wrongly so. There is no such thing as a collection of individuals recruited on the basis of an identifiable characteristic called *tsav*. The *tsav* is always something attributed to others, and is only objectively discovered after death, through an autopsy. If illness or misfortune take on epidemic proportions, the head(s) of the afflicted concession(s) will invite the *mbatsav* who may be the cause of his/their ordeal. The *mbatsav* do not form a group that would gather of their own accord when summoned by their representative because the *mbatsav* have no representatives, always being mandated by a presumed victim or by an elder of that victim. The *mbatsav* who would meet at night to eat human flesh (Bohannan P. 1957, pp. 2–3) are a chimera invented from scratch by those who believe themselves the victims of others' *tsav* (Abraham 1940, pp. 51–57; East 1939, pp. 242–245), just like the witches' sabbath of our own collective imagination. We would be deluding ourselves if we considered the *mbatsav* the spokespersons of a minimal *tar* aggregated in religious matters.

Neither the *utar* nor the minimal *uipaven* can lay claim to the title of a corporation or a group aggregated in political, ritual or other matters; and yet they are described as the minimal segments of an imposing military segmentary architecture. How do we reconcile these facts? Once again, by disentangling aggregation from alliance. Concessions are sovereign in both war and peace. Within the minimal *tar*, they weave a dense network of non-segmentary alliances that looks like aggregation. Beyond that, they activate the classic dynamics of Nuer-type segmentary military alliances.

The minimal *tar* is the land where the 'natural coalition' formed by the minimal *ipaven* can live in peace[28]. It is also the land

---

[28] In reality, mystical aggression is common within the minimal *tar*, where physical violence is more or less suppressed. The Tiv seek to increase their political power beyond their residential precincts, and this rise in power is always interpreted in supernatural terms, as the acquisition and growth of *tsav*, which to me admirably expresses the paradox of a social formation based on the concessions' sovereignty. A Tiv will not acquire *tsav* by intimidating or bullying others, or by becoming inordinately rich. He will only do so by controlling his behaviour, acting with wisdom and sagacity, and joining as many *akombo* groups as possible.

In other words, competition reaches its supernatural peak among those who cannot aggress one another physically, i.e. members of the same minimal *tar/ ipaven*, and the Tiv counter this mystical threat by seeking support and backing in another type of alliance. In my view, this explains the relationship between *igba* and *ityo*. In *Justice and Judgment among the Tiv,* Paul Bohannan manages to demonstrate that the *ityo* can be defined as the set of living agnates whose *tsav* Ego fears (i.e. those whose *tsav* can affect Ego). *Ityo* is unique in that (a) it is defined in relation to Ego, and (b) it is essentially relative. As a set of individuals to whom Ego attributes a *tsav* that can be fatal to him, *ityo* will overlap with sets of differing scope from one individual to the next, although there is always some measure of unanimity of public opinion about those who have *tsav*.

Even more important is the fact that *ityo* must also vary in genealogical depth as the individual gets older. On the supernatural level, a young man is potentially the victim of a large number of agnates who, on the other hand, cluster more or less around the concession where this young man lives and are not genealogically very distant from him. As a man grows older, on the other hand, he extends his network of acquaintances to concessions further away. The people whose mystical powers he fears diminish in number as his own power grows, but these potential aggressors are scattered over an ever-wider area, making up an ever deeper genealogical whole. I thus believe that *ityo*, as an Ego-centred category, varies in its lineal and lateral extension, as well as in its geographical extent, as Ego gets older and becomes increasingly powerful himself. This relativity of *ityo* would explain that of *igba*.

Igba has two main meanings. Firstly, Ego's *igba* comprises all those who belong to his mother's *ipaven* (and possibly *tar*). In another context, *igba* are those with whom Ego allies himself in his fight against the mystical aggression of where the *ipaven* seeks to guarantee its members' access to land, which it cannot do if land is too scarce. When there is not enough land left, the minimal *ipaven* must be ready to grab the land of neighbouring *utar*. As they vary in size, minimal *utar* will only attack neighbouring ones if their numbers are more or less equal. It is this mechanism, the same that we found among the Nuer, the one that draws this illustrious configuration of 'segmentary alliances and oppositions'. As with the Nuer, the so-called equilibrium is not one of lineage segments or aliquot parts, but a numerical equilibrium, a system of coalitions in which groups of roughly comparable size ally and oppose each other, without which the sovereignty of concessions and the equitable distribution of land between *uipaven* would be pure utopia.

In a famous study of Tiv genealogies, Laura Bohannan emphasized the distinction the Tiv introduce between a 'segment-by-segment' genealogical construct and a 'father-by-father' one, to illustrate the distinction between groups and networks, descent and kinship, relationships between corporations and relationships between individuals (Bohannan, L. 1958, pp. 42–44). To me, these two types of genealogical constructs shed light on a very different reality. If the two genealogical calculus do not coincide, it is because one (father-by-father) operates on genealogical links that Tiv believe to be real, that truly connect individuals, whereas the other (segment-by-segment) is merely a political calculation combining groups of unequal sizes into coalitions of vaguely comparable ones. The two calculus reflect the dissociation between genealogy and demographic size, and Laura Bohannan's

---

his *ityo*. When a deliberating council is convened, the depth and laterality of the *igba* invited must equal the depth and span of the *ityo* accused (Bohannan, P. 1957). The victim, or the elder representing him, will call for help from an *igba* (always drawn by the mother) of equal laterality and generational depth to that of the accused *ityo*, so as to oppose an equal force to that of the aggressor. Only such a balance of power can force a settlement. The system of segmentary alliances therefore operates at the level of both physical aggression and mystical violence, but the network is traced differently in the two cases: through the father in the case of physical attack, through the mother in the case of supernatural attack.

text makes it clear that some *uipaven* linked by genealogy are nonetheless separated in the order of 'segmentation' because of their different sizes[29], without daring to draw the obvious consequences.

As with the Nuer, existing alliances dictate who they will aggress; thus a minimal *tar* will attack neighbouring *utar* more distant in alliance terms and, therefore, in terms of segment-by-segment reckoning. The kinship they recognize as 'real' influences the orientation of alliances, without fixing it completely. Minimal *utar* and *uipaven* who have split will remember their earlier unity and, presumably, feel more strongly allied to those from whom they have recently separated than to those whom they have heard belonged to the same *tar* as their forebears, in the vague and distant past. In Tiv country, as in Nuerland, kinship is used to build alliances, but other alliances are created through friendships and political interests, which are also translated into the language of agnatic kinship (Bohannan, L. 1952). In short, we find in these minimal *utar* and *uipaven*, which amalgamate into progressively larger *utar* and *uipaven* according to the groups they confront, the segmentary *alliances* of the Nuer type. Like the Nuer, the Tiv have neither descent groups nor lineages.

The Tiv case is of particular epistemological significance because of the historical interpretation it also suggests. Before the Bohannans' fieldwork (late 40s and early 50s), the Tiv had already undergone a long colonial experience, and no solid historical insight can be gleaned without a mass of historical and ethnographic information that simply doesn't exist. Dorward, a historian of the Tiv, had already made giant strides in dissecting the complex relationships between the Tiv and their colonial

[29] The idea of equality in numbers and demographic balance is so deeply rooted in Tiv thinking that it was also expressed in their matrimonial practices. In the past, the Tiv obtained their wives by exchanging sisters, and ensured demographic parity by stipulating that they were not exchanging people, but their fertility. If the sisters exchanged did not give birth to an equal number of children, the imbalance was evened out by giving the disadvantaged husband new rights over one of the daughters of the most fertile sister.

administrators (Dorward 1974). Despite his commendable effort a detailed social history of the Tiv has yet to be made, and I am not competent for that. Nevertheless, the painstaking and colossal task of historical reconstruction should not paralyse ethnologists, who should venture down the path of social history when anthropological documents lend themselves to it. The administrators and missionaries who described Tiv society before the Bohannans, for example, emphasized the political role of cult groups, a role almost entirely neglected in the otherwise rich ethnography of the Bohannans. That those two types of documents diverge so widely can be interpreted in a number of ways: personal prejudices, theoretical interests of the time, lack of professional training, without excluding the possibility that these testimonies reveal historical transformations. This is the avenue I will explore.

Downes, East and Abraham, all without ethnological training but all with a long experience in Tiv country, speak of an arbitration group in disputes between concession heads (Downes 1933, pp. 74–76; East 1939, p. 131; Abraham 1940, p. 17). One of the administrators identifies this group more precisely as the minimal *ipaven*, whom he also depicts as the owner of the ancestral *imborivungu* (Abraham 1940, pp. 36, 41). The *imborivungu* is a cult object, the femur of a minimal *tar* ancestor which, decorated and placed in his skull, is deposited in a special altar, the *poor*, the spiritual centre of the minimal *tar* (Downes 1971, p. 56). The *imborivungu*, it should be noted, belonged to the innumerable *akombo* ('fetishes' in missionary vocabulary) that Downes divides into two main categories,

> "[...] the great *akombo*...; those we call the *akombo sorun tar* (the *akombo* that have the power to restore things to their natural order in the *tar*) and who work for the well-being of the family (*ityo*), of the social group. The others, the *akombo a kiriki* (the little *akombo*)... work for particular ends [...]" (Downes 1971, p. 76).

There are several varieties of these two types of *akombo*, and each type is associated with an independent cult group that individuals join after an initiation ritual.

Of all the cults devoted to the great collective *akombo,* the *akombo biam*, or cult of ancestral *imborivungu*, surpassed all others. It recruited only the 'true sons of exchange marriages' (Downes 1971, p. 61) who, by definition, descended in direct line from the ancestors whose skulls lined the *poor*, but who had to undergo initiation before they could join. It was *ingol*, it will be remembered, that married its members by exchange, and it is *ingol* that is associated with *akombo biam* and a number of other cult groups. Initiation into the *akombo biam* was prohibitively expensive (Downes 1971, p. 61), and only middle-aged men could afford it. Initiates of one *akombo biam* also joined other *akombo* cults and, over the years, some of them accumulated ritual and religious knowledge that made them cult leaders, so that a single individual could cumulate spiritual leadership of several cults. In the older generation, one of the most important cult leaders, a man whose *tsav* was disproportionately greater than the average person's, conquered leadership of the *akombo biam* cult and responsibility for rites to the ancestral *imborivungu* to 'repair the *tar*' (East 1939, pp. 213–14; Abraham 1940, p. 155; Downes 1971, pp. 31, 59), thus improvising himself as the *tar*'s spokesman during mediation rituals.

These same ethnographic testimonies tell of concession heads of the same minimal *tar,* members of one and the same minimal *ipaven*, which would have *ipso facto* constituted one and the same cult group in the worship of the *imborivungu*. The master of the *akombo biam* would have led the *tar* through his leadership and spiritual charisma, would have received the funeral honours reserved for 'tar leaders' and his bones (his femur and skull), consecrated *imborivungu*, would have joined those of the previous leaders in the *tar*'s ancestral *poor* (Downes 1971, p. 59). The link between minimal *tar* politics and the *akombo biam* cults was so intimate that the Tiv spoke of the splitting of a minimal *tar* and the creation of a new one in terms of the fission and creation of new *akombo biam* cult groups (East 1939, pp. 107–108).

Before 1927, when the colonial government abolished marriage by exchange, most concession heads also headed an *ingol* and communed in the same *akombo biam* cult. In religious matters, they belonged to a corporation and ritual group whose representative (the *or kombo biam*) also acted as religious head - *or sorun tar* -, or '*tar* repairer'. Members of the same cult group, these concession heads could not afford to let their quarrels go unresolved, for fear of 'defiling the land', and they invited their fellow *akombo biam* members to act as mediators. In the light of these testimonies, should we speak of an aggregation of concessions into a minimal *tar*, prior to colonial domination? No, because the concession heads gave the *or sorun tar* no authority to convene a judicial council or a legislative assembly, and even less to judge or legislate on his own. By analogy, we can imagine heads of state who are members of the same Masonic Lodge, committed to ensuring peace between their nations without having to invoke a supranational aggregation.

If this historical reconstruction is plausible – and in this respect, I repeat, only detailed historical research will be able to rule – it reveals profound transformations in Tiv society between the end of the 1920s (the period dealt with by the administrators) and the period of the Bohannans' fieldwork. Before 1927, the wealthiest Tiv managed to marry by exchange and, as sons of this preferential marriage themselves, could dream of initiation into the *akombo biam* (East 1919, pp. 131–132, 191–194). They also married later (East 1939, pp. 106, 123, 141), and only a few men could hope to meet the necessary conditions to create new concessions, so concessions probably reproduced at longer intervals and reached a larger size. Devotees of the *akombo biam* cult of the *imborivungu*, these concession heads 'reigned' over the minimal *tar*. In 1927, the colonial authorities outlawed marriage by exchange, advocating marriage with bride price. This freed young men from their elders' control. The young Tiv could then go to work for wages and quickly amassed the sums needed to get married. They married earlier than their elders, and the *akombo biam* lost much, if not all, of its relevance, especially as the Pax Britannica made it easier to create new concessions. The incidence of polygyny, traditionally low, increased (East 1939, p. 313); the population exploded (East 1939, p. 131). In short, everything conspired to draw the same scenario; the abolition of marriage by exchange favoured younger generations (East 1939, pp. 162, 168), removing them from their elders' control, and exacerbating the competition and individualism latent in Tiv society to the point of awakening those quasi-anarchic conditions which the Bohannans observed.

CHAPTER FIVE

Translating the Iqar'iyen ethnography[30]

Raymond Jamous studied the social organization of the Iqar'iyen, a Berber-speaking community of the Moroccan Rif through the themes of honour and baraka (Jamous 1981). The Rif is that part of Morocco at the extreme north-east, next to Algeria and along the Atlantic coast. These Berbers from the Rif, although located in a nation state, were so isolated at the periphery of Morocco that they still more or less operated in the 1970s as they did under the sultanates.

Jamous presents their social organization in a 'segmentary' model. In the classical framework of segmentary lineages, we would expect to find lineages all the way to the most inclusive level. But this is not how things work among the Iqar'iyen:

> "Here, six levels can be distinguished, from the confederation [highest level] to the house, composed of a restricted or extended family. The segments of levels one to four (from the top down) are exclusively territorial units, and it is from level five onwards that patrilinearity and territoriality are articulated to one another. In other words, the members of the confederation, of each of the five tribes, fractions and

[30] I did not previously publish this reanalysis. I sketched it in the framework of a seminar I gave in French on my operationalism (hence the choice of a French book). And as Jamous' ethnography is greatly inferior to that of the Nuer, Tallensi, Tiv, or Yao, this operationalization was much more difficult and therefore scantier.

> territorial communities do not recognize any common kinship, nor do they claim to be the descendants of an ancestor who founded the corresponding territorial group. It is only at the fifth level, that of the district, that the inhabitants recognize an agnatic kinship" (Jamous 1981, p. 29, *all translations are mine*).

What does a 'territorial segmentary structure' mean, according to Jamous? Does it imply that beyond the lineage we find aggregation on the basis of territoriality? If so, we should expect chiefdoms or something similar. If not, we are not dealing with either lineages or chiefdoms, and there is no answer to that question. Jamous further concludes that territoriality 'encompasses' kinship, since the most inclusive groups are 'organized' "according to the 'principle of territoriality'" (p. 29). The most inclusive groups would therefore be territorial but, for this to be, there would have to be title-holders at the highest levels. As we shall see, there are none. The question thus remains unanswered.

In the alleged segmentary cases I have already reanalysed (the Nuer and Tiv), segmentation operates together with leadership. Jamous also finds leaders among the Iqar'iyen, and this leads him to postulate a hierarchical relationship between segmentarity and authority. The segmentary model would "encompass the authoritarian model" (p. 187), a most obscure statement that calls for an operationalisation. For this, I will start with chapter two, where the author presents the backbone of his so-called segmentary structure.

Patrilineages and other segmentary structures

In this second chapter, the presentation follows the classical pattern of moving from top to bottom. At the lower levels of this so-called segmentary architecture, within what he calls the 'neighbourhood' ('quartier' in French), Jamous discovers 'segmentary' groups organized agnatically. He calls them patrilineages. But are there really patrilineages among the Iqar'iyen and, if so, to what level(s) of grouping do they correspond? To answer, we need to reverse the order of analysis and start with the least inclusive groups.

The smallest level of grouping is the house, about which Jamous writes very little. We learn that there are architectural structures identifiable as houses, that these houses are scattered on ridges and almost fortified (p. 41), though some are closer together and separated from other similar 'constellations' by land. He calls these clusters of dispersed houses 'quartiers' (we should rather say 'dispersed hamlets', since the notion of quartier gives the idea of a nucleated habitat, which this is not). These houses may comprise a single family (monogynous or polygynous – a 'nuclear family'), or a man, his wife(s), and all or some of his married sons and their children – an 'extended family'.

These houses are individually owned by the household head. Whoever owns a house generally also owns land within the land of the 'territorial community' (level 4 of Jamous' diagram). These houses are said to be first and foremost residential groups. Daughters leave the parental home at marriage, while most sons stay home if the father is still alive. In fact, the father remains household head even if all his sons are married. As long as their father lives, the sons seem to be subordinate to him if they stay at home. In short, the iqar'iyen house does have a representative (its 'head'). As for its composition, it is mainly agnatic, but includes all the wives of married male agnates. In fact, as we shall see, it is actually more complex.

What do the household members do? We can only surmise. We can safely assume that some members perform economic and domestic activities, and that domestic chores are mostly carried out by women, but we know nothing about economic activities. Are women involved? Impossible to say. But we can also assume that in domestic and economic activities, these groups are simultaneously minimal and maximal; in other words, everything begins and ends there, there is no nesting of these houses into more inclusive groups in agricultural activities, animal husbandry and domestic activities (housekeeping, childcare, processing of agricultural and animal products, domestic crafts, consumption, and so on). We do know, however, that household heads are involved in some activities at a higher level. I will come back to this later.

Is the household the minimum judicial group? Almost everywhere, and especially in so-called patriarchal societies, household heads normally settle conflicts within the household and this seems more than likely in the in iqar'iyen environment. However, it is also commonly accepted that we treat conflicts within the household as domestic problems, not judicial ones. I admit that this is arbitrary, and we can here consider the household as a minimal judicial group. We will see that it does not change the analysis.

The house is thus represented by a headman, who seems to enjoy great authority over his dependents (including his wife or wives). This group can also be considered a minimal judicial group (the question of its nesting remains open), partially overlapped by a production group and the various groups assigned to so-called domestic activities. In the case of all these latter activities, we can safely suppose that they form minimal groups that are not nested. There is therefore no aggregation in these contexts (as far as we actually know from the majority of ethnographic cases).

It is from what he calls the 'neighbourhood' (quartier) and above that we get to know more. In fact, his case studies on the foundation of so-called patrilineages are ethnographically revealing. I will rest most of my conclusions on them.

Some houses seem to be grouped into neighbourhoods, and the houses in these neighbourhoods are linked by an agnatic genealogy which, to Jamous, makes them patrilineages. But to conclude to the existence of a patrilineage we need to answer several questions, some of which can be found in the very genesis of the constitution of what Jamous calls a patrilineage. He writes that "patrilineage stories and other narratives highlight, first and foremost, the protected status of the group's founding ancestor" (p. 45). Moreover, "any individual or group arriving in the iqar'iyen territory, or leaving one community to settle in another outside the confederation, does not have to ask permission from the higher-level segments. All they need to do is find a lineage group, *and in particular a household head willing to welcome him or them* (italics added). The immigrant becomes this man's protégé and supports him in all circumstances. In return, this protector will defend him if he is ever attacked, and give him housing and work" (pp. 45–46). Since the iqar'iyen population seems to be constantly in a state of migratory flux, this situation must be common.

We do not know exactly where the immigrant(s) is/are housed. The case histories suggest two types of scenarios: first, the immigrant lives in the home of his protector: "These people (protected immigrants) have the status of protégés and choose, in coming to settle in the neighbourhood, a household head with whom they will live and on whom they will be dependent" (p. 44). On the other hand, the case of Mohand Moh (pp. 46–47) shows us that he immigrated with his wife and young children a first time and, on a second immigration, "built a small house where he installed his family" (p. 47).

Thus some households, in addition to affines (wives), include non-affines who seek protection, and work as a horribly exploited Lumpenproletariat (they work on their protector's land and keep for themselves and their family only one fifth of their production). Moreover, it seems that individuals often have to leave their neighbourhoods, and look for protectors, whom Jamous often describes as 'grands' ('great men'; we will have ample opportunity to come back to the 'grands', or *amghar*, below). Whether they are *amghar* or not, those who take in these protégés increase the number of their dependents and, by extension, their influence. We already come across a whole dynamic whereby individuals seek out protectors, and others seek people to protect, in order to assert their 'greatness' and increase their influence.

Even if we were to presume complete neighbourhood endogamy (which is not the case), the neighbourhood does not only include households whose heads are agnates: "In any case, the neighbourhood's inhabitants are not all related. The patrilineage is the most numerous and dominant group. Only its members own houses and land" (p. 44). We should perhaps rather say: only its members have the right to own land. In fact, we should move away from the concept of neighbourhood.

Since we are really talking about a hamlet with scattered settlements, I would rather refer to it as a 'local group'.

Immigrants are second-class citizens, allegedly barred from owning land (thus making it difficult for them to own houses), yet they are the source of the so-called new patrilineages. How can this be? Let us take a closer look at Jamous' data, especially at Mohand Moh's story. The scenario seems typical: Mohand Moh works hard to support his family and discreetly amasses a small nest egg. He is survived by two sons, who continue to live together; they themselves have several sons, whom they marry off as soon as possible to multiply the number of their descendants. Then, "after much effort, [the two brothers] buy a few plots of land" (p. 47). At their death, the two brothers leave numerous descendants, they own some land and take advantage of a conflict with the original protector's group over the purchase of land to assert their independence and move to an abandoned locality. And that is it! A new 'patrilineage' was born because the sons and grandsons were able to remain united and multiply, while the host group weakened due to internal dissensions.

In short, concludes Jamous, "settled patrilineages seek to increase their strength and numbers, not only by accepting immigrant families, but by enticing them to settle near them [...] The support [received by the head of the family who becomes its protector] strengthens his lineage at the expense of the others" (p. 47). Some households within a local group compete for influence and authority, which derive fundamentally from the number of their dependents and the land they own. But this has a double effect. Over the generations, the host group can weaken when its 'lineages' seem to be in constant rivalry, while the immigrant group can slowly swell and, after one or two generations, acquire land. If the descendants of the first immigrants remain united and multiply, they can challenge the descendants of their former protectors and assert their independence. They then form their own local group, and the cycle begins again.

Within their own local group, agnates who no longer cohabit may compete to assert their superiority, so that some household heads can become 'great men' (*amghar*), in their neighbourhood and beyond. Is the so-called neighbourhood (local group) a patrilineage? For a patrilineage to exist, there must be aggregation, and for aggregation to operate there must be a tenured position at each level of nesting. The household head is the tenured position corresponding to the house. But what about the local group? Is there a single activity in which the various houses of the hamlet are united, under the tutelage of a 'district chief'? In the case of neighbourhoods under the tutelage of an *amghar*, it may seem so. I will leave these cases aside for the moment and will first look at local groups without an *amghar*. Jamous insists that all ownership of land, livestock and houses is individual. In the context of this type of ownership, the local group does not form a corporation. But he further adds that a so-called patrilineage can be challenged "in its common patrimony (roads, wells, silos) [...]" (p. 109). In the case of this type of property, the local group therefore could form a corporation. This is the only mention Jamous makes of this type of property in the entire book; we cannot measure its importance, and it is also impossible to know how this 'infrastructural' property is managed. We must therefore satisfy ourselves with declaring the local group a land-owning corporation in this context, and this context only.

Moreover, if quarrels arise within the local group, they seem to be settled by the *ayraw*, or 'assembly', whose composition and functions, Jamous explains, "are analogous to those of the assembly of the territorial community" (p. 36). We must therefore examine the composition and functions of the territorial community assembly:

> "All the men in the community can attend, but only the heads of households who own land have the right to speak. Others may speak only with their permission. The functions of this assembly are very diverse: appointment of the Sheykh el Jami, distribution of tasks for the upkeep of the mosque [...], settlement of disputes between the patrilineages making up the community. The assembly does not rule by customary

> law. It makes circumstantial decisions. These are not voted on. Moreover, this concept has no meaning here. There are no rules of procedure in these assemblies. Discussions are very lively: either they lead to unanimous agreement on a particular decision to be taken, or they lead to nothing at all" (p. 35).

Anything to do with the mosque does not apply to the local group. All in all, at this level there is no incumbent empowered to resolve conflicts or to summon a small group to resolve them, and therefore no aggregation, either by descent or territoriality. In terms of religion (or, more specifically, the practice of Islam), there seems to be no activity that unites members of the neighbourhood exclusively. My conclusion is therefore unambiguous: the local group (or 'quartier', always without the presence of an *amghar*, let us remember) is made up of households, the majority of whose heads, it seems, are those agnates carrying out some administrative and judicial activities. But this makes it neither an agnatic group (wives are included, as are protégés), nor a group aggregated by descent. What shall we conclude? According to my conceptual framework, it is quite clear that the various household heads are not aggregated into a patrilineage within the local group. They are allies, and this alliance follows agnatic kinship, or simple dependency (of protected immigrants), even though these allies form a corporation with regard to some types of property. Is there aggregation at higher levels?

From Jamous' perspective, patrilineages form part of a segmentary architecture which is organized according to the 'principle of territoriality' beyond patrilineages. In other words, patrilineal descent would aggregate houses into patrilineages, since we are talking about patrilineages, but what does territoriality do? Jamous has no clear answer to offer with his notion of territoriality. In an operational perspective, the so-called patrilineages are not aggregated in territorial groups, as I shall demonstrate.

Very simply, the various local groups are said to form 'territorial communities' in a 'segmented' way (still without really knowing what this means). Here, I would prefer to speak of 'communes', because of the ambiguity attached to the term 'territorial'. What do we know about these communes? Very little. First of all, although some communes own land on the plains, not all of them do. All of them, however, own land in the mountains, and this land forms "a compact, one-piece territory in the mountains" (p. 39). In short, the lands of the local groups are intermingled, but those of the communes are not, at least the lands that the communes own in the mountains. Is it a land-owning corporation? Absolutely not, as nowhere in their case does Jamous speak of a common land patrimony (the mosque not being a land patrimony). However, this formation of compact land is a concerted effort by a collection of local groups to keep their mountain land as a whole, presumably for political and defence reasons. These local groups are not linked by any ancestral genealogy; Jamous assumes them to be brought together according to territoriality, and according to segmentarity. What this means is completely obscure to me. We can at least ask the question: would local groups be aggregated into a commune on the basis of territoriality? Two sets of elements allow us to answer this question.

On pages 39–40, Jamous describes the genesis of such a community to explain an anomaly, and it seems that we find at the level of the so-called territorial community what we encounter at the level of what he calls the neighbourhood: that various local groups seek allies in various contiguous communes to sometimes form new communes. When this happens, the land is untangled so that the new commune has a single piece of land. Why would communes split up and create new ones? I am convinced that it is a political manoeuvre, that from time to time a local group wants to establish its pre-eminence by creating a new commune. This would suggest that not all local groups are "'aliquot parts' or 'similar', repetitive units [...] [defining themselves] by their structural relativity," (p. 29) as the segmentary theory would have it, any more than the houses are. Why all the land in one piece? That could have been a protective measure that evolved over time. But this genesis tells us something else: just as the households in a given neighbourhood do not appear in any way aggregated, but simply allied, it is clear that local groups are not aggregated into a commune, but simply allied. These allies are not linked by agnatic kinship, and they form a 'territory' with precise boundaries, a closed geographical block.

Interestingly, the so-called territorial community is the first level above the home where we find elements that would suggest aggregation. The inhabitants of this commune not only own land gathered into a compact block, but they also erect mosques and enjoy a special institution, the *ayraw* or 'assembly', to regulate their affairs (p. 34). In short, the commune emerges as a group in the context of religious and judicial activities. Let us deal with them in that order.

Jamous could not be more explicit on the subject:

> "The mosque is built communally and used by all the members of the different patrilineages of the *dshar* (commune). All household heads must provide an equal share of work to build and maintain the mosque. To distribute the various tasks and organize the work they delegate their power to one of them, called *Sheykh el Jami*, or the one responsible for the mosque. This man is also in charge of recruiting the *fiqh*, a Muslim scholar who leads the prayer, teaches the Coran to children and takes care of the mosque. This position does not confer any prestige nor any particular right. The *Sheykh el Jami* cannot take any decision without consulting the other household heads" (p. 35).

As a 'temporal asset', the mosque appears to be the corporate property of the commune, which from this point of view also forms a corporation. It also seems that the commune represents the minimal group in terms of Muslim practice; there is an apparently titular post, but no authority. We can therefore conclude that there is no aggregation in terms of religious practice (in any case, Islam is a religion without a 'Church', so to speak, and it is impossible to speak of aggregation).

What then is the *ayraw*? We have already seen that the composition and functions of the local group and commune assemblies are similar (p. 36), from which we can conclude that there is no aggregation; the *ayraw* merely expresses the alliance of these local groups into a single territorial community. In other words, an operational translation reveals that, although the commune forms a corporation with respect to the mosque, and a minimal group of Islamic practice, it has no representative and cannot, therefore, form groups of groups. Can we nevertheless speak of a 'composite corporation' (see my Tallensi analysis)? I hesitate to conclude this. In the Tallensi case, the 'composite (or aggregated) corporation' was defined with reference to the same property as its components. Here, however, the local groups form corporations with regards to a type of property, especially land (wells, roads), and a different corporation with respect to the mosque, together with the local groups in the same commune. This is why I prefer to stick with the following formulation: the local groups form a corporation in reference to one type of property and the communes in relation to a different type, without one being included in the other. There is no aggregation.

In short, if we temporarily set aside the case of the *amghar* we cannot discern any real authority beyond that of the household head. The genesis of the *dshar* thus provided us with the right elements: the local groups formed a corporation with regard to the ownership of the mosque and were allied in religious matters (the practice of Islam) and in judicial matters. Their alliance is distinguished by the fact that they occupy a contiguous territory, perhaps a relic of nomadic practices: "*Dshar* is the equivalent of the Arab term *douar*, which originally meant a circular camp delimiting a certain territory, among the nomads" (p. 34). Allies, then, allies who seem to cultivate an ideology of equality (everyone can speak, decisions are taken unanimously) but which are fundamentally unequal ones.

Indeed, let us reflect on the idiosyncrasies of this Berber case. Jamous does not provide any census, so that it is impossible to know the composition of residential groups. Furthermore, he says nothing about polygyny but, from what we know about North Africa, it was very uncommon, especially in the 1970s, and limited to the richest people.

This has serious repercussions. From my reanalysis, I conclude that residential groups are not aggregated at all. According to my definitions, this would make them sovereign, although I agree that this slightly stretches the notion of sovereignty. But let us stick with it for the moment. If we assume that marriage and monogyny were almost universal in the 1970s, it follows that those groups are immensely sensitive to the vagaries of demography. From Moroccan censuses of the 1970s for rural Morocco, we would expect married women to have on average 7–8 children, of whom only 4–5 would survive to maturity. By definition some will be childless, perhaps as little as 5 percent, and a few would have only daughters. And, admittedly, some will have many more that 8 children, and many sons. Without the compensating influence of polygyny and great variations in the age at marriage, *inequalities are thus demographically built in the organization of social formations based on the sovereignty of residential groups.* In this context, the case of Mohand Moh is quite revealing. Jamous mentions explicitly that his sons stayed together with the father, suggesting that sons do not automatically stay with fathers, especially if there is not enough land for all. Furthermore, he mentions that he also had many grandsons. In brief, his ascension is greatly due to his having many sons and grandsons. These demographic inequalities would also explain the migrations, presumably of sons whose fathers could not keep them at home for lack of land. And he doesn't mention what happens to households with only daughters. Would the sons-in-law first come in as protégés, and some eventually married a daughter if they proved reliable? None of this is mentioned but I am convinced that it explains both the frequency of migrants seeking protectors, and the success of some protégés who have many sons. Finally, since non-polygynous residential groups are the smallest 'sovereign' groups that exist, the great variability in their size dictates the greatest need for alliances.

These conclusions about the commune (lack of aggregation) also apply beyond. Between the territorial community and the tribe lie the 'fractions'. Each tribe is divided into five fractions. No activity, either judicial or religious, seems to be associated with this so-called 'level of segmentation', except that some markets 'belong' to a fraction or tribe. We are also informed that each fraction owns a portion of territory in the mountains and in the plains (except in the case of the Ait Bu Yafar tribe, who are confined to the mountains – p. 37) but "that these portions are not always contiguous" (p. 37). In fact, the whole question of 'fractions' remains obscure. So little is said about it that it is almost impossible to extrapolate but nothing, however, indicates that the communes were aggregated into a single fraction. No incumbent is suitable to head these fractions, from Jamous' account. Once again, if the so-called fractions have any reality, it is that of an alliance. The fact that they are made up of communes that are sometimes dispersed (since the communes occupy a closed geographical area, whereas the territories of the fractions are not contiguous) suggests that they can probably operate to counter the tendencies of the tribes to split. But we must leave fractions aside, with the certainty, however, that no aggregation will be found in them, either by descent or territoriality.

What about the 'tribe'. Composed of five fractions, the tribes nevertheless occupy a single territory, and all have a maritime border. What do they do? Nothing, it seems. They have no titular representative; if this is how the *qaid* might appear, it is an error of perspective. The *qaid* is an official sent by the sultan to collect taxes, not a 'tribal chief'. On the other hand, Jamous states that "[for] the Iqar'iyen, the word 'tribe' designates on the one hand a political unit, since it acts as a single body against whatever threatens it [...]" (p. 33). What are we to make of this statement?

It takes us right to the heart of the problem. Jamous is very clear on this subject: "The segmentary units of the three levels considered so far only exist in relation to each other. Iqar'iyen against external tribes, tribe against tribe, fraction against fraction" (p. 34). Relational identity, union in conflict: this is the purest

Evans-Pritchard. This proves beyond any doubt that there are no aggregated groups at that level but only alliances, alliances that manifest themselves in and through conflict beyond the commune (the commune forming the last level where we find an alliance coupled with a corporation); beyond the tribe, this alliance is reflected in the very terminology that Jamous chooses to designate it, namely a '*confederation* of tribes'.

But if we find alliances from the household all the way up to the confederation, what kind of alliances are they? If we call 'segmentary' those alliances "balanced in such a way that the opposing parties in a conflict can call upon a force equal to that which opposes them" (Verdon 1991, p. 255), are they segmentary alliances? I do not think so. Not every iqar'iyen alliance is segmentary. In fact, from the household to the commune, alliances must be seen on two different levels, one judicial, the other military (or defence). Households form alliances into a local group, and local groups into a commune, within the framework of judicial activities (and religious activities in the latter case). There is nothing segmentary about these alliances. They seem to follow the channels of agnatic kinship at the level of the local group, but this may simply be the counterpart of the fact that agnates tended to build their houses fairly close together (to form an easily discernible 'dispersed hamlet'). Beyond the local group, the alliances followed the channels of local contiguity. At both these levels, alliances are coupled with the fact that these groups of allies also form corporations, and carve out visible geographical units (the dwellings in the case of the local group, and the fact that the mountain land forms a single block in the case of the commune).

When it comes to violent activities, however, the alliances play out in a very different way. Within the local group nothing is very clear as Jamous barely mentions it, but the existence of assemblies (*ayraw*) suggests that conflicts are rare, as they should also be within the commune, also regulated by an assembly. In fact, I do not think that segmentation follows the channels that Jamous mentions, but emerges where the *amghar* operate (there are very many instances of conflict between fractions, and none, to my knowledge, between tribes). This raises two questions: (1) what are fractions, tribes and a confederation, and what should we call them, and (2) what should we conclude about the *amghar*?

From households to tribes, we follow a logic of nesting, based on neither descent nor territoriality. Since there are alliances, they are what I call 'territorial' alliances, alliances based on occupations of land, without speaking of segmentation. In Jamous' text, apart from one case of feud involving fractions (and it does not seem that this case can be extended to a 'fractional accounting' as he suggests), there is no case of tribes opposing each other. It goes without saying that if an army threatened a tribe, or a tribe threatened to invade another tribe, there would be alliances at that level but not necessarily confrontation between tribes in even numbers. They would look for the allies they could find, to counter their adversary with equal strength of course, without this turning into an organization of segmentary alliances. And since there is no mention of one tribe attacking another, the question remains academic. What distinguishes a tribe, in my opinion, is the fact that it occupies a single geographical area. We might think that tribal alliances were a way of ensuring access to different ecological zones (mountains, plains, sea), which they seem to do in a nomadic environment. So, at the lowest level we have agnatic alliances, and higher up we have alliances based on local contiguity, but alliances which, in my opinion, are in no way segmentary.

Now what can we say about the 'grands'? At first glance, the emergence of an *amghar* may suggest the appearance of a position of authority, a titular position. Indeed, Jamous writes:

> "The *amghar* is the one who unifies his lineage under his authority and exports violence outside his group. The patrilineage can no longer split up to exchange violence, as is the rule in the absence of a 'great one'. Any conflict between agnates must now be resolved peacefully. Murder within the group is forbidden" (p. 107).

And:

> "We say that the authority of the 'great man' comes from having been delegated and recognized the right to represent the group. It is consensus, not coercion that enables him to occupy this position" (p. 109).

He repeats this elsewhere (pp. 119, 146, 185). On page 109, the previous quotation continues in the following terms:

> "In fact, as we shall see, power is far from negligible among the Iqar'iyen. The 'great man' has real coercive power. But everything must happen as if the agnates were handing over to him, voluntarily and of their own free will, the right to guide and govern them" (p. 109).

When we closely follow the career of one of the *amghar*, we realize that this individual achieves his position through violence. This violence is first and foremost that of robbing his agnates, while giving them the impression that he is helping them. In short, the *amghar* takes advantage of the misfortune of others to put them in a position of indebtedness. Once indebted, impoverished, his agnates are practically deprived of the source of their honour; they become, more or less, like those who seek the protection of another. They go from being autonomous individuals to dependent ones. By creating economic dependence, the 'great' creates political dependence.

Incidentally, as Jamous does not write anything about polygyny, we are left to surmise. However, I strongly suspect that the rise of *amghar* could be linked to polygyny. At what stage do they start marrying more women, no one knows, but if they marry more than one wife, we will find a case where part of their ascension is due to their very progeny, especially if they have many sons. And even without polygyny, I believe that their position is due to their demographic circumstances, notably their male progeny.

The *amghar*'s career thus consisted precisely in transforming alliances between equals into a kind of more or less captive clientele. This is a form of clientelism, as the *amghar* did not hold a permanent position. His position was constantly under threat, he could fall or be assassinated at any moment and, what is more, his position was not transmitted. "The title of 'great' is not inherited, it is acquired" (p. 100). In short, he is a political entrepreneur who owes his political position to his gifts for economic manipulation. For want of a better term, I will call him a 'leader'. 'For want of a better term' because a political leader does not necessarily use as much coercion, but the fact remains that, even if he rises above his allies through his manipulations and cunning, "he will never become a lord *and will remain first among equals* (italics added)" (p. 185). *Primus inter pares*, that is basically what the *amghar* is, ally turned leader, transforming his local group into his personal domain, rallying all his allies to his cause, and speaking on their behalf. He represents them, yes, but as a leader.

And in this social formation, leadership is as important as the alleged (and false) equality of allies. In my opinion, it is leadership that calls for a segmentary organization, not of local groups, communes, fractions and tribes, but of the *leff*. I argue that it is the *leff* that functions in a segmentary way, not the nesting of the household all the way up to the iqar'iyen confederation.

What are *leffs* and why are they important? *Leffs*, or what Jamous calls 'political leagues', are alliances between *amghar*. The leagues mobilize and intervene essentially to moderate conflicts between two *amghar* of the same territorial community, to stop bloodshed (p. 164). And yet,

> "Massacre is [...] a way for a group to get rid of a rival in order to settle a group of immigrants on its land, in other words a new group of dependents. It is a political operation linked to the quest for power. The winning group will be able to show its pre-eminence and, subsequently, prove that it has the strength to uphold its honour and reputation" (p. 84).

In short, the *amghar*'s ambitions do not stop at his local group, but extend beyond. And if another *amghar* stands in his way, the conflict can escalate to the point of bloodshed. To stop him, one of the *amghar* calls in his *leff* and the two leagues clash. Shots are exchanged, followed by mediation by the *chorfa* (the religious sheriff) as soon as someone is injured or killed. What is interesting is that the leagues extend beyond the borders of the tribe, and that their "number is always even and greater than two, generally four or six [...]" (p. 162). In other words, it is really in the context of conflicts between *amghar*, and consequently in the context of political leagues, that attempts are made to mobilize forces that are balanced. If there is a segmentary defensive (or military) organization, this is where it is to be found. And that is why mediation is so important. Because of this balance, and because of the size of the forces involved, the battle would inevitably lead to bloodshed without the intervention of conciliators (the *chorfa*). And this has sometimes happened.

In other words, the iqar'iyen segmentary organization seems to be a corollary of leadership. If no one was trying to climb the leadership ladder, the vendetta would stop at the blow for blow. It is the despotic impulses of some individuals that endanger the lives of others and force a segmentary defence. Jamous' argument could therefore be reversed, and we could argue that segmentation depends on the leadership inherent in this social formation. And that is what I shall try to demonstrate.

Rethinking the Iqar'iyen social formation

Let us go back to where I started. I first demonstrated that there was no aggregation beyond the household. In my conceptual framework, this is equivalent to declaring the household sovereign. I then briefly analysed the position of the *amghar*, and discovered that he was no title-holder, but a leader. So I concluded that even in local groups with *amghar*, we are not dealing with aggregation, but leadership. Whether or not an *amghar* 'rules' within a local group, there is no aggregation anywhere. This forces us to rethink everything.

In his formulation, Jamous has to postulate the priority of one element over the other: segmentarity (equality) or power (inequality). The two seem incompatible and he concludes that one encompasses the other. This is utterly meaningless. Furthermore, like all theorists of political anthropology, Jamous gets bogged down in the notorious category of 'acephalous societies': he has to explain a lack, so to speak, an absence. But let us suggest the opposite: that most iqar'iyen adults strive to achieve sovereignty and political independence, but some want more. The result is a clientelistic social formation: you either have dependents, or you may be dependent yourself. And the greater the number of dependents (and therefore the greater the wealth), the greater the power. It is only within his household that an adult man is sovereign, but it should be noted that his dependents, especially his adult sons, do not necessarily take kindly to his tutelage. So fathers invoke a 'divine law' ordering the sons to be subordinate to their father. This is the Iqar'iyen universe. But this universe is also one of inequality. Few sovereigns have 'kingdoms' of equal size. Some will have more or less land, others more or less children. Inequality is written into the very constitution of the 'kingdom' which the household head 'rules', and this inequality fluctuates over the course of a lifetime. Hence the primary rule, much more important than the elusive segmentarity, that most 'rulers' seek to increase their domain, and that they can only do so at the expense of others.

There is therefore a whole set of coexisting rules, none of which takes precedence over the others: (1) that sovereignty stops at the domestic level (i.e. the head of the household is sovereign over a 'kingdom' consisting of his house, his lands and his dependents); (2) that this sovereignty is founded on inequality, since very few sovereign rulers have equal kingdoms; (3) that any sovereign with a superior kingdom tries to take away from the kingdom of others, or tries to increase his kingdom, which he can only do at the expense of others; and (4) that to protect their sovereignty, sovereigns must therefore surround themselves with allies. This is the universal rule of all politics.

In a word, beyond the house everything is a matter of alliances, but within these alliances some individuals seek to be leaders. Or rather, the allies will sometimes tend to follow a leader because they themselves are too weak, or too weakened. Briefly, wanting to grow at the expense of others is as much a rule of this social formation as domestic sovereignty. Domestic sovereignty leads to equality (we are all sovereign, so we are all equal) whereas the desire to grow at the expense of others leads to clientelism and leadership (but some of us are more equal than others – Orwell's famous statement!). In conclusion, there is no acephalous society or segmentarity: there is domestic sovereignty, inequalities, and therefore alliances (alliances of all kinds, some of them segmentary), clientelism and leadership.

In a nutshell, all we have to do is postulate domestic sovereignty (and therefore equality) and the basic inequality of these 'sovereign' residential groups, and everything else follows, or nearly so (religion is thrown in to make things a little more complex…). This formulation fits in much better with the famous code of honour. Honour and baraka are products of opinion: a man only has honour if he follows a precise course of action. Similarly, the sheriff (religious leader) completely depends on opinion and, for him to be recognized as having baraka (spiritual power due to divine blessing), it is absolutely essential that he succeeds in his negotiations when called upon to mediate. On both sides (the secular and religious), opinion creates reputation, and reputation generates status. It is thus all a question of opinion, of how others see you. You are not someone because of some intrinsic attributes – being the eldest, being from the oldest generation – but because of what you do. The doing is what defines the being, but this doing is closely prescribed: honour on the one hand, and baraka on the other. It is understandable that the baraka is necessary because the code of honour is somewhat brutal, especially when embedded in the leadership system that leads to the emergence of *amghar.*

In brief, honour, to use Bourdieu's felicitous expression, is a kind of symbolic capital, anchored in real 'possessions'. Through marriage, the husband acquires an 'asset' (his wife), subject to multiple prohibitions. Then, when his father dies, he acquires land, another capital to which his honour is attached. But why? Is there any advantage in describing all this in terms of honour/'domain of the forbidden' (*domaine de l'interdit*), as Jamous does? In this perspective, honour is what is attached to the source of all prosperity for the layman. To undermine one's honour it is to undermine his very life, since life is growth. In short, honour is the ability to maintain control over the main sources of social advancement. Honour is not measured by its effects, but by the individual's ability to maintain it. In brief, one enjoys a quantum of honour through marriage and inheritance, through women and land, a quantum that one attempts to increase. One has it, or rather obtains it through marriage, filiation and work (not to mention cunning). Through the quantity of land and the number of children, one tries to have dependents, a clientele, people who are indebted to the honourable man. So one climbs the ladder by accumulating the numbers of those below, and this game is of equal importance to the inviolability of 'domestic sovereignty'. In essence, iqar'iyen honour is linked to something one possesses, to the source of prosperity, i.e. women and land. Possession is a source of honour, while success is proof of baraka. But honour must be defended, because it seems to be under constant threat. The baraka is threatened from within, so to speak: if the cherif does not succeed, he has quite simply lost his baraka. If there is no manifestation of its effects, the force can no longer exist. But the same cannot be said of honour. If a challenge is not met, honour is lost.

How does one lose one's honour? By demonstrating one's inferiority. The code of honour thus refers to power relationships. Anyone who fails to defend an attack on his honour loses it. This is both interesting and paradoxical. For if honour were exclusively linked to possessions, the person who does not respond to the challenge (if it does not involve murder) has not necessarily lost anything. If a stranger talks to my wife, I certainly have not lost that 'possession'. This imposes a refinement. Honour is not linked to possessions, but to controlling access to these possessions. This is where the notion of prohibitions (*interdits*) comes in. If it is forbidden to most men to talk to my wife, it is to assert my control over her. If you break this rule, you are questioning my ability to control her, my ability to defend my 'domain'.

Let us go further. If I am assassinated, it goes without saying that it is not I who has lost honour, but my close agnates, if they do not avenge my death. But why my close agnates? How am I an integral part of their honour? They have no control over me, how am I part of their prohibitions? When I get married I acquire a certain domination, but I am always under that of my father. So, if I am killed, it is him whose honour has been attacked. If he is dead, it is my brothers who are dishonoured if they do not strike back. Why should I be part of the honour of my brothers and first cousins, and they of my honour? We can only conjecture, but I would leave the notion of control to look at alliances.

In such a system, one can only maintain one's sovereignty (as in any social formation, moreover), whatever its degree, through a network of alliances. However, one's closest allies (but also one's fiercest competitors) are first one's brothers and half-brothers, then one's first cousins. This encompasses most of the local group. One depends on one's close allies (this close alliance being mainly defined by agnatic kinship) as much as they depend on me, because our 'sovereignties' are reciprocally dependent on one another. However, if one kills one of my close allies, he directly undermines those who guarantee my sovereignty. If I do not respond, that means I cannot even defend my closest allies. I am therefore a poor ally, a 'little one' and my smallness has been demonstrated. To make things right, I must take revenge. So I show that I was worthy of their alliance, of their trust, and that I am greater than anyone thought. Everything is a balance of power. I will accept compensation if I believe that the forces present are too unequal, but as soon as a certain numerical balance is re-established, I will strike. This is the logic of this social formation.

CHAPTER SIX

The Yao of Malawi: a matrilineal chiefdom?[31]

In 1956 Clyde Mitchell published *The Yao Village*, a brilliant monograph that soon became a classic of British anthropology and the ethnography of matrilineal societies. In it, Mitchell described with great mastery and detail the matrilineal organization of this population of the Protectorate of Nyasaland (now Malawi) and the integration of their villages into chiefdoms. Since then, ethnographers have considered the Yao among the populations traditionally organized into matrilineal chiefdoms. It is this demonstration, and the conceptual framework within which it is embedded, that I here examine in an operational perspective.

In 1951, in a collection of texts written by ethnographers working at the Rhodes-Livingstone Institute, in Zambia (Colson and Gluckman 1951), Mitchell published a first ethnographic sketch of the Yao. In this brief presentation (around sixty pages), he described the social organization starting with its minimal units, the smallest matrilineal segments, and working upwards to the most inclusive one, the chiefdom. In 1956, in *The Yao Village*, he reversed the order of presentation and first traced the contours of the chiefdom before moving down through villages to the minimal matrilineal segments. Why? To understand we need to evoke the classic framework initially devised by Rivers and perfected by

[31] Originally Verdon 1995.

Fortes and Evans-Pritchard, namely the distinction between the 'political' domain, – that of relations between so-called 'corporate' groups – and the 'domestic' domain – that of relations internal to these corporate groups (Rivers 1924; Fortes and Evans-Pritchard 1940)[32]. Nevertheless, the Yao facts were somewhat resistant to this distinction and, rather than a decal, we should look upon it only as an inspiration[33]

The Yao: Mitchell's 'corporatist' model

Let us briefly sketch out this quasi-Fortesian model of Yao social organization[34]. In the purest tradition that led Evans-Pritchard to write *The Nuer*, followed by *Kinship and Marriage among the Nuer*, Mitchell starts his analysis with a description of inter-village relations, which he openly calls the 'field of political relations'[35]. These villages, by far the most important groups, he presents both as the minimal political groups organized into chiefdoms, and as the field within which kinship predominates[36].

---

[32] For details of the evolution of this conceptual and analytical framework, see volume 1.

[33] Where 'descent theorists' contrasted interpersonal relations (internal to the smallest so-called political group, i.e. a lineage segment or a local group) to relations *between groups*, Mitchell isolates the Yao village as a minimal political entity but, within these villages, he does not write of domestic relations, but of a lineage system, of relations between matrilineal lineage segments ranging from a minimal segment (a group of uterine siblings, the *mbumba* – we will come back to this) to the village matrilineage via an intermediate level, the section. Let us not delude ourselves, however, for in order to describe this intra-village lineage mechanism with its segmentary appearance, he will have to talk about relations between siblings, between father and son, between maternal uncle and uterine nephew.

[34] This presentation is based exclusively on the 1956 monograph.

[35] Where dates only appear without author's name, these will be Mitchell's publications; where dates do not even appear but only page numbers, these will refer to his classic 1956 monograph, *The Yao Village*.

[36] Note that in 1951 he used the term village in a generic sense, and distinguished between hamlet and thorp (an archaic term designating a small village): a hamlet consists of a single *mbumba* (the smallest matrifiliative group, or sorority), whereas a thorp contains several (1951, p. 313). I will try to follow this terminology. When I

Great slave traders and great slave owners, the Yao had long been organized into chiefdoms and had probably invaded the Nyasaland region (in present-day Malawi), which they occupied after the British conquest. Their alleged invasion, however, was not of a military nature; they infiltrated the region in small matrilineal nuclei who settled among the Nyanja (the natives). Taking advantage of the dissensions that divided their hosts, they then subjected the area to their domination. This invasion was already complete by the time of Livingstone's visit in 1866, and the first documents confirm the importance of the villages and of their organization into chiefdoms. Even before the British conquest, the village would have appeared as a corporation represented by its chief (headman, or *asyene musi*) vis-à-vis the external authorities. Whatever the identity of the culprits in a conflict, responsibility fell on village headmen to mediate when the protagonists belonged to the same village. Responsible for arbitrating conflicts within his village, the *asyene musi* had to defer to higher authorities for inter-village disputes, or for very serious offences, up to and including the Paramount Chief (*asyene cilambo*). Even before the British invasion, village chiefs were subject to the authority of intermediate chiefs and the Paramount Chief; within the village, slaves were subject to free men, and the latter lived under the authority of their elder brother and the village warden.

Despite this hierarchical organization, the villages enjoyed a great deal of autonomy; Mitchell observed and even described this in some detail, without really incorporating it into his analysis. I will come back to this later. In addition, new villages were created quite easily when a matrilineal section, dissatisfied with its lot under the authority of the *asyene musi* (village headman), decided to go and beg a plot of land from another *asyene musi* in order to set up a village. The size of these villages could increase according to the warring (and economic) fortunes of their chief, who could thus rise in the hierarchy. This process even encouraged chiefdoms

discuss a village community in the generic sense, I will speak either of a local group or of villages, and I will use hamlet in the precise sense of his 1951 text.

to split when an ambitious and successful *asyene musi*, surrounded by a powerful clientele of slaves and a large progeny from slave wives[37], challenged the Chief's authority and emerged victorious. In this way, the chiefdoms would frequently split up.

The prohibition of slavery and the British invasion brutally interrupted this dynamic of growth and reproduction of chieftaincies, so that the chiefdoms of the colonial period present a frozen image of the state of political relations at the end of the nineteenth century; it is this post-conquest organization that Mitchell describes in the rest of the book. At the time of his fieldwork, from 1946 to 1949, the relationships between the various village chiefs would have been defined by the history of their conquest and by their kinship. By the history of their migration and invasion, first of all, in that the *asyene musi* belonged either to the category of aboriginal chiefs (sic) or to that of invaders or newcomers. Insofar as the natives (of Nyanja origin) had been displaced, the fundamental principle of the Yao hierarchy was based on simple anteriority in time: the first to settle in a place claimed to be its chief. Their hierarchy was also based on kinship, as bonds of 'perpetual kinship' linked the new villages to the old ones; this kinship was supposed to reflect that which linked the two *asyene musi* when the new village was founded. Some *asyene musi* thus found themselves in a perpetual relationship of maternal uncle to uterine nephew, son to father, or even paternal uncle to brother's son. Finally, rank was also determined by the fact that a man had to ask another *asyene musi* for a plot of land in order to found a new village, thereby recognizing his pre-eminence. All in all, Mitchell concludes, "under the Paramount Chief of a chiefdom all the other village chiefs rank *in a relatively fixed pyramidal hierarchy*" (p. 77, emphasis added), a hierarchy he had previously described in the following terms:

> "In any place, chosen at random in a chiefdom as large as Kawinga, for example, there are likely to be two or three

[37] In a matrilineal society, the sons of female slaves had no choice but to remain in their father's village.

villages that recognize the primacy of one of their own. The headman of that village will be called upon to settle disputes over land or personal quarrels [...]. But this superior chief will recognize as his *superior the person who occupied this place before him* [italics in text]. This system extends to larger and larger areas, each headman in turn recognizing the pre-eminence of another headman who was there before him, until in the final analysis the same principle establishes the primacy of the invading chief over all the other headmen" (p. 63).

At the top of this pyramid sits the Paramount Chief, the representative of the chieftaincy, the maximal political group whose unity he expresses through his prayers to the ancestral cults that give him power over the rain and, consequently, over the fertility of his chieftaincy. This unity of the chiefdom would also have been embodied by the right to impose fines in the event of disputes involving bodily harm and arson. In the past, he would also have been supreme judge for all serious disputes within his chiefdom.

After presenting this 'relatively fixed' pyramidal hierarchy, Mitchell describes another hierarchy that is anything but static, a social formation where village chiefs compete with one another to acquire power and prestige, and rise to the top of the political pyramid. According to Mitchell, this would have been the very essence of the Yao political process. This competition would have been expressed through constant struggle for the various symbols of prestige. In the past, the diacritical signs of prestige consisted, for example, in special clothing, or the type and size of dagger a chief could wear; today, the main signs of prestige include, in order of importance, a) the right to wear a scarlet turban, b) the right to perform initiation rites for boys, c) the right to perform initiation rites for girls. The number of combinations of these signs is limited and, by weighing them, Mitchell obtains a precise gradation defining the place and rank of the various types of village chiefs under the authority of the Paramount Chief.

Having described this hierarchical pyramid from top to bottom, Mitchell concludes his analysis of the political field with a study of the village chief himself. Representing a corporation (the village) of which he is the 'possessor' or 'guardian' (Mitchell uses the two terms synonymously on page 110; we shall return to them later), the position of the *asyene musi* in the political structure reflects the history of the dominant matrilineage in his village. Responsible for some rituals (libations to the spirits of the ancestors), the village chief occupies a relatively uncomfortable position, caught between the bark and the tree. On the one hand, he must defend the interests of the members of his matrilineage; but the Yao, who are matrilineal, also practice uxorilocal residence, and the villages are mainly made up of the female members of the matrilineage, their young male children and their husbands. Consequently, the *asyene musi* must avoid dividing the village by alienating the husbands.

In conclusion, powerful centrifugal factors constantly threaten to break up the villages, and the *asyene musi* must counteract them. Conflicts, both between lineage segments and between lineage members and spouses, are chronic and constantly give rise to accusations of witchcraft, confirmed or disproved by regular visits to the diviners. The *asyene musi* must fight relentlessly to preserve the unity of his village, which he can only do by showing himself to be an impartial judge and a fine psychologist, capable of detecting virtual conflicts and nipping them in the bud. Otherwise, he runs the risk of seeing a large part of his village split off to found a new one far away. This sketch concludes the analysis of the more strictly political sphere. Chapter VI begins with an analysis of the matrilineal lineage system within the village.

Admittedly, when villages split up, the dissenting matrilineal segment retains perpetual kinship links with the mother village, which situates the villages in relation to one another in the political hierarchy, but the precise genealogical links are forgotten after one generation. It is therefore within villages that the 'principle of matrilineal descent' operates fully. These matrilineages, according to Mitchell, are of a genealogical order comparable to what Fortes identified as inner lineages among the Tallensi: from the eponymous (female) ancestor to the last-born the genealogy does not span more than five or six generations. In a group calculation, the genealogies presented by Mitchell show matrilineages that do not exceed G+2 or G+3[38].

The Yao matrilineage would be localized, forming the backbone of the village, and the matrilineage's elder would *ipso facto* occupy the position of *asyene musi*. The matrilineage would support its members in their disputes, in sickness (consultation of soothsayers) and in death (organisation of funerals). In the past the lineage elder would have prayed to the dead on behalf of this community. This solidarity, however, is infinitely precarious because matrilineages, initially divided into sections (branches descended from female ancestors in G+1), fragment into minimal segments consisting of a group of sisters and their children, under the guardianship of their elder brother (the *mbumba* or sorority group). Each of these sorority group is opposed to the others, each dreaming of forming the embryo of what will become a matrilineage capable of establishing itself elsewhere; each *asyene mbumba* (head a sorority group) is therefore seeking to become an *asyene musi* if the number of his siblings and their offspring constitutes a large enough political clientele for him to consider secession.

Mitchell sees the sorority groups amalgamated into sections[39], and the sections into a localised matrilineage. Here we find, on the one hand, the classical interweaving of lineages and, on the other, the continual process of segmentation whereby sorority groups, over generations, seek to become major sections and, ultimately, autonomous matrilineages capable of establishing themselves elsewhere. According to Mitchell, this interweaving creates a segmentary matrilineal lineage. And this segmentary dynamic, in the classical perspective, would explain the relationships between uterine brothers, between maternal uncles and uterine nephews, and between fathers and sons. The process of segmentation is repeated at each generation, as men reach adulthood and try to gain

---

38 What he himself explicitly states elsewhere (1951, p. 331).

39 Where there are sections. An eponymous ancestor who had only one daughter, leaving numerous descendants, would be at the summit of a matrilineage that would not be differentiated into sections.

control of their *mbumba*, and this segmentation not only divides matrilineages and villages, but also generates a whole dynamic that seems to extend beyond the villages to the chiefdom. From the minimal uterine group (the sorority) to the chiefdom, we find the same scissiparous tendencies, multiplying the lineage segments, the villages and, in the past, the chiefdoms themselves. And at every level of grouping, the *asyene* must work to counter these tendencies, to unite those who seek to secede.

Some conceptual problems

This summary obviously does not do justice to Mitchell's wealth of case studies, but it suffices to pinpoint the issues that concern me. *The Yao Village* is implicitly torn between two opposite poles, never reconciled because never recognized as such. We can easily discern the strong language of descent theory: on the one hand, an interlocking of groups, from *mbumba* to chieftaincy, described as corporate, each possessing symbols of its own unity. On the other hand, we find an internal differentiation, segmentation levels in which each segment opposes segments of the same order, giving lineages a segmentary appearance. This is the backbone that could be called static, despite the image of segmentation, static because it assumes an arrangement of segments within the local matrilineage, as well as a relatively fixed hierarchical pyramid within the chiefdom. On the other hand the rich case analyses – and they make up the greater part of the volume – point to an entirely individual dynamic that is not to be found among either the Nuer or the Tallensi (not to mention countless other cases of so-called segmentary societies), a dynamic of lineage segments that aspire to become autonomous villages, of villages that strive to grow in order to compete for prestige and rank and even, in the past, to challenge the authority of the Paramount Chief and, if successful, to form new chiefdoms altogether. Although Mitchell attempts to integrate this dynamic into a corporatist model, he fails, and for one simple reason: whereas the segments of classical theory simply perpetuate groups from below, so to speak, the various Yao allegedly corporate groups seek, on the contrary, to rise to the top by amalgamating other groups. At most, we could say that a *mbumba* aspires to become a chieftaincy, if God gives it life. This antinomy is revealing in that it confronts us with the limits of anthropological discourse, and brings us directly back to the title of this article: "Did the Yao form matrilineal chiefdoms (at least before the Conquest)?", a question that raises two others: in what way did they form chiefdoms, and in what way were they matrilineal? A spontaneous answer to the second question would be: they were matrilineal because a set of increasingly inclusive lineage segments traced a common ancestry to an eponymous ancestor, exclusively through the female line. We will come back to this 'evidence' after a detour to the first question: how did the Yao constitute chiefdoms?

The answer can only be guessed, because Mitchell provides no definitions and leaves us in the dark as to what he means by the term. So I will stick to the interpretation that seems most likely.

In Anglo-Saxon literature, two main trends have dominated reflections on chiefdoms. On the one hand, an American tradition, inspired by the work of Julian Steward and carrying on mainly in the works of Service (1962), Fried (1967) and, above all, archaeologists[40], is overtly evolutionist and locates chiefdoms among the 'levels of cultural integration', somewhere between the tribe and the state (or kingdoms); but these reflections post-date Mitchell's work. Among the British, on the other hand, we can detect a more typological reflection which, while concealing an implicit vision of political evolution, carefully avoids mentioning it and ingenuously presents itself as a mere classification. This is the famous typology that Fortes and Evans-Pritchard elaborated in their introduction to *African Political Systems* (Fortes and Evans-Pritchard 1940). Although Mitchell makes no mention of this introduction either in *The Yao Village* or in his main ethnographic sketches, it is hard to imagine an Africanist working in the field in

[40] See Earle (199la) for a complete synthesis and bibliography.

the 1940s who had not read it. I will therefore base my reflection on this classical text.

Let us briefly recall their main conclusions. Fortes and Evans-Pritchard dissociated 'primitive states' from stateless societies. Primitive states encompass societies that "have a centralized authority, administrative machinery and judicial institutions – in short, a government – and in which cleavages of wealth, privilege and status correspond to the distribution of power and authority" (Fortes and Evans-Pritchard 1940, p. 5), while stateless societies lack them. More fundamentally, these two types of societies are opposed in the way they organize relations between their territorial segments. Indeed, in this 1940 publication, where Evans-Pritchard's ideas further fertilized those of Fortes, both authors perceive a universal constant: all societies are ultimately composed of what they call territorial segments (Fortes and Evans-Pritchard 1940, p. 10), and the way in which these territorial groups are amalgamated into more inclusive units is what distinguishes primitive states from stateless societies. In state societies, 'administrative organization' "primarily regulates political relations between territorial segments" (p. 6), so that administrative and territorial divisions overlap completely: "In the societies of Group A [primitive states], the administrative unit *is a territorial unit*" (p. 10, italics added), making the chief "the administrative and judicial head of a given territorial division [and... the) head of state is a territorial ruler" (p. 10). These primitive states, where rank and prestige dominated social life, were often culturally heterogeneous societies (p. 9), centralized and pyramidal (rather than segmentary), distinguished from acephalous societies by their organized use of force (p. 14).

While Fortes and Evans-Pritchard clearly contrasted primitive states and stateless societies, they were completely confused when they lumped kings and chiefs together among state societies. In some passages, chiefs emerge as those in charge of the main territorial and administrative divisions of the same kingdom, while in other contexts they themselves sit at the head of distinct social formations that we might call chiefdoms. Paradoxically, this muddle contained the seeds of a distinction between kingdom and chiefdom, a distinction that Mitchell probably intuitively grasped when he wrote, in 1951, that "the available historical documentation suggests that there has never been a strong central Yao state" (1951, p. 347). The Yao would be like primitive states in their pyramidal administrative centralization, in the importance of rank and prestige, in their cultural heterogeneity and in the fact that, in the past, the ruler's power was largely based on force, but they would be different from kingdoms in that this centralization was not developed and the Yao states did not persist, subject as they were to frequent splits. Hence the implicit equivalence: kingdom = strong state, chiefdom = weak state.

In a personal communication, Fortes admitted to me that this introduction to *African Political Systems* was mainly his own composition, and that Evans-Pritchard had practically only endorsed it. A thorough knowledge of the work of both authors lends great credibility to this assertion, for despite the reference to the famous segmentation and its implicit cultural relativity, this text gives us a very Fortesian image of so-called segmentary lineages (see volume 1). If the lineage system articulates the relationships between allegedly corporate segments, then we must assume – and this is exactly what Tallensi ethnography teaches us – that at each level of inclusion there should be a representative of this more inclusive segment, an elder appointed because of his genealogical position or because of some specific criteria.

In fact, the Fortesian model of lineage requires an important clarification. In any social organization, it is necessary to dissociate what we might call 'titular positions' – offices that exist even if no one occupies them at a given moment, and which presuppose the existence of specific criteria of accession – from what we might call a leadership position. You do not become the holder of a leadership position, because a leadership position is created and must be defended at all times. Without a political clientele (followers) who believe in his leadership qualities, a leader is nothing but a boastful braggart. So let us retranslate my previous statement: at each level of inclusion in a lineage whose segments are said to be corporate, we should logically find an office, usually that of lineage elder[41].

In a Tallensi or Abutia lineage (Verdon 1983, 1991), some levels of inclusion can be delineated, from the minimal segment to the maximal lineage. At each of these nesting levels we find a representative, normally the eldest of the oldest generation, an individual who owes his office to his position in an ancestral genealogy and who enjoys a particular set of jurisdictions. Let us assume three levels: minimal, intermediate and maximal. If disputes arise between members of the same minimal segment, the case is referred to the eldest member of the segment; if disputes arise between members of different minimal segments of the same intermediate lineage, the representative of that intermediate level arbitrates. And so on up to the maximal level. Again, all these representatives are title-holders, not leaders.

Rather than lineages, according to Fortes and Evans-Pritchard, an 'administrative apparatus' governed relations between corporate territorial segments in primitive states. So let us simply substitute territorial administration for lineage organization. In Fortes' logic, we should also be able to discern a nesting of local groups: minimal local groups should themselves be aggregated into increasingly inclusive territorial units on the basis of this administrative apparatus, all the way to the top of the pyramid. Each level of grouping should similarly be represented by an individual in a position of authority. For the sake of simplicity, let us again assume three levels: villages, groups of villages amalgamated together into what we might call a district, and groups of districts merged into a larger unit, in our case the chiefdom. Just as we might expect to find tenured elders at every level of a lineage organization, we should encounter village chiefs, district chiefs, and a Paramount Chief at every level of this administrative organization. And, as we

[41] It is interesting to note that an operational reading of the Nuer reveals no lineages, a conclusion implicitly reached by Holy (1979), whereas the same reading retains the Tallensi's lineages. And while the Nuer have leaders, the Tallensi have none.

can observe in our own state societies, some types of disputes would fall exclusively under the jurisdiction of the village chief, others under that of the district chief, while some would have to be referred directly to the Paramount Chief.

This presentation of lineage and administrative organizations presupposes that we have solved a problem that was latent in Fortes and Evans-Pritchard's introduction and that would only come to light later, namely the total confusion surrounding the notion of lineage. Let us go back to the 'obvious' definition given earlier of the Yao's matrilinearity (assuming for now that they have matrilineal lineages); the Yao would be matrilineal, I wrote, "[...] because a set of increasingly inclusive lineage segments traced a common ancestry to an eponymous ancestor, and did so exclusively through women's progeny" (p. 139 above). This definition obscures the dimension I have just highlighted, in that its reference to the 'inclusion' of segments does not allow us to dissociate the genealogical referent (each level representing a different generational level) from the properly social referent, so to speak (the fact that each level of inclusion also presupposes a titular position). The result is most saddening because, in the final analysis, any group whose members recognized a common ancestry (beyond the immediate family) could claim the title of descent group and, consequently, be declared a lineage. In some texts, descendants of the same individual in G+1 form a descent group, and Mitchell even extends the definition to descendants of the same mother (the *mbumba*), whom he presents as a lineage segment. However, according to Fortesian theory, lineage segments are synonymous with descent groups and, in the same literature, descent group and lineage are also synonymous. It therefore becomes impossible to separate so-called segmentary lineages from any group of agnates or uterine relatives descended from the same ancestor, and ethnographers have consequently seen lineages everywhere. As I argued earlier, this problem can be solved by dissociating groups from aggregated groups.

I will use my operational framework to answer my initial question: do the Yao form a matrilineal chiefdom? Within my framework, it goes without saying that there can be no lineage without an aggregation based on descent. As my own work on Abutia suggests (see above, chapter 1) and the literature testifies, I would initially assume that there cannot be a chiefdom without a territorial aggregation. Let us refine further. In Abutia, if the three villages had been aggregated, the territorial organization would have capped lineages. But other chiefdoms have no lineages and are aggregated all the way through territoriality. But are all chiefdoms aggregated in one way or the other? The notion of chiefdom intimates a pyramidal social formation, with a Supreme Ruler at its apex. But is territorial aggregation necessary? If we find a pyramidal social formation but without aggregation, what are we then dealing with? To answer, we will explore Yao chiefdoms to assess if the villages were aggregated on the basis of territoriality into districts, and those aggregated further into a chiefdom.

An operational reanalysis

Any reanalysis of the 'traditional' organization of societies that have suffered colonial rule is fraught with serious difficulties, amplified when colonial conquest has frozen relatively fluid relationships. We must therefore assume that ethnographic work reveals some features of the pre-conquest organization, even if the imposition of a colonial regime has transformed political relationships. I will therefore base my analysis on the chiefdoms observed by Mitchell, and then raise the question of pre-colonial political organization.

Within an operational framework, I will initially seek to identify the contexts (i.e. types of activity) in which the authority of the Paramount Chief manifests itself. In his testimonies, Mitchell suggests that the Paramount Chief acted as the representative of an aggregated group in judicial, religious and land tenure contexts. Unfortunately, his ethnography here suffers from serious shortcomings, and I will have to conjecture. I will broach the judicial question last; it is both the most complex and the one about which we are best informed.

Let us turn first to the Paramount Chief's religious activities, i.e. what Mitchell calls 'cults to the spirits of the ancestors' and, secondly, initiation rites for boys and girls. Since not all village chiefs have the right to celebrate these rites, but all officiate at ancestor cults, I will begin my reanalysis with the latter.

It seems that only village chiefs enjoyed this prerogative, which would lead us to believe that the village formed a religious category as a group of individuals whose well-being depended on the benevolence of the *asyene musi*'s ancestors. Insofar as the *asyene musi* prayed to his ancestors in the name of the village, could we say that in this context villages were aggregated into groups of villages, and ultimately into a chiefdom?

What would we find if there was aggregation in this field? Above all, an ancestral genealogy linking the different villages. Villages A, B, C[42], for example, would claim to be descended from the same ancestor (i.e. X), villages D, E, F, would claim to be descended from the same ancestor (i.e. Y), and all these villages would claim to be descended from the same ancestor at a higher level (i.e. Z). When sacrificing to the intermediate ancestors (X or Y), all villages descended from the same ancestor would form a single aggregated group, and their chiefs would all gather, under the tutelage of one of them, to participate in the cult. Finally, this aggregation could only be based on descent, since an ancestor cult automatically refers to ancestral generations and their genealogical relationships. If this were the case, the Paramount Chief would not sit at the top of a chieftaincy, but rather of a maximal lineage. But we know that this is not the case. Mitchell tells us that the Yao suffer from genealogical amnesia, and that villages are not linked by the memory of an ancestral genealogy; he explicitly confines lineage organization to villages. Between villages, he implicitly refers to territorial aggregation[43].

---

42 Where A, B and C represent both village names and the names of eponymous female ancestors, assuming for the convenience of the demonstration that villages take the name of the mother or sister of the man who founded the village.

43 "The Chiefdom in the old days was distinctly a territorial unit..." (p. 47).

In conclusion, there is no aggregation at work in ancestor worship. Village chiefs worship their own ancestors on behalf of the villagers for their well-being, and the Paramount Chief (*asyene cilambo*) prays to his own for the same purpose; no genealogy encompasses them. The Paramount Chief's ancestors are only relevant to the well-being of his *musi*, except in matters of rain and initiation. Initiations include people from some neighbouring villages, who depend on the *asyene cilambo* in these matters, as their own chiefs do not have the right to celebrate these rites. The Paramount Chief, on the other hand, had exclusive power over the rain, a power he inherited from his ancestors and could not delegate to anyone else. How is this power to be interpreted, if not in terms of aggregation? To answer this question, we will have to take a long detour through land ownership. In some places, Mitchell writes of the village chief as the 'owner' (*asyene*) of a village (*musi*), and of the Paramount Chief as the owner (*asyene*) of the chiefdom (*cilambo*). So what is an *asyene*? Fortunately, Mitchell sheds some light on the subject in his 1951 article. Pointing out that Yao dictionaries translate *asyene* as 'owner', he corrects:

> "This is a mistranslation if we use the word 'owner' to imply the possession of property rights over an object. A closer translation of the word *asyene* would in this case be the person with whom an object is identified. The word is also used to indicate an emphatic form of the personal pronoun, so that *asyene* in this sense would be translated as 'he himself' […] Therefore I propose to translate the term *asyene mbumba* as 'warden' of the sorority-group" (1951, pp. 318–319).

And what applies to *mbumba* extends to *musi*, since Mitchell often refers to village headmen as 'warden'. In short, the main idea behind the notion of *asyene* is that of a 'guardian', an individual responsible for a given community. But does the *asyene*'s responsibility come with ownership of the land? This is where things get complicated. Mitchell relates that an *asyene mbumba* who wishes to create his own village goes to another *asyene musi* for land, and that the parcel given is irrevocable, as long as the *musi* remains. In other words, if the village community and its *asyene* move elsewhere, the land granted to them will revert to the person who donated it. It should be noted that a dissident wishing to leave the chiefdom in which his native village was established can apply for a plot of land from any *asyene musi* in another chiefdom, without first seeking permission from the *asyene cilambo*. Any *asyene musi* therefore seems to have the right to distribute plots of land that he is said to 'own'. If this really is ownership, what kind of ownership are we talking about?

Our own Roman understanding of property severely narrows the categories of our discourse on the topic. However, whether culturally influenced or not, we cannot do without categories, and I will inventory some of them here. In the Roman sense of bare ownership, as our culture understands it, we can dissociate individual ownership from 'corporate' one[44]. However, the English term corporation refers to two different realities: the corporation aggregate, or 'a legal entity made up of several individuals', and the corporation sole, or 'a legal entity made up of a single individual'. The Queen of England, for example, occupies an office; the Crown lands are not her individual property, but belong to the office.

Let us examine land ownership in Yao country in the light of these categories. Is it a case of individual ownership by the *asyene*, of corporate ownership but of the aggregate type, corporate ownership but of the sole type, or is it something else altogether? To answer these questions, it is a good idea to remember that each of these types of property carries with it some rights. In the case of collective corporate ownership, for example, no *asyene* could

[44] It is important to note here that this is in no way a contrast between private and collective property, a sad trap into which most ethnographic writings fall. By definition, all property is private, in that it necessarily excludes non-owners; non-private property would by definition be non-ownership. This property is either that of an individual (individual property), or that of a set of individuals which, in this context, defines itself against the rest of the world. In the latter case, we are dealing with 'corporations'.

distribute land without the prior consent of the *musi* concerned. However, the *asyene musi* can act without prior consultation, on his own initiative, so that the idea of collective corporate ownership can be dismissed out of hand; neither *musi* nor *cilambo* are aggregate corporations, which leaves us with only one alternative: individual ownership or personal corporate ownership (corporation sole)?

In the case of a corporation sole, the holder of the office has a right to the property's usufruct. British Crown lands are not the property of the Queen, but she does enjoy the income she derives from them. The *asyene cilambo*, on the other hand, can no more claim usufruct of his chiefdom's lands than the village chief can of those of his *musi*. Is there, then, a possibility of individual ownership of the land, either by the village *asyene* or by the Paramount Chief? The very idea is absurd, because individual ownership, even when subject to some servitudes, is accompanied by prerogatives that extend far beyond those enjoyed by a corporation sole. A Paramount Chief who held individual bare ownership of the chiefdom could rent out all the land, or even sell it, in order to earn an income, which he is radically forbidden to do[45]. We are left to suppose that there is no ownership of land corresponding to our Roman categories, and that the very notion of ownership appears metaphorical.

How can we overcome this difficulty? In the case of the *cilambo*, the key to ownership lies in the power of the *asyene cilambo* over rain. To grasp the link between rain and ownership, it is relevant to dissociate the earth, as inert object (or commodity in our cultural conception), from the earth as living matter, plant and animal life; without this life, human labour is useless and cannot counter the threat of famine and death. It is in fact this living, animated aspect of the soil for which the Supreme ruler is directly

[45] We know that the Paramount Chief could carve out an estate within his *cilambo*, which he would cede to a village chief who asked him to do so. Insofar as he nonetheless remained *asyene cilambo*, he could not be considered the 'owner' of the Chiefdom, since vast plots within it 'belonged' to various *asyene musi*.

responsible (or guardian, i.e. *asyene*), and he is so through his supernatural power over the rain.

What then of the village chief's ownership of the land distributed to him within the *cilambo*? It is safe to assume that it is of the same type. It should be noted that ancestral spirit worship had all but disappeared by the time of Mitchell's fieldwork, so his ethnography remains painfully silent on the *asyene musi*'s religious responsibilities. Yet it is clear that the *asyene musi* enjoyed his status in the name of his forefathers, whose priest he was. Moreover, Mitchell adds that he was responsible for the well-being of the community under his jurisdiction. Yet it is hard to imagine that this well-being did not extend to the general 'health' of the group. Although he had no power over rain, it is easy to imagine that the *asyene musi* also possessed power over harvests, or reproduction, through his privileged relationship with his ancestors. In short, insofar as the *musi* is more a territory than a community (as Mitchell often repeats), the village chief is, of course, responsible for it on a judicial level, insofar as he is the first to be affected by the conflicts that wreck his community, but he is also responsible for it on a more global, demographic level, we might say, through the responsibility over the living properties of the soil that his position confers to him.

It is therefore no longer a question of property in the sense in which we understand it. To a certain extent, we here come across some of the obstacles that European history must contend with when confronted with Frankish law in the study of feudalism (see, for example, Augustins 1989). To a certain extent only, because African property possesses a spiritual dimension that is absent from feudal law. In both cases, it might be useful to avoid the notion of property and invoke another one, that of 'potestality'[46]. In the Yao case, as in that of many African (and even South American) chiefdoms, this

[46] Insofar as all property presupposes power, it is also potestality. I attach no special importance to this particular concept, but only to the idea that property in the Roman sense must be separated from a different relationship to land. It is perhaps the notion of land that needs to be refined, rather than that of property.

potestality is exercised over men through the living properties of the soil. This would explain why every newcomer must recognize the pre-eminence of an *asyene*[47], otherwise his crops may be cursed. On the other hand, an *asyene* rarely refuses land to anyone wishing to settle under his jurisdiction, if there is land available, and there always seems to be[48].

It is in this sense that the notion of ownership can be said to be metaphorical. By allocating plots of land to individuals with a sizeable following who come to him, the Paramount Chief is not exercising his power as owner of the soil, but as guardian of its vital potential, so to speak. On this plot of land, the *asyene musi* will be responsible for the well-being of the inhabitants, and the *asyene cilambo* bequeaths part of his supernatural power rather than donating bare ownership of the land. In his village, the headman's forebears are the guarantors of the *musi*'s well-being, and only a vague power over rain subordinates this well-being to the Paramount Chief. In short, the village chief acts within his village as the chief does within the chiefdom with regard to land tenure, so that neither the *asyene cilambo* nor the *asyene musi* hold individual ownership of the land attached to their 'domain'.

Having examined ancestor worship and the power over rain, let us move on to the second religious activity around which villages could rally: initiation rites. Superficially, the situation seems more complicated, because some village chiefs cannot perform these rites, while others have the right to initiate girls only, others boys only, and some boys and girls. But the question that concerns us is a simple one: is there aggregation when it comes to initiations? In this respect, the differential distribution of rights to initiation rites forbids us to consider the village as a minimum unit; shall we then consider the entire chiefdom as a minimum unit? The

---

[47] Those who come to settle in a village that has already been founded recognize the pre-eminence of the *asyene musi* and that of the *asyene cilambo* because of this superimposition of spiritual potestalities, that of the *asyene cilambo* adding to that of the *asyene musi*, so to speak.

[48] Note that Mitchell does not mention a single case of refusal.

proposition is untenable; if the Paramount Chief can initiate boys and girls from his village and surrounding ones, other chiefs subordinate to him share this privilege. Let us then demonstrate by the absurd: since neither villages nor chieftaincies are minimal units, the very idea of minimal unit in the context of this activity is meaningless, and negates that of aggregation. Indeed, village chiefs who obtain the right to perform initiation rites in one chiefdom retain them when they move to another.

There thus seems to be no aggregation in religious matters. But what about judicial ones? This is where the evidence is most convincing, since the *asyene cilambo* heads a Supreme Court where cases that escape the jurisdiction of village chiefs are judged. Nevertheless, it is also in this area that the influence of British administration on pre-colonial judicial organization has been most acutely felt, and that the gap between Mitchell's corporatist vision of the Yao organization – which is no stranger to colonial interpretation – and his case studies reveal a very different dynamic.

Let us briefly take stock. For there to be judicial aggregation in the case of disputes that escaped colonial administration and still fell within a so-called traditional framework[49], some types of conflicts would have to fall exclusively under the jurisdiction of village chiefs, others under that of intermediate ones, and still others under that of the Paramount Chief. Let us take a closer look at Mitchell's evidence.

By declaring the Yao village the first level of political organization, Mitchell opens the door to a spontaneous interpretation – which we shall see is erroneous –, namely that the first level of the judiciary would begin at village level. The facts, of course, belie this interpretation. In reality, what is the minimum

[49] If I qualify the term 'traditional', it is because it is absurd to use the term in the study of populations subjected to colonial experience. Indeed, what appears traditional is an interpretation of the pre-colonial situation, both by the agents of colonization and by its victims, to justify their political claims. By definition, this interpretation is always a distortion, and does not accurately reflect pre-colonial organization.

judicial unit? At first glance, it seems to be the 'sorority group' (*mbumba*)[50]. In fact, every unmarried man is under the guardianship of either an older brother or a maternal uncle, who acts as *asyene mbumba*. When this bachelor marries, he is assigned two 'marriage sureties': a junior one, usually a uterine brother, and a senior one, usually a maternal uncle. This maternal uncle will sometimes combine the roles of senior matrimonial guardian, *asyene mbumba* and even *asyene musi* when the village is made up of a single matrilineage. When the eldest brother is *asyene mbumba*, he will often be the younger guardian of many of his sisters, and the older matrimonial guardian of his uterine nephews. However, in all the case histories presented – and there are many – the majority of disputes between villagers are between sisters-in-law, spouses, or uterine relatives and affines – and the first to settle these disputes are none other than the matrimonial guardians, including of course the *asyene mbumba*.

However, when we study the village genealogies presented in the appendix, we can clearly see that what Mitchell calls matrilineage is differentiated into various lineages, or sections, each descended from a different ancestor, sections that occupy different quarters or hamlets of the same village. Mitchell himself mentions these sections on several occasions. From his examples, it also appears that within each of these sections there is an elder to whom disputes are often taken, probably those that cannot be arbitrated by matrimonial guardians, or perhaps those involving uterine relatives within the same lineage, though none of this is mentioned. Finally, some of the disputes are arbitrated by the village chief himself (who is also representative of his lineage and the localized matrilineage that forms the backbone of the village), while others are judged outside the village. Nevertheless, it would be possible to salvage Mitchell's thesis, deny that the village is the minimal judicial group, claim that the *mbumba* plays this role, and thus obtain a more coherent formulation. In judicial matters, the

[50] This is what he wrote in his first sketch (1951, p. 319).

mbumba would stand out as a minimal group, aggregated on the basis of uterine descent into a lineage, which would similarly be aggregated into a localized matrilineage[51]. We would still be dealing with matrilineal descent groups, i.e. matrilineages.

But is it really so? A woman, in her relations with her husband and children, must be able to count on the support of a man, normally her uterine brother if he is old enough (and assuming she has one), or her maternal uncle. Let us imagine three adult sisters, living in the same village (that of their female ancestor) with their husbands (the marriage is uxorilocal). Let us also assume that this village is represented by an individual who is not their own maternal uncle but a more distant uterine relative, and that they have adult brothers living in their wives' *musi* (which may be in neighbouring villages). We can already see that if the *mbumba* itself is not localized, neither is the matrilineage. But let us overlook this minor difficulty. These sisters have only young children, and one of them has quarrelled with an affine; the case must be reported to the *asyene mbumba*. If there are several brothers, which of them will play this role?

This is where things get more complicated. Despite an open preference for the oldest brother, all the case analyses reveal that it will be the uterine brother who cares most and best for his sisters who will be chosen (pp. 149–151) and, in the course of their lives, these sisters may change their choice several times. It is their manoeuvring, their favouritism for one brother or another, which underpins the rivalries between uterine brothers and fuels the endemic conflicts that perpetually threaten the Yao villages with fission. And this movement of the Yao organization, as well as the antagonisms it provokes, can be found at every level.

In fact, a dominant feature of this legal system is that, in the event of a dispute, relatives are called in from all sides! When a dispute arises between individuals of different sororities, even within a lineage, there is no obligation for the protagonists to

[51] Beyond that, the village would be aggregated on the basis of territoriality into a complex chiefdom.

submit their case to the eldest of that lineage. One can defer to the village chief, or to another village chief in a perpetual kinship relationship with the village; one can also appeal to an influential uterine relative living in another village, or simply to a neighbouring chief of higher rank[52]. Finally, this neighbouring chief may belong to a neighbouring chiefdom[53]! Even when the village chief gets involved, chiefs or elders from neighbouring villages are constantly invited to arbitrate. And it is the same at every level! When a dispute involves two village chiefs, influential chiefs or elders in a position of perpetual kinship are called in, and when a very high-ranking chief or even the Paramount Chief turns up, it is usually because he has been invited. This, of course, has to be seen in the context of the colonial situation.

Thus, this complete interweaving of all levels characterizes the 'traditional' Yao judicial system of the colonial period. There seems to be no category of litigation that automatically must be submitted to the *asyene musi*, and others that should be passed on to the *asyene cilambo*. Individuals can play one chief off against the other, so there can be no aggregation of *mbumba* into matrilineages on the basis of matrilineal descent, nor aggregation of villages into a chiefdom on the basis of territoriality[54].

These facts confront us with an interesting conceptual and ethnographic puzzle. If we declare the *mbumba* the minimum judicial unit, and that we have not identified any cases of aggregation beyond the *mbumba*, our definitions require us to declare it sovereign! How can we reconcile this conclusion with the existence of the village as a clearly delimited entity, both physically and socially, and with the existence of the *cilambo*?

This can only be done through a much finer analysis, and by putting the notion of sovereignty back into perspective. A more detailed analysis would indeed reveal that it is erroneous to consider

---

52 See, for example, the conflict between Cikumba and Mpeta (p. 128).

53 See for example the case of Ciwalo (p. 52).

54 It is interesting to note that Mitchell admits that among the Yao, "there is no clear-cut district organization as among the Zulu and Bemba" (p. 63).

the *mbumba* the minimal judicial group, because its borders are most often blurred. Remember that each individual has two matrimonial guardians, one of whom is likely to be the mother's *asyene mbumba* (her own maternal uncle) and the other his uterine brother, who in many cases will also be his *asyene mbumba*. So, before a brother has acquired the status and influence over his siblings necessary to claim the title, his sisters will still occasionally turn to their former *asyene mbumba* (the maternal uncle), and whoever wants to rule his *mbumba* will have to fight both his brothers and his maternal uncle. What is more, in his disputes a married person can appeal to both his elder and younger guardians. Since authority is often divided, the boundaries of the *mbumba* are all the more blurred.

It is only with the death of the maternal uncle or through physical separation that the *mbumba* can assert itself as a group with more precise boundaries, led by a more or less uncontested *asyene*. Finally, the *mbumba* is rarely localized and, to assert his claim to the title of *asyene mbumba*, a man will have to move closer to his sisters, either by marrying a woman from his own village[55], from a neighbouring village, or by convincing his wife to follow him[56]. To be precise, most *mbumba* overlap, and the *mbumba* is not a minimal judicial group. We can therefore better appreciate how Mitchell could see the Yao village as a minimal political entity.

This correction raises two new questions: if the *mbumba* are not aggregated into matrilineages, then what are we dealing with; and, is the village after all a minimal judicial group? To answer the first question, let us consider an experimental scenario. Let us imagine that a man has uterine sisters who have children, that their maternal

[55] This is possible insofar as some lineages are linked by patrilateral ties and several cross-cousins often live in the same village. Emigration can therefore be avoided by cross-cousin marriages, which seem to be very frequent.

[56] In fact, a wife must follow her husband (if she so wishes) if he gains a title. If he is already titled at the time of her marriage, the wife will come to live with her husband.

uncle has died, that this man has returned to live in his sisters' village and has succeeded in establishing himself as their *asyene mbumba*. Let us call this *mbumba* a localized sorority. This localized *mbumba* may break away from the *musi* to found a new village, or to join another *musi*; in this process the *asyene mbumba* acts not so much as the titled holder of a position of authority *but as a leader*. Now, if a village chief is himself the *asyene* of his own *mbumba* (which he should normally be) and if the new *asyene* of a localized *mbumba* chooses to stay in his sisters' village, how can we imagine the coexistence of these two *mbumba* within the same *musi*?

Better to understand that logic, let us argue in reverse. If the *asyene mbumba* is a political leader who can become *asyene musi*, we can consider that his decision to remain in a village represents a case of alliance (always assuming the *mbumba* is localized) and that the coexistence of leaders within villages constitutes a case of political alliances. But let us beware! This is not to say that secession from the *asyene* of a localized sorority during the formation of a *musi* constitutes a breach of alliance. To appreciate this, let us look at the dynamics of village growth and reproduction. The leader of a *mbumba* who succeeds in expressing the political sovereignty of his sorority group by creating his own village seeks to create a 'name' by associating his village with his ancestors (the details of this process are never described to us). The leader thus enthrones himself, so to speak, and creates a title of which he becomes the holder. Over the years, as his uterine nephews take charge of new *mbumba* and assert themselves as potentially rival leaders, the titled village chief remains their elder generationally, as he is linked to them by uterine kinship. In this way, some *mbumba* leaders will choose to stay with a maternal uncle or village chief who represents an older lineage, but their decision is to ally themselves with this chief. This alliance, however, is that of a junior in generational and political terms; it is an alliance of people in unequal relationships, and therefore a *hierarchical alliance*.

In my opinion, this formulation is the one that best captures the specificity of this village political organization; in my terminology, it would be a *clientelistic chiefdom*, distinct from the more classical aggregated ones. I have constructed this experimental scenario of a localized *mbumba* to better grasp the idea of hierarchical alliances; in reality, most *mbumba* are not localized. Many *asyene mbumba* live in a different village from their sisters and, if they dream of autonomy, they will seek to localize their *mbumba*, not within the village where it is already located, but by forming a new village. Hence the crucial importance of the *musi*; indeed, it is only by locating his *mbumba* through the creation of a local group that a leader of a sorority can exercise his authority more discontinuously. The founding of a village is therefore the crucial stage in the expression of the *mbumba*'s virtual sovereignty. By becoming *musi*, the *mbumba* defines its social boundaries, until adult uterine nephews challenge the authority of the maternal uncle who founded the village. Can we conclude from this that beyond the villages we are no longer dealing with alliances but with aggregation?

I have already demonstrated the absence of aggregation; the mere fact that village chiefs can easily break away from one *cilambo* to join another, and that they occupy a more or less equal rank in the *cilambo* to which they emigrate, would suffice to prove the absence of aggregation. In the absence of aggregation, we necessarily find alliances, and everything indicates that beyond the village, these alliances are also hierarchical. This explains why the *asyene musi* suffers, albeit to a lesser degree, from the same difficulties as the *asyene mbumba*. It is in the very nature of hierarchical alliances that they do not allow for any precise division of authority and jurisdiction, and that the various levels overlap. Admittedly, the *asyene musi* enjoys greater autonomy than the leader of a non-localized *mbumba*. However, he too must contend with the emerging authority and influence of his own uterine nephews, who seek to establish a leadership position in their own *mbumba*, as well as with the authority and influence of those who have preceded him, those who have ceded him land – in short, those above him in the hierarchy. Because this hierarchy is not the classic interlocking of aggregation, because all are leaders competing in the struggle for rank and prestige, spheres of influence and authority overlap[57]. At no level can we properly speak of a minimal judicial group or, by definition, a maximal judicial group, since overlaps are as much horizontal as they are vertical.

That answers my second question: no, the Yao village is not a minimal judicial group either. In conclusion, where no minimal group clearly stands out in political activities and, by definition, where aggregation is impossible, political autonomy, or sovereignty, is expressed in degrees, according to the balance of power present. A hierarchy of leaders corresponds, as it were, to a hierarchy of autonomy, so that the very notion of sovereignty is here of dubious use.

This could explain the strange combination of leadership and tenure that characterizes the position of *asyene musi*: insofar as it is only through the foundation of a village that the head of a *mbumba* truly asserts the strength of his leadership, he freezes it, so to speak, in physical and social space[58]. The title places him more openly in the inter-village political hierarchy and, in subsequent generations, the eligibility criterion becomes more automatic. In theory, the title will pass to the eldest of the eldest branch's uterine nephews (i.e. to the *asyene mbumba* of the line descended from the eldest female ancestor) but, despite his title, the new *asyene musi* will face the same challenge of keeping his inferior allies in his village, which he can only achieve through his leadership qualities.

In reality, the village chief needs his lower allies as much, if not more, than they need him, because in a network of hierarchical alliances, a village chief can only hope to climb the hierarchical ladder by increasing his political clientele. The *asyene musi* is thus dependent on his clients, because he remains a leader in spite of his accession to the title, and a leader is only entitled to this designation if those who follow him recognize it. If, on the other hand, he succeeds in keeping, and even multiplying, his inferior allies

[57] In 1951, Mitchell referred to the *asyene musi* as leaders (1951, p. 339).

[58] Social through the creation of a title, as well as ties of perpetual kinship with the mother village, through the forefathers.

among his clientele, he will be able to exert pressure to be granted rights to initiation rites, and thereby reach a higher rank.

This pyramid has an apex that corresponds, Mitchell explains, to the personal enterprises and alliances that punctuated the Yao invasion. The sum total of *asyene* who perceive themselves as allies in the same hierarchy and who *ipso facto* recognize themselves as clients of the same leader (the Supreme Leader) form a *cilambo*. This is the 'country' of all these allies, under the supernatural supervision of the *asyene cilambo*. In a sense, to admit that an individual possesses power over rain is to define oneself as a member of the network of alliances woven by one's predecessors. It is thus possible to discern constellations of hierarchical allies occupying well-defined areas, where one of them, *primus inter pares*, holds power over the rain and seems to rule the territory. 'Seems' only, because he appears to have no real power over his allies in the 'traditional' organization under colonial rule[59]; if he is given a certain pre-eminence, some economic and even cultural privileges, it is simply because he sits at the top of a hierarchy. Thus, read operationally, the Yao of 1949 knew neither lineages nor

[59] Note that even the Yao language supports this hypothesis, given our current state of knowledge. Indeed, the few reanalyses made so far all demonstrate an important coincidence between language and social organization. Generally speaking, if we are dealing with different types of groupings, the vernacular uses different terms to designate them; in this case, we have three specific terms, namely *mbumba*, *musi*, and *cilambo*, and the analysis must respect what the language suggests. But what also emerges from previous analyses is that the same term designates positions that share the same criteria of eligibility. Take the case of Abutia. Where eligibility is defined by generational and chronological seniority, we speak of *ametsitsiwo*, literally 'elders'. But when the incumbent is the priest of a deity and the criteria differ considerably, we speak of *fia* (Chief). In short, despite the level of grouping, the presence or absence of aggregation and the type of aggregation, we can assume that there is an identity of criteria in the choice of successors to these positions. However, in the Yao case, we always speak of *asyene*, from the simplest to the most complex levels of grouping, which suggests an identity in the eligibility criteria. First, all *asyene* are male and elders but, above all, they are all leaders who are wardens of their clientele. By definition, we would then be dealing with a social formation based on leadership, which consequently excludes aggregation and revolves entirely around political alliances.

territorial groups (aggregated chiefdoms or kingdoms). They had these matrifiliative groups known as *mbumba*, some of which shared a uterine origin that could serve as a basis for their political alliance if they decided to live in the same village; but *mbumba* were nowhere aggregated on the basis of descent, and villages nowhere aggregated through territoriality.

What about the pre-colonial political organization? On the one hand, there is no reason to believe that religious aggregation (ancestor cults and initiation rites) took place during this period; everywhere in Africa where such aggregation operated, colonization generally left it more or less intact. Politically, however, things changed abruptly and, in this context, pre-colonial organizations were transformed. But in our case, to what extent?

In the past, positions of authority (certainly that of *asyene cilambo*) were almost exclusively commercial and military in origin (the slave trade being the source of military power): one imposed one's authority because one had both the men and the firepower to do so; so, this too was a form of leadership[60]. Of course, as a military leader, the *asyene cilambo* could probably coerce his allies much more directly and severely. Nevertheless, Mitchell wrote: "From MacDonald's description [MacDonald was a missionary who observed the Yao before the colonial invasion] it appears that each Yao chiefdom was a congeries of almost autonomous villages" (p. 31). Moreover, there is every reason to believe that the same political competition between potential leaders operated, since the *asyene* could not rely on their uterine relatives and tried to increase their clientele through the number of their slaves and the number of children their female slaves could give them. What is more, disgruntled relatives could leave one leader to join forces with another or form their own village. To consider secession, they may have needed a more powerful clientele, both demographically and militarily, but the same dynamic existed.

[60] Again, Mitchell writes specifically of commercial and military leaders in his earlier text (1951, p. 347).

By eliminating slavery and military force, the colonial invaders certainly transformed the growth and reproduction processes of political groups. Before the colonial era, an ambitious village chief could hope to rise in the hierarchy and even create his own *cilambo*, and these reorganizations of alliances injected greater mobility into the reproduction of maximal political units (hierarchical sets of alliances). At grassroots level, on the other hand, it is possible that the *asyene mbumba* may have met stronger opposition to their secessionist aspirations. A dissident group was likely to face not only threats of witchcraft, but the real danger of physical sanctions far more tangible because based on military might. By fixing alliances on a given territory, colonial conquest interrupted the reproduction of *cilambo*, but may have accelerated that of *misi* (sing. *musi*). However, it remains the most plausible hypothesis that this was not a matter of aggregation but of hierarchical alliances; the whole dynamic of political group reproduction bears witness to this.

In fact, we could inverse the reasoning. Coming from countries with a political organization based on the territorial aggregation of nation states, colonial administrators seem to have acted in one direction, and one only: they imposed aggregation where none existed, because aggregation (and especially territorial aggregation) was the language they understood. But, to my knowledge, they have never imposed an organization based on fluid, shifting leadership where a pre-colonial social formation was based on aggregation. In their administrative superstructure, the British gave the Yao the interpretation of a society where local judicial groups were aggregated on the basis of territoriality. Nevertheless, insofar as they neither imposed nor invented this 'traditional' organization we have just examined, and insofar as this organization could only reveal some elements of an earlier reality despite the distortions due to the colonial experience, this reality was most likely composed of hierarchical alliances. To conclude, the Yao were neither matrilineal nor did they have aggregated chiefdoms; they had clientelistic ones!

CHAPTER SEVEN

Translating Australian Aboriginal ethnography[61]

Long before the emergence of the ethnography of segmentary societies, Radcliffe-Brown had developed the foundations of structural functionalism and descent theory (see volume 1). He is among the first, if not the first, to have adopted Durkheim's sociology. Almost immediately after his fieldwork in the Andaman Islands (1906–1908), Radcliffe-Brown moved to Western Australia, where he studied and wrote extensively on the Australian Aboriginal 'tribes', which culminated in his classic *Social Organization of Australian Tribes* (1930), and these writings dominated Australian anthropology of Aborigines to this day. It is this literature that we here want to explore and investigate.

From the 1950s onward, ethnographers of Australia increasingly questioned Radcliffe-Brown's understanding of Aboriginal social organizations. Some, mostly committed to ecological models, have rallied to the master's posthumous defence, and to this day (1982) the debate about the Australian 'horde' still rages. We look back on Radcliffe-Brown's views, as well as those of his critics, to show that beneath disputes over the composition of local groups and their movement is a deeper level of 'discord'. Inability to provide a generally acceptable interpretation of Aboriginal social organization

---

[61] This article was written in collaboration with Paul Jorion. Unlike my previous reanalysis, this one was not based on one author, but on a whole field of anthropology, namely Australian Aboriginal societies.

might in fact stem from limitations intrinsic to the very notion of 'group' which underlies the various ethnographic accounts. If it were possible to transcend these limitations thanks to Verdon's operationalism, it might be equally possible to suggest new solutions to problematic areas of Australian ethnography.

The debate

In 1913 Radcliffe-Brown adopted Howitt and Fison's (1885) distinction between groups defined with respect to local contiguity (local groups) and groups defined with respect to kinship and marriage (social groups), only to reach conclusions different from theirs – namely, that the tribes he studied (Kariera, Ngaluma and Mardudhunera) were all patrilineal, an observation he later extended to the whole of Aboriginal Australia. In this same paper he described local groups as 'owning a defined territory' (1913, p. 145), as well as owning the group's very members: "It is impossible for a man to leave his local group and become naturalized or adopted in another. Just as the country belonged to him, so he belonged to it" (1913, p. 146). This formulation anticipated by more than twenty years his famous definition of corporate groups (Radcliffe-Brown 1935; see footnote 66). In 1913 he clearly depicted the 'local group' as the main corporate group of Aboriginal society, bounded both in territory and membership. Since recruitment was through the father, these local groups were certainly patrilineal, and normally exogamous, he claimed; if not, they greatly favoured out-marriage[62].

In the second part of his essay, Radcliffe-Brown proceeded to investigate the 'relationship organization' (kinship terminologies and marriage practices) of these three tribes, and found that people of the same local group were also genealogically connected in

[62] Radcliffe-Brown noted, however, that the local group could not be regarded as a hunting or food-collecting group. He acknowledged that in these activities Aborigines often moved in separate families, and sometimes gathered with the families of other local groups in times of affluence.

specific ways. He therefore suggested the "use of the word 'clan' to denote a social division of this kind, *of which the Kariera local group is an example,*" (our emphasis), adding that: "A clan by this definition consists of a body of persons who are closely related to one another in one line and who are clearly marked off in some way from the similar divisions of the same society. Each clan is marked off from every other by the possession of its own territory, and by other features as well [including totems and rituals]" (1913, p. 159). He concluded: "The local group thus forms what we may call a 'clan', with male descent" (1913, p. 160).

In 1913, Radcliffe-Brown thus equated 'local group' with 'clan', regarding both as owners of the territory. Five years later he abandoned the concept of local group, to replace it by that of 'horde' (originally applied to local groups in Howitt and Fison 1885). He designated the horde as a 'well-marked social division' with the following characteristics:

> "It consists of a number of persons who regularly live together in one camp and share a common life.
>
> The horde is the *primary land-owning group,* each horde owning and occupying certain area of country.
>
> Each horde is independent and autonomous, and manages its own affairs by means of the camp-council, often directed by one headman.
>
> A child belongs to the horde of the father – i.e. descent is strictly in the male line. A woman, on marriage, joins and lives with the horde of the husband.
>
> The horde acts as a unit in its relations with other hordes of the same or other tribes (1918, pp. 222-223, our emphasis).

In contrast, the clan was a 'social group' marked off in some way (as by a name) from other similar groups, consisting of a number of persons who regard themselves as being closely in one line (1918, p. 223). Horde and clan still overlapped completely in membership, but the clan no longer functioned as a land-owning unit; it was rather represented as a group defined in terms of 'cognitive differentiation' and internal cohesion rooted in descent. The horde, on the other hand, was shaped through daily interaction and ownership of the land.

It was contradictory to equate horde and clan in terms of membership, since the horde included wives and excluded adult daughters. Radcliffe-Brown tried to solve this problem in 1930 by reverting to an earlier usage, calling the horde once again a 'local group', but adding a further characteristic. He now claimed that the horde "consists of (1) male members of all ages whose fathers and father's fathers belonged to the horde, (2) unmarried girls who are the sisters or daughters or sons' daughters of the male members, (3) married women, all of whom, in some regions, and most of whom, in others, belonged originally to other hordes, and have become attached to the horde by marriage" (1930, p. 35).

This definition dissociated horde from clan and Radcliffe-Brown adjusted his position by stating that "in the Kariera tribe, *connected* with each horde is a Clan" (1930, p. 59, our emphasis). Clan and horde still overlapped, without being coterminous; the 'local clan' appeared henceforth as a localized sub-set of the clan, and not the localized clan of earlier publications[63].

[63] Much of the confusion surrounding the interpretation of Radcliffe-Brown's position stems from his later opinions at variance with earlier statements. In a letter posthumously published in *American Anthropologist* (1956), Radcliffe-Brown asserted that he had always meant the clan to be a 'unilineal descent group' engaged both in collective action and in the ownership and occupation of a territory, whereas he regarded the horde only as a collection of parental families regularly co-operating in the food quest. He further claimed that the unity of the horde derived from the fact that its members are also members of the same clan, the horde being only a 'quasi-domestic group', adding that "[...] all the married men of a given horde are members of one particular clan" (1956, p. 365). Yet, in 1918, 1930 and even 1935 it was clearly the *horde* (and not the clan) which he regarded as a corporate group engaged in collective action and land ownership, its unity being fostered by these very facts. The clan he had described as a group united by male descent and cultural insignia marking it off from other groups. Of 'quasi-domestic groups' there was then no mention.

These views came under serious revision in the wake of the ethnographic work initiated by Elkin (1938). Berndt later elaborated a new model of the articulation of clans and local groups in Aboriginal Australia (Berndt 1955, 1959, 1964). He recognized two types of social units: the ‘local descent group’ and the ‘horde’. The ‘local descent group’ owns a totemic site and the stretch of territory surrounding it, recruits members on the basis of patrifiliation and is exogamous. The ‘horde’, on the other hand, is not exogamous, and occupies the land of many local descent groups for the primary purpose of collecting food. Berndt later wrote:

> “As my evidence suggests, the same personnel are involved in each; they have complementary functions to perform, which express two basic and interdependent concerns of Aboriginal life - the religious and the economic. In that sense, the local descent group is the land-renewing and land-sustaining unit; the ‘horde’, the land-occupying, land-utilizing or land-exploiting unit” (1976, p. 135).

This evidence, complemented by Meggitt’s rich ethnography of the Walbiri (1962), prompted Hiatt to question Radcliffe-Brown’s position, arguing (1) that recruitment to local groups is not confined to patrilineal descent, so that one finds members of more than one clan in a given local group (horde); (2) that the movements of these groups in their quest for food is not constrained by any territorial boundaries, and (3) that the clan (and not the horde) is the land-owning group (Hiatt 1962).

Hiatt re-stated his position in 1968, claiming that “there is no quarrel with Radcliffe-Brown’s statement about the […] patriclan as a land-owning unit. The argument is about the horde - more precisely about residential associations, exploitation of resources, and group movements” (1968, p. 99)[64]. Hiatt shifted the debate by

[64] In this statement, Hiatt might have construed Radcliffe-Brown’s position as that of 1956.

introducing the concept of territoriality, implying that the whole question rests on assumptions about the manner in which *Homo sapiens* occupies a territory, whether by delineating it or not. He thus reduced the discrepancies between his and Radcliffe-Brown's opinions to a question of boundaries. If territoriality implies strict delineation, the marking off of boundaries, it would then follow that individuals owning a territory would move only within its boundaries and that clans would not mingle in the occupation of their bounded territories. This view would be RadcliffeBrown's. If one denies that such delineations exist, on the other hand, clans will indeed mix in the occupation of their territories. This would be Hiatt's position. He now claims that the question of local group composition and movement, the main bone of contention, ultimately derives from assumptions about human territoriality.

These views came under attack from two veteran ethnographers and ecologists of Australia who argued that Radcliffe-Brown was right, if one only took care to distinguish the social from the ecological dimension of human territoriality (Stanner 1965), and also kept in mind the perturbing implications of white settlement on Aboriginal society (Birdsell 1970). The scrambling after Aboriginal land by white settlers, according to Birdsell, easily explains discrepancies between Radcliffe-Brown's observations and those of more recent ethnographers.

In a reply to Birdsell, Berndt contrasted their positions: where Birdsell links ownership to occupation he himself, and presumably those whom Birdsell collectively labelled the 'Sydney school', (Berndt, Elkin, Hiatt and Meggitt) separate the two. He (Berndt) ties land ownership to the group which owns the totemic sites, a group not coterminous with the unit which exploits or utilizes the territory (Berndt 1970). The problem thus seemed to have been reduced to the question of finding out whether it is the group occupying the land which, because of an instinct of territoriality, also owns the territory, or whether it is the group having exclusive mythico-ritual ties with the totemic sites located on the territory which also claims ownership of that land.

In 1971, Piddington replied to Birdsell's criticism of his (Piddington's) fieldwork, adding the most interesting remark that "[…] Australian land tenure […] was based on spiritual rather than economic or legal conceptions" (1971, p. 240), and using the analogy of 'gravitational fields' to understand Aboriginal land ownership. A similar idea was later taken up by Shapiro, who tried to reconcile Stanner's concept of 'estate' (the recognized locus of a patrilineal descent group) with Hiatt's and Berndt's notion of 'ritual group' (Shapiro 1979). Within the estate, Shapiro distinguishes between a 'core area', which consists of the totemic sites and the land immediately adjacent, and the surrounding land, "whose identity is increasingly uncertain with distance from the core" (1979, p. 17). To complete his resketching of the problem, Shapiro abandoned the notion of patrilineal clan and replaced it with that of 'ritual lodge'; he also dropped the concepts of horde and local group altogether, substituting 'residential group' instead. Changes of terminology only solve problems if they presuppose a change of model, and Shapiro does provide a new model, by treating the residential groups in developmental terms. Shapiro and Piddington seem to have gone the farthest in a new direction. Other publications have touched upon the problem of boundaries (Tindale 1974; Peterson 1976; Doolan 1979) but none has produced an interesting alternative. In our opinion, the debate is still wide open, and turns on Radcliffe-Brown's original representation of social organization.

In his 1930 essay, Radcliffe-Brown indicated what he understood by 'social organization', that is, the manner in which groups are formed: "Individuals are united together into groups on the basis of sex and age [in Australia], of community of language and custom (tribe), of possession and occupation of a territory (horde), and on the basis of kinship and marriage (family, clan, section, moiety)" (1930, p. 63). He thus defined groups by the elements which bind their members together, elements such as sex, language, territory, the various 'social glues' which generate different types of groupings. 'Patrilineal descent', for the clan, and 'territory', for the horde, are both elements which generate solidarity or internal cohesion and thereby act to form groups and to differentiate them from other groups. This representation, admittedly, made it difficult to find any *raison d'être* for the existence of the clan, except that of increasing the horde's (presumably loose) unity through additional means. Superimposed onto the horde, the clan only fostered the local group's solidarity through descent and symbolic representation[65]. In our opinion, this understanding of social organization in terms of solidarity and differentiation blurred the articulation between clan and horde, and also led Radcliffe-Brown to a relatively rigid position on the problem of boundaries as necessary to generate differentiation[66].

Elkin, Meggitt, Berndt and Hiatt have implicitly introduced a different representation of social organization by defining groups, not in terms of 'binding elements', but with reference to specific activities in which these groups are involved – or the 'functions' they perform – such as ritual, food seeking, residence, and so on. By shifting the focus onto activities, the 'Sydney anthropologists' have succeeded in dissociating clan from local group, and describing their articulation in more plausible terms. Yet their

---

[65] In 1966, Hiatt wrote that if clan and horde meant the same thing in Radcliffe-Brown's writings, his work would not make sense. Up to 1930, we contend that horde and clan did refer to groups which had coterminous *membership*, but whose unity was generated by different means. He disconnected their membership in 1931 only but still conceptualized their main difference in terms of the elements which serve to bind them.

[66] Radcliffe-Brown later complemented this definition of group with his elaboration of the concept of 'corporation' (1935). Trying to understand how groups perpetuate themselves, Radcliffe-Brown represented society as being composed of 'corporations' which own an 'estate' consisting of (1) a territory and (2) the statuses of the individuals forming the corporations (that is, the rights and duties which characterize their positions in specific social relationships). For the corporation to continue over time, Radcliffe-Brown added, *its estate must be bounded.* If there were constant disputes over territory and membership, the group could hardly reproduce itself. Corporations must therefore possess their members exclusively, thereby defining their own social boundaries. Since every child has two parents, one of the parental corporations (the father's in patrilineal societies, and the mother's in matrilineal ones) will therefore 'own' the children to the exclusion of the other. Interestingly enough, Radcliffe-Brown chose no other paradigmatic instance for his demonstration than the Australian horde!

achievements have not been crowned with complete success, as the occasional ecological rebellion testifies, and we would attribute this partial failure to the limitations of their notions of group and social organization. If our assessment is right, a more accurate description of Aboriginal social organization would ultimately depend upon a systematic broadening of the concept of group which has already enabled Australian ethnographers to overcome limitations in RadcliffeBrown's interpretation. By using a conceptual framework which seeks to transcend the limitations of this functional notion of group, we hope to clarify the analysis of Australian Aboriginal social organization a bit further.

In brief, the points to clarify revolve around the representations of ownership and boundaries. In view of the deadlock reached in this matter, we apply Verdon's operational framework.

Operationalizing hordes

In the light of the considerations in ownership developed in Chapter 1, let us now re-examine some of the more debated areas of Australian Aboriginal social organization. Were there corporations in traditional Australian society and, if so, what were their estates composed of?

When ethnographers write of the violent death inflicted upon those who dared transmit their totem's sacred songs to non-eligible members (Wheeler 1910; Strehlow 1970; Shapiro 1979), we are unequivocally dealing with a type of resource owned by a collectivity of individuals who distinguish themselves from the rest of the world by specific criteria. These resources consist of a religious knowledge – namely secret myths, rituals and songs – and one finds a rare consensus among ethnographers of Australia that this group (variously identified as the 'patrilineal clan', 'ritual group' or 'ritual lodge') defines itself with reference to the ownership of religious resources, and recruits members on the basis of a specific criterion, namely ancestral insemination or reincarnation. Since the 'inseminating' ancestors are normally those of the father (and in a few societies, those of the mother), ethnographers have designated these groups as ‘patrilineal’ or ‘matrilineal’. We would rather speak of patrifiliation or matrifiliation as being their criteria of membership, and regard these groups as corporations owning a religious estate. For the sake of convenience, let us designate them as ‘totemic corporations’.

None of these corporations, however, is further aggregated into more inclusive units on the basis of descent. In general, the term ‘clan’ has been unfortunately associated with two types of collectivities: (1) simple ‘religious corporations’, such as the one we are dealing with, and (2) groups of lineages aggregated into a more inclusive unit on the basis of putative descent. In view of this confusion, we temporarily relinquish the concept of ‘clan’, and label these Australian totem-owning units patrifiliative (or matrifiliative) totemic corporations[67].

The real question, however, is to find out whether land is owned corporately or not. Ethnographers of Australia seem to assume as much, but disagree over the identity of that corporation. Some (early Radcliffe-Brown, Birdsell, and even Hiatt 1965) contend that the horde (or local group) owns the land whereas others (later Hiatt, and the so-called Sydney school) see the totemic corporations as land-owning corporations. Let us examine these two claims more closely.

The name ‘horde’ was not, after all, such a misnomer, since Aboriginal local groups seem to have no restrictive criteria of membership. From the available evidence, it seems that permission to hunt or collect food on the land surrounding the totemic sites of a given totemic corporation could not be refused to spouses, affines or kin of the members of that corporation. Since kinship and affinal recognition ranged far and wide in Aboriginal Australia, all newcomers fell within one of these categories (except complete

[67] Shapiro reached a similar conclusion when he contrasted the notion of patrilineal among the Australian Aborigines and the ancient Semites (1979, pp. 13–14). For want of a more encompassing model, Shapiro has been unable to formulate the distinction beyond the simple caveat that ‘patrilineal’ means different things in these two contexts.

strangers, who would have no logical ground for asking permission to use the land, unless they were seeking political asylum). As a result, virtually any individual from friendly neighbouring populations was eligible to come and exploit the land surrounding the totemic sites of a totemic corporation. Criteria of membership were so open as to be unrestrictive (and therefore non-existent) and we would thus compare the Australian local group to the land-utilizing crowd of the east-African cattle-herders. Lacking in any criteria of membership, the horde could not constitute either a group or a category and could not *a fortiori* form a land-owning corporation (all that its members really have in common is a common activity, that of exploiting resources in a given area). This is not to deny that the individuals forming the horde actually have rights in the land but, according to our model, these rights are collective and vary in intensity.

If the horde cannot stand as a serious candidate for corporate ownership of land, the totemic corporations certainly could, by virtue of their very constitution, if it could be shown that they claimed the land as part of their estate. But did they? Ethnographers are of one mind about the fact that 'patrilineal clans' or 'ritual lodges' are defined with respect to the ownership of a religious heritage. Only some among them have contended that those who owned the totems also owned, by extension, the land surrounding the sites where the ancestor-totem left evidence of his deeds. However, all who want to postulate corporately-owned real estate immediately run into the problem of boundaries; Radcliffe-Brown and the ecologists (Tindale, Birdsell) simply posit their existence, against much evidence to the contrary. Others acknowledge that the land is not 'jurally bounded' but still wish to regard it as an 'estate', thereby creating unsurmountable difficulties. Hiatt's definitions illustrate this.

Hiatt associates the nineteen local groups of the Gidjingali with defined clusters of named sites and adds that "the clusters of sites were not circumscribed" (1965, p. 16). Despite the absence of jural boundaries, he decides to regard each of the nineteen groups as "owning a cluster of sites *and the surrounding countryside"*

(1965, p. 14, our emphasis), and he adds: "I shall call these groups 'land-owning units' and their territorial possessions 'estates'" (1965, p. 14).

These definitions, however, only created more trouble since "disputes over land did not arise, and it was therefore difficult to discover the attitudes of owners towards their estates" (1965, p. 16). Hiatt finds it difficult to comprehend ownership and estate in the absence of jural boundaries, and he is led to assert that ownership is defined in terms of shared knowledge rather than proprietorship (1965, p. 16)[68].

According to our model, the conclusion is simple: if there are no boundaries there is no estate, and if there is no estate there cannot be a corporation. We therefore assume that land can be occupied without being subject to territorial claims, if territory presupposes jural boundaries[69]. This, admittedly, only begs the question of defining boundaries. We do not dispute that some Aboriginal Australian societies do have jurally bounded estates (and land-owning corporations), and we also assume that every population knows of a certain number of barriers which are rarely crossed and can be spoken of as 'boundaries'. These are, for instance, linguistic boundaries, class boundaries, ethnic boundaries, and so on, some of which may coincide with geographical division

[68] Even acquaintances, or friends, including anthropologists, were absorbed into the 'class system' (see Bates in Salter 1972).

[69] To regard totemic corporations as land-owning corporations seems somewhat contradictory. Ethnographers are quite explicit about the exclusive possession of the totem's esoteric knowledge. Why would Aborigines, who form such exclusive corporations with respect to their religious estate, then form completely inclusive ones with respect to their land? It is difficult to see how the same entity (a corporation) can simultaneously be defined by complete exclusion and complete inclusion (that is inclusion of all those who belong to one's 'world')! Corporate ownership does imply a measure of exclusion which would be contradicted by the very openness and lack of restriction in the use of the resources. Membership of local groups (hordes) is so unrestrictive because the land is not owned corporately and this, in our view, appears to be a response to environmental conditions. Where resources are such that their exploitation requires access to very large tracts of land, it is better that they remain 'unbounded' and withheld from corporate ownership.

(as when people separated by a river do not intermarry and speak different languages). This coincidence, however, cannot be taken to mean that the geographical feature is a boundary demarcating the estate of a corporation. No society allows interaction to take place in any direction and, for any Australian group, there are obviously limits beyond which its individuals do not interact. Beyond that limit (which can coincide with a geographical feature) people are strangers, barbarians, 'wild Blacks', feared because they are unknown, because there are no channels of communication. Thus, when Tindale (1976) writes of 'tribal trespassers' who were killed, he fails to make a crucial distinction: the trespassers were not slain because they used an estate without permission, but because they were 'outside society' and belonged to another world. Their intentions were not known, and they were therefore feared[70]. Crossing a social or ethnic barrier can indeed be much more dangerous than trespassing on a jural one. Moreover, most of the land in Aboriginal Australia will also be delineated to a certain extent because cognitive mapping is necessary for communication

---

[70] Ecologists believe that territoriality necessarily accompanies the occupation of a given geographical area and that the defence of a *bounded* area is necessary for the definition of a territory. Although we would not query the fact that occupation of land will give rise to claims and consequently to defence of threatened resources, we would certainly question the assumptions of the cultural ecologists involved in this debate and, in this, find support among animal ethologists themselves: "A territory, a defended piece of land, is formed under rather specific ecological circumstances [...] The territory thus protects rare, defendable resources. It does not occur in species exploiting shifting resources, unless, during the breeding season, a stable resource can be exploited for the young. Where resources cannot be defended, such as when they are highly concentrated or highly dispersed, not active but passive means of selection are selected for. This includes better roaming and food-finding ability, such as is reflected in light body weight, upright stance, and appendages evolved for roaming; in the genus *Homo,* for instance. For a territory to arise, the resources must be defendable. Thus, the year-round territory can be found only in relatively specific ecological situations, as in subtropical and tropical plant communities of moderate productivity, such as tropical rain forests" (Geist 1978, p. 232). And also: "Territoriality in humans, therefore, has at best a cultural base, but not a biological one akin to that in territorial mammals, and we cannot invoke nature to justify territoriality in man" (Geist 1978, p. 234).

and transmission of knowledge, so crucial in an environment where a detailed ecological knowledge is a condition for survival. Yet mental maps and social barriers should not be confused with the jural boundaries of a corporation's landed estate.

Landed estates did exist in some Aboriginal Australian societies (the Tiwi being the foremost instance – see Hart and Pilling 1960, p. 11), the tendency to form land-owning corporations varying with ecological and demographic conditions. Nevertheless, wherever jural boundaries have been reported to be fluid or non-existent, we contend that the land does not form an estate and is not corporately owned[71]. Aborigines do own their land, but neither individually nor corporately; in order to make sense of this 'ownership', we follow up one important idea of Piddington (1971), that Aboriginal land tenure is expressed in a religious idiom.

Australian Aborigines are extremely concerned about the continuity of creation, about re-creating their world at regular intervals. In fact they regard themselves as ancestral re-incarnations, and their worldly odyssey can be construed as a recapitulation of ancestral deeds, performed in order to ensure the perpetuity and continuity of the created world. It is as if they had been entrusted with the task of transmitting the genetic programme of animal and vegetable species, together with atmospheric and physical events typical of their environment which rank among the species; a failure to transmit it would lead to the species' extinction, and a faulty transmission would produce lethal mutations. The living ones, re-incarnations of the ancestor-totem, must therefore possess the ancestral knowledge which will empower them to regenerate the species of their environment. This knowledge, moreover, must be enacted at specific places, where the ancestor-totem left his

[71] One of those who, together with Tindale, have asserted the existence of 'boundaries', also acknowledge that 'trespassers' were feared because they were believed to be criminals in their own tribe (Dixon 1976, p. 214), and not because they infringed proprietary rights. Having stated that "trespass was a crime which has been defined as greater than woman stealing" (Tindale 1976, p. 20), Tindale can only adduce two sources, namely Fawcett 1898 and his own ethnography.

mark, so that the environment can be compared to a minefield, dotted with spiritually 'explosive' places. This danger, however, varies in intensity as different sites are variously associated with the totem (see Biernoff 1978).

These 'degrees of spiritual danger' are further matched by 'degrees of esotericism' in the religious knowledge owned by the totemic corporations, and we could represent this variation by a series of concentric circles. The inner core of that knowledge would consist of that part of the knowledge which is most closely associated with the totemic sites, and which empowers its 'knowers' (the native theologians, or scholars) to reproduce the species. This knowledge is the most esoteric, and is strictly reserved to those who are ancestral reincarnations, who have been initiated and who are the closest to the ancestor in their life-cycle (that is, the closest to death, when the ultimate fusion with the ancestor-totem takes place). Those who have access to the inner core also have access to the less esoteric knowledge. Individuals outside the totemic corporation are excluded from the inner core knowledge, but they can be taught the knowledge contained in outer rings[72]. To be accurate, we must consequently modify our earlier statement, and mention that the totemic corporation is defined with respect to the ownership of the most esoteric knowledge only; other degrees of knowledge, while under the corporation's control, can be imparted to outsiders.

What, then, qualifies an individual to share in one type of knowledge instead of another? In our opinion, this is assessed according to the individual's 'ontological distance' from the ancestor-totem. Those who were born after 'insemination' of their mother by a particular ancestor-totem are almost merged or fused

[72] Jorion also found parallels in the location of in-shore fishing grounds in Brittany, which were subject to different levels of knowledge. Knowledge of the exact location of fishing grounds is the most esoteric, is owned individually and is transmitted from father to son. The knowledge of the location of the 'dangerous spots', such as sandbanks, wrecks or rocks, is more exoteric and can be communicated to a fellow villager, but not to a pure stranger who threatens the local resources (Jorion 1978).

with it and their ontological distance from it is close to nil; they alone have a claim to the totem's most esoteric secrets. Other individuals are only separated from the ancestor-totem by one or a few links; others still are not related at all.

These considerations can be linked to our earlier assumptions about rights of ownership which do not form the basis of corporations. This ontological distance which governs access to the various levels of religious knowledge is also used as a scale to measure a 'gradient of rights of ownership' which stem, to a certain degree, from occupancy and use of the land surrounding the totems. In Aboriginal Australia, land ownership is thus complicated by the religious nature of the environment. One can only occupy and exploit the resources of a given area if one knows where the 'mines' (the dangerous places) are, and can avoid spiritual accidents. The problem thus has two facets: on the one hand, ownership is associated with intensity of use and occupancy, and on the other, this use and occupancy depend upon a prior religious knowledge, the rights to which are measured by an individual's ontological distance from the ancestor.

In other words, all who exploit the land 'own' it, in the sense that they enjoy a privileged access to it, but some own it more than others. Those who own it the most with respect to the criterion of occupancy are, at the same time, those ontologically closest to the ancestor whose sites are located on that land, and who can therefore claim to have occupied the land since its creation. And this set of individuals (the totemic corporation) *appears* to own the land 'corporately'; in fact, their land is not jurally bounded, their ritual control over the totemic species extends to the land surrounding other totemic clusters, beyond the land they allegedly own corporately, and their 'ownership' is also shared by other individuals.

People who want to use the land surrounding the totemic cluster of another totemic corporation will acquire a certain amount of religious knowledge from the members of that corporation according to their ontological distance from the ancestor whose totems are situated there, but they can only do so through concrete association with land. However, if individuals exploit land not associated with their own totem and remain in close association with the land for many years, more religious knowledge will be passed on to them as the length and intensity of their association increases. In other words, the criterion of ontological distance overrides that of length of association, but the intensity and length of association can also be transmuted into ontological distance. Above all, all individuals from friendly neighbouring hordes have a right to the minimum knowledge necessary for exploiting the land without danger.

In the light of our model, we therefore contend that members of totemic corporations do have the strongest claims over the land surrounding their totemic sites, but that this ownership is also shared with others occupying this land; their various rights vary in intensity along a gradient measured by ontological distance from the ancestor-totem. This ontological distance springs from 'genetic' closeness to the ancestor, or from a close and intense association with the land, translated into ontological closeness through the revelation of increasingly esoteric knowledge. This dual source of ownership would therefore explain why ethnographers have believed both types of collectivities, the totemic corporation and the horde, to own land corporately.

A different analogy emphasizes this point. Let us assume that the ancestors acquired a 'patent' over the 'fabrication' of species by creating them and that, like a patent, it specifies how to build the invention and instructs people how to operate it. Let us further imagine that there exists an intermediary level of knowledge, that of repair, between fabrication and operation. According to their ontological distance from the original inventor and patent-owner, some individuals learn how to fabricate, repair and operate, others are only taught how to repair and operate and others still, only how to operate. Through a long and close association with the 'manufacturers', however, simple operators are eventually taught how to repair, and repairmen may also be told the secrets of fabrication[73].

[73] The absence of jural 'boundaries' to land is further supported by the fact that "the members of the kangaroo, euro, emu, carpet snake, grass seed, and other

The same analogy helps us to understand the proxemic boundaries which delineate the land surrounding totem clusters. The patent-owners have to follow carefully the patent's specifications and instructions in order to reproduce annually the species created by their totem. Their wanderings are thus constrained by these specifications which require them to be at certain totemic sites at certain times of the year. Their movements are regulated and the area they cover is necessarily circumscribed by the necessity of not straying too far from the centres which they must reach at specific dates. Roaming is thus predetermined by a series of 'ritual appointments'. With this knowledge of the ritual specifications will also come an expert ecological knowledge, so that the elders who possess both types of information emerge as headmen, and appear to own the land surrounding their totemic centres[74]. Depending upon ecological conditions and the stage that they have reached in their life-cycle, however, individuals may choose to hunt and collect food on land far from their own totem's sites, and on these neighbouring lands they also enjoy a privileged access.

---

totemic clans were regarded as having the power of bringing about the increase of their totemic plants or animals *not only within their local group area, but throughout the adjoining areas as well*" (Strehlow 1970, p. 104). In a book dedicated to 'tribal boundaries' one reads on the verso of the title page that maps are not completely accurate, because boundaries in Aboriginal Australia are not clear-cut (Peterson 1976). The editor also warns us that "it is clear from the foregoing that the term boundary is used by the contributors as a shorthand term, like tribe, and that many so-called boundaries are not boundaries at all, in a strict sense" (Peterson 1976, p. 6), and he further adds that "it is clear from the papers that boundaries move, that they are permeable and that they are sometimes hard to define precisely" (1976, p. 8). The fact that ethnographers have never witnessed or heard of disputes over land, disputes being about women, witchcraft or sacrilegious transgressions, does tend to support our hypothesis.

[74] An example of more 'exoteric' knowledge can be found in Coward Springs, Mound Wedge and Pitaldi Rock (Mountford 1978, pp. 29, 40, 58), where Aborigines believed waterholes to be inhabited by rainbow serpents who killed strangers not knowing the proper behaviour to adopt. Such knowledge was obviously transmitted to all 'friendly neighbours' who wanted to use the waterhole.

Operationalizing classes

In addition to being equated with land-owning corporations, the totemic corporations have also been regarded as 'ritual groups', and we disagree with both postulates. Their religious knowledge is certainly meaningless without the accompanying rituals which also form part of the religious estate, but it is nevertheless analytically incorrect to merge the patrifiliative (or matrifiliative) totemic corporations with the ritual groups. The individuals which form totemic corporations do redistribute themselves, for purposes of ritual and initiation, into various units which have been called moieties, sections and subsections, and which unquestionably act as ritual groups. However, ritual groups overlap only partially with corporations owning religious (including ritual) knowledge.

Among the Kariera, for instance, a child is a member of his grandfather's 'section' or ritual group; it is thus both agnation and alternate generation (not 'descent', see Verdon's definitions) which operate as criteria of membership to ritual groups, whereas it is patrifiliation which defines membership of the totemic corporation (or more accurately, 'ancestral insemination'). Patrifiliative totemic corporations are thus divided into agnatic ritual groups of alternate generations, but these ritual groups cut across corporation membership and include members of different corporations. Analytically speaking, totemic corporations in general thus differ from ritual groups; the former are defined with reference to ownership and the latter with respect to an activity, and their respective criteria of membership also differ.

These ritual groups have also been labelled 'classes' (moieties, sections, subsections) and their study has been flawed from the beginning by the assumption that they constituted 'matrimonial classes', that is, groups involved in the exchange of women. The very manner in which Aborigines formulated their marriage regulations (such as Banaka marry Poronga) encouraged early evolutionists to view them as 'group marriages', an intermediary stage between complete promiscuity and polygyny (Howitt 1891; Spencer and Gillen 1898). This interpretation was abandoned at the beginning of the century, but the idea survived that sections had a major role to play in the allocation of brides. After unsuccessful attempts at classifying Aboriginal marriage systems on this basis, Radcliffe-Brown himself ultimately adopted a sceptical position on the role of sections or classes in marriage regulations (1951).

In Aboriginal society, marriage prescriptions actually bear on specific categories of individuals defined with respect to Ego – bilateral cross-cousins, matrilateral cross-cousins, second cousins of the MMBDD type, and so on – and the association between marriage prescriptions and the sections is in fact a by-product of the manner in which ritual groups and totemic corporations recruit members. At birth, patri- or matrifiliation allocates children to totemic corporations, which overlap with ritual groups but only partially. A child always belongs to the ritual group which overlaps with his or her totemic corporation, but also to a group different from that of the parent through whom he or she gained membership of the corporation. As a result, if men have a right to marry their bilateral cross-cousin, for instance, it so happens that all the women in this category will belong to one and the same ritual group (or class, or section), and all the men who are their potential spouses will also fall within one single section. Among the Kariera, where such a marriage is practiced, if all these men belong to T and their bilateral cross-cousins belong to U, it then appears as a useful cognitive short-cut to state that 'men of T marry women of U'. This, however, is simply the aggregate result of a prescriptive rule which bears on specific categories of individuals defined with respect to Ego. It is also symptomatic that in those Australian societies where marriage rules are expressed both in terms of kinship categories and in terms of classes, children use the latter formulation only. Moreover in the whole of Australia there is no society in which marriage rules are expressed in terms of classes only, whereas there are some where they are formulated in terms of kinship categories only.

We contend that it is heuristically useful for both actors and observers to describe the operations of the system *as if* it took place between aggregate entities but that, in fact, the regulations involve only specific categories of kin. Indeed, it is always possible to designate specifically an individual's potential brides in terms of kinship categories (that is, marriage is determined), whereas it is impossible to do so on the basis of a man's class membership alone (that is, marriage is here *under-determined,* to use the language of set theory). Moieties and sections do not exchange wives; if they did, some individuals would be entitled to act as representatives of the group in marriage negotiations, and marriage payments would presumably be passed from group to group.

Australian societies do vary, however, in the emphasis they put on the 'regular' marriage being transacted, that is, in marriage taking place between the prescribed categories of kin. All societies with prescriptive rules, Australian ones included, must allow for second choice marriages with women belonging to a category (and hence in Australia to a class) different from that of the 'proper' wife. With some, such as the Aranda, the children issuing from such marriages will belong to their father's totemic corporation, whether the wives belong to the proper category or not. Among the Tjingili, on the other hand, the children can only belong to the totemic corporation of their mother's prescribed husband. If men cannot find spouses in the prescribed category and marry outside it, their children belong to the corporation of their wives' prescribed spouses.

Moreover, marriage rules cannot always be translated unequivocally in class terms. This is especially true of prescriptive marriage with the MBD, practised among the Murngin, who have puzzled generations of anthropologists. Briefly stated, the Murngin system operates as follows: if a man is T, his MBD will belong either to U or to V, and this is a mechanical by-product of the type of marriages contracted by T's father and mother's brother (his eventual father-in-law).

Finally, if Aboriginal marriage is regulated in terms of kinship categories, and we contend it is, it then follows that the number of sections (two, four or eight) cannot determine the number of potential spouses for a man or a woman. By regarding ritual groups as matrimonial classes, Yengoyan has calculated the number of potential spouses to be 9.45 in moiety societies, 4.725 in section societies, and 2.3625 in subsection societies (Yengoyan 1968: 196). This conclusion is unwarranted if one understands Australian marriage rules as bearing on kinship categories rather than matrimonial classes[75].

Conclusion

In applying operationalism to the Australian data, we believe we have provided an ideal etic description which mirrors more closely the actors' own views, the so-called emic perspective.

[75] For a solution of the Murngin puzzle, see Jorion and De Meur, 1982.

CHAPTER EIGHT

Concluding remarks

Reflections on segmentarity

We have followed Evans-Pritchard and Fortes through their inconsistencies, watching them become entangled, one among lineages that do not exist, the other among clans devoid of reality, and both among localities balanced on a segmentary genealogy. Translated in my new operational language, the Nuer lineages disappear, and the Tallensi lineages split up, unscrambling themselves from the locality around which Fortes had wrapped them, escaping the contradictions to which his analysis had doomed them. The incongruities diminish, many vanish, and with them the central idea behind all this ethnography, behind the theory itself, that of Segmentary Lineages.

How could we ignore for so long the inescapable fact that the very category of segmentary lineage is a contradiction in terms? Evans-Pritchard showed territorial segments to have no reality or permanence other than that given by opposition to segments of the same order. Fortes read the same segmentation in Tallensi lineages, in segments that were in reality permanent and identifiable at any given moment. Like eighteenth-century chemists with phlogiston, or nineteenth-century physicists with ether, twentieth-century ethnographers noted the contradiction without being able to do without the theory. It was necessary. Segmentary lineages had to be preserved at all costs, at the cost of coherence and plausibility. And they cooked up a solution. They postulated that lineage segments can only be identified in complementary opposition, while simultaneously acknowledging that other conditions operate, giving some of these segments a corporate outlook and generating Tallensi-type lineages. Other circumstances work in the opposite direction, depriving the segments of all corporateness, as is the case with the Nuer. So you always win! Tallensi and Nuer remain close cousins, they keep that segmentary family resemblance that everyone seems to recognize.

What is to be made of this segmentation that I have torn from the lineages? Is it the inclusion of smaller groups into larger ones (nesting)? No, because lineages, territorial groups and aggregated corporations are nested. Could it be the incessant proliferation of new segments, with the normal reproduction of the polygynous family, as Evans-Pritchard and Fortes suggest? No, because an operational reanalysis, and even Calhoun's reinterpretation, reveals that the reproduction of Namoo lineages takes place at the intermediate level, where genealogical memory is easily distorted. New segments are created from the top, at intermediate levels, and not from the bottom, as the segmentary theory assumes. This segmentation as 'creation of new segments' is what we can modestly call 'group reproduction', provided we take care to specify the level of grouping at which this reproduction takes place (whether it is the minimal groups, or the aggregated groups of intermediate levels that reproduce; for a demonstration, see my Abutia ethnography (Verdon (1983)). In short, all that is left of segmentation is the meaning I kept from my scrutiny of the Nuer, that of the so-called 'complementary opposition and fusion' that describes, not a lineage organization, but a special form of political *alliance*. This is the specific meaning I give it.

When *descent* does aggregate groups, however, I seriously doubt that there are more than two levels of nesting at the most: minimal lineage aggregated in intermediate ones, and the latter aggregated in maximal ones. It is obviously not the case with territorial aggregation. Also, as in Abutia, descent groups can be aggregated in a territorial group, but the reverse is impossible. Furthermore, where there is aggregation, by descent or territoriality,

I find that this is reflected in the indigenous terminology, a different term designating every different level.

Additional thoughts on segmentarity

In his great 1968 synthesis on the tribe, Sahlins reinvents Hobbes. The 'tribe', that fundamental category of cultural ecology which Sahlins once embraced, now became synonymous with segmentary organization; and segmentary organization, synonymous with Hobbes' war of all against all. Sahlins recognized Hobbes because, behind all Sahlins' political anthropology, Hobbes' shadow always lurks. The Hobbes who suddenly reveals himself to Sahlins is the Hobbes that ethnology had already placed in the depths of the social (see volume 1). It is not surprising to find him at the end of the road.

Before extending the notion of segmentary organization to the very idea of tribe, Sahlins had proposed a general theory of segmentary lineages: the segmentary lineage would have been the instrument of expanding societies, acephalous but imperialist, egalitarian but predatory (1961). Strangely enough, the Tallensi and Lugbara, to name but a few so-called segmentary societies, escaped Sahlins' net. Elsewhere, Fortes saw an almost necessary link between segmentary lineages and ancestor worship. Yet, just as enigmatically, his cogitations focused on the Tallensi and Lugbara cases, but left the Nuer and Tiv out. A curious divorce seems to separate the Tallensi and Lugbara, on the one hand, and the Nuer and Tiv (and many others) on the other. A singular ontological rift that ethnological theory never managed to transcend, but which it refuses to acknowledge by compressing both into the same category of segmentary societies, imposing an identity that reduces all disparity to the presence or absence of corporateness. This venerable antinomy, this theoretical impotence, disappears in an operational crucible, like a simple lexical error.

It is hardly surprising, then, that Sahlins or Fortes should have failed in their efforts to generalize, since the Tallensi (and Lugbara, as an operational translation would demonstrate) differ from the Nuer and Tiv as lineage societies from societies without lineages and, consequently, no single theory can encompass them all. And if we believe that the Tallensi's cult of individual, named ancestors supports the complex aggregation of their lineages, it naturally follows that in the absence of lineages, as with the Nuer or Tiv, such cults have no raison d'être. Simple (and perhaps even complex) lineages can exist without ancestor cults, and some forms of ancestral worship will spread in lineage-less societies, but we can provisionally accept that a Tallensi-type ancestor cult is accompanied by a lineage organization. And if, on the other hand, we believe that Nuer or Tiv imperialism has something to do with their recognized military configuration, it follows quite naturally that this so-called segmentary configuration is incompatible with a lineage-based organization, and that it excludes lineage-based societies but includes lineage-free societies with segmentary alliances. Solid intuitions, such as those of Sahlins or Fortes, but which had been disfigured by the virulence of exceptions, take on a new look after an operational surgery.

Further thoughts

If it eradicates false problems and revives theories thought to be dead, an operationalization gives new foundations to intuitions still vacillating, and suggests new ones. Let us turn once again to Africa, this time Bantu South Africa.

Exasperated by the contradictions of Bantu ethnography on the subject of clans and lineages, Kuper concluded that if we can't agree on what constitutes Bantu lineages and clans, it is simply that nothing of the sort exists (Kuper 1982). However, the classical ethnographer might reply that these various lineages and clans, despite their diversity, always bring together communities of agnates. According to accepted definitions, these are all groups whose members share a common ancestry and a sense of solidarity (corporateness). In short, they would be descent groups, whether you call them lineages, clans, sibs or whatever. Kuper would have nothing convincing to say to this rejoinder, because he deduces negatively the absence of lineages and clans by a process of elimination, so to speak, whereas his thesis calls for a positive demonstration, based on a new, more solid vision of descent groups. As things stand, Kuper and his detractors might seem equally right. From an operational point of view, only Kuper is right. The Southern Bantu have groups that are partially recruited by agnatic kinship (partially, in that other criteria come into play here and there) but nowhere are these groups aggregated on the basis of descent. Some are aggregated on the basis of territoriality, but none on the basis of descent. The Southern Bantu have no descent groups, let alone lineages or clans.

Let us explore this further from more general considerations about descent groups. Of all the seven societies I have studied (including the Abutia), the only two with descent groups, namely the Abutia and the Tallensi, are fundamentally agriculturalists who own land corporately. Let us develop this idea. From what I know of African social formations, I am pretty convinced that corporate ownership of land is necessary for descent groups to emerge; necessary, but obviously not sufficient.

This severely limits the number of lineage-based societies. Let us take land: before the colonial invasions there was to my knowledge no private ownership of land in Africa. And where land was the main means of production but not owned corporately, it was either owned 'collectively', as I argued for the Nuer or, as I demonstrated for the Yao, land itself was not owned, but its vital potential was, through power over rain. In both types of social formations, land was not owned corporately and I demonstrated that there were no descent groups in those two societies, as there are not any with the Tiv or the Australian Aborigines.

Let us turn to cattle. I am also convinced that cattle are not owned corporately. I will thus assume that, in most African pastoral social formations, cattle are owned individually. This takes us back to Kuper, in that it would exclude most African pastoral social formations from societies with descent groups. That would mean an almost complete absence of lineages in most of East and Southern Africa, including the Bantu. An operational reading transforms the ethnographic landscape: in sub-Saharan Africa, societies with lineages would henceforth be the exception rather than the rule. In primary forests (literally jungles, never felled), there is no agriculture but only hunting and gathering. In secondary forests people might have small animals (sheep and goats) but no cattle because of the tsetse fly. Those areas would be agricultural, and thus areas where descent groups can emerge, together with areas of thick savannah (as in Abutia) and dry savannah with more agriculture than cattle-herding (like the Tallensi and their neighbours, the Gurunsi), where lineages have emerged.

Let me re-emphasize. ALL the six societies I have re-analysed were described as descent-based. After an operational translation, only ONE has descent groups, namely the Tallensi. Admittedly, many other populations surrounding the Tallensi also had lineages, as many Ewe village leagues seem to have done, and many other ones presumably existed in the parts of West Africa covered with secondary forests and savannah. Otherwise, they seem to be few and far between.

There are some potentially interesting consequences to that, and I will again confine myself to mentioning a few of them for sub-Saharan Africa. Drawing on African ethnography, Eisenstadt argued that age groups appear where descent groups are too weak to perform important political and military functions (Eisenstadt 1956). Let us look at Eisenstadt's African sample.

A brief overview of his sample reveals two types of society: alleged 'segmentary lineage ones' and so-called 'chiefdoms'. In my view, all the societies that Eisenstadt classifies as segmentary are, like the Nuer (since segmentary lineages are a contradiction in terms), without lineages. There is no case of a true lineage society. Interestingly, the Nuer had important age-sets, as did the Zulu and Masai, among many others. Moreover, Kuper's analysis suggests that all the 'chiefdoms' mentioned by Eisenstadt also lack descent groups, as chiefdoms would by my definitions, be they truly aggregated or clientelistic. If my intuition is right, it would mean that African age-sets seem to be linked to the absence of descent groups. Let me be clear about this. Obviously, the absence of lineages does not imply the presence of age-sets, as there is a vast number of social formations without lineages (our own societies for instance) and without age-sets. But let us turn the argument around: where there are important age-sets, I believe there are no descent groups.

Let us assume this to be true. It could be partly explained by the demographic circumstances of these societies. Indeed, the smaller the number of individuals on which the reproduction of a given group depends (household, locality), the greater the probability that its size will vary greatly. The size of minimal lineages, for instance, can fluctuate greatly but their aggregation neutralizes this variability to some extent since the size of maximal lineages shows less variation than that of minimal lineages (see Verdon 1983). In the absence of descent groups, residential groups or local groups can differ greatly in size, and age groups can neutralize if not equalize this variability, since an age group size can be fixed by adjusting its recruitment period. Ritter supports this thesis when she writes that age groups develop or are borrowed from neighbouring societies often engaged in warfare where the size and composition of local groups fluctuates through the year, or where large numbers of men live at some distance from permanent localities (Ritter 1980, p. 98). There would thus definitely be an important connection between age-sets and lineage-less societies. That will help us with a different case.

Shipton's equations

In two extremely brilliant articles of superb comparative analysis, Parker Shipton contrasted two types of societies of Eastern Africa: the Luo to the north (including neighbouring Gisu and Gusii, western Kenya), typical of descent-based, segmentary lineage societies according to him, practicing intensive agriculture in a pattern of land tenure in 'strips'. Almost all their land seems to have been occupied, and much of it was inherited. As a result, he found relative scarcity of land and correspondingly high population densities.

To the south (western and northern Tanzania, and Malawi) he selected the Nyamwezi, the Sukuma and Yao, all social formations without lineages, based on locality and forming hierarchical chiefdoms, with much less intensive agriculture based on a land tenure system of 'patches'. Land was abundant, there was very little or no cattle, and they practiced itinerant agriculture. People could move to various lands across the chiefdoms. He also discovered concomitant low population densities.

The articles add a host of clever elements to this contrast but such contrasts, unfortunately, are only as good as the initial distinction: lineage-based segmentary Luo versus lineage-less, territorial Nyamwezi and Yao. I have already reanalysed the Yao. There was no territoriality at work there, and the reference to 'locality' shows the greatest part of the problem. According to my definition (see above, chapter 1), locality is an *activity*, not a 'principle of social organization'. And to Shipton, lineages and descent are also principles of social organization. Let me repeat: principles of social organization are Aristotelian and disappear from an operational viewpoint. This is the main flaw of this antiquated ethnography. But we also face another critical question: did the Luo in any way corresponded to what Shipton wrote about them? I am afraid not.

Let us take a closer look. Just a few generations before the British ethnographic surveys of the 1930s, at the end of the 19th century (let us say 1875 for convenience), the Luo were essentially pastoralists (cattle was still very important in the 50s), constantly expanding their land, but on rich areas. This expansion was obviously taking place at the expense of neighbouring populations, through the use of force (border skirmishes). We know that they were originally from the Nile region, where some Luo are still known there as Shilluk. They were once neighbours of the Nuer which, we saw, were involved in a similar dynamic. I therefore surmise, as my reanalyses suggest, that they then had no lineages and formed clientelistic social formations of segmentary *alliances*. How can I prove it?

I find a first clue in their relationship to land. Shipton mentions that in their expanding phase, the Luo treated land in a purely utilitarian way. This is logical. In herding societies (societies which perceive themselves as such), all the symbolic, cultural, ritual and other emphases revolve around livestock. This stands out in Evans-Pritchard's ethnography. Among pastoralists, all the importance and value of livestock is normally accompanied by a utilitarian relationship with the land. The land produces food, of course, but it is fundamentally the support for the people and livestock. If crops fail, people fall back on their cattle (see the Nuer). It is the livestock that must live because, in the final analysis, they are the ultimate source of survival. If agriculture suffers, people can feed on cattle: their milk, blood and meat.

There are other hidden contrasts between the two zones. Shipton doesn't mention it, but we should note that the Luo and their type of agriculture are found on some of the best lands in sub-Saharan Africa. For that very reason the British colonised Kenya and monopolised vast tracts of the best land, on which they developed plantations and commercial agriculture on a fairly large scale from the first half of the twentieth century. However, on the rather mediocre land in the south, nothing similar seems to have happened. Consequently, from the beginning of colonisation until the 1950s, the Luo had undergone major transformations. They had to halt their territorial expansion and settle down. This showed in their increased dependence on agriculture and, presumably, a reduction in the size of herds and the importance of livestock. Once again, this is reflected in the relationship to land: very quickly, land became more or less the ultimate asset. It was not valued in the spiritual way of the Yao, but by anchoring land rights to specific strips. They did this by developing a relationship to the land through the ancestors: it was the ancestors, the first to have occupied and cultivated a given area, who actually conferred titles to the land. If a genealogical link could be traced through the agnatic descendants to the ancestor who first settled the land, then they had an inalienable right to that land.

This new link to the land was not lateral but lineal: the Luo ignored lateral transmission (between siblings) and favoured patrifiliative one. Where land is owned corporately, transmission is normally lateral. Patrifiliative transmission thus suggests no corporate ownership of land, and therefore no lineages. What kind of ownership do we find? There is not enough information for me to assess. It raises an interesting question: if not corporate and, presumably nor individual, what kind of ownership is it? No answer can be found from Shipton's articles.

In addition, lineages operationally defined are headed by title-holders who owe their position solely to their genealogical position: they are the oldest of the oldest living generation. When they die, it is not a son who replaces them but the next in line in that generation, or the oldest in the next generation if the incumbent is the last of his generation. The transmission of power is lateral. Shipton never mentions office-holders among the Luo. He only writes about 'leaders' and 'council of elders'. But leaders depend on a clientele and operate in clientelistic social formations, not in lineage-based ones.

Also, marriage practices lead to the same conclusion. Like the Nuer and other herding populations of this type, the Luo practice leviratic marriage: when a man dies, his wife marries his brother (or a close agnate if no brother is available) but the wife's children do not belong to the new husband. They remain the children of the deceased brother. I have never come across this practice in lineage societies and, the more I think about it, the more it seems to me to be completely at odds with lineage logic, where descent is paramount. Finally, in the light of my cogitations above, the Luo, Gusii and Gisu, like the Nuer and Dinka, all have age-sets, which I believe related to the absence of lineages. In the light of all these facts, I would conclude that the Luo and similar groups did not have lineages and did not develop them. But what did they develop?

Since Shipton simply summarised elements drawn from various ethnographies and presents his data from top to bottom, it is difficult to establish how things worked in 1875. Let us therefore accept that they formed segmentary alliances. It should be noted that segmentary alliances operate where the sovereign group is relatively small: a hamlet among the Nuer, a concession among the Tiv, and scattered homestead among the Luo. It is this small size of the sovereign group that forces them to forge alliances with other sovereign groups that pit groups of equal size against each other if there is conflict, in order to balance the forces present. Since their sovereign groups are small, these alliances disappear with the inclusion of these social formations in a state, in this case the colonial state, then the independent country. So segmentary alliances probably disappeared in the first thirty years of the 20th century. Moreover, I know of no cases of segmentary alliances becoming lineages. How could this happen? These sovereign groups, certainly among the Nuer and Luo, are groups of clients (affines, matrilateral relatives, others, see Nuer reanalysis above, chapter 2) around a leader. There is no corporate ownership of anything. How could it develop lineages? The clients are not even agnates of the leader. Nor can the leader claim individual ownership of the land. In short, the disappearance of segmentary alliances is just that: the end of one type of alliance. It does not mark the end of clientelism. Clientelism continued among the Nuer and I believe it continued among the Luo. Our problem, which I cannot solve, is the type of alliances they developed after they became sedentary, and the type of relationship to land.

Africa and beyond

I believe we can extend the area of lineage-less societies to North Africa. Let us take Berber Morocco, supposed to have segmentary lineages. The case of the Berbers from the Rif makes it clear to me that there are none there. From what I have read about the Moroccan Berbers (and from the work that one of my doctoral student did; see Paulin 2014), they have no descent groups but social formations with leaders (sheikhs), like Moroccan Arabs. Another one of my doctoral student's work in Tunisia also reveals an absence of lineages there (Latreille 2006). East of Tunisia, we find much of the same. The case of Libya is more complex. As can be expected, Evans-Pritchard found segmentary lineages among the Sanusi of Cyrenaica but his student, Emrys Peters, had serious misgivings. He could not contradict the master; he kept the segmentary lineages but he was perplexed by the Bedouin dealings with homicide.

Above all, Holy's reanalysis of Peters' ethnography shows clearly to me that there were no descent groups in Libya (Holy 1979b), and the fact that they were camel-herders clinches the case. Egypt might be an important exception, but too little serious ethnography there allows to conclude. East of Egypt, the ethnography of the Rwala Bedouins who dominated Syria, Jordan and the north of Saudi Arabia also shows no lineages but the rule of sheikhs (Lancaster 1981), which extends in fact to the whole of the Arab world. Further east, apart from Iran perhaps, we find the same absence of descent groups, as Barth's work on the Swat Pathans testifies (Barth 1959). Similarly, I don't believe there are descent groups in Afghanistan and Pakistan. India is too vast to write anything about lineages, but Leach's work on Burma (Leach 1954) also showed the absence of descent groups and the presence of leaders. If we include all the primary forests of the world, we are left with very few areas where lineages have evolved. India and China could obviously have developed them. But when we look south, there are none in Aboriginal Australia and, I believe, none in Papua New Guinea (where 'big men' rule), nor the islands of the South Pacific, starting with the Trobriand (Malinowski 1922).

Overall, where ethnologists saw lineages everywhere, I turn things upside down. From what I know, few societies have descent groups operationally defined, and most have various types of alliances. The overwhelming importance of alliances follows from the fact that I see sovereignty in most traditional societies associated with relatively small groups since I rarely find descent. The smaller the sovereign groups, by definition, the greater the need for alliances. As a result, most of them are based on leadership. I define these as clientelistic social formations.

Looping the loop

I close this peregrination where it started, with Evans-Pritchard. It is an extraordinary occurrence in the history of social anthropology that this segmentary wildfire, so to speak, started with one man, Evans-Pritchard. He definitely influenced Fortes in his work on the

Tallensi, despite the orientation that Fortes gave to descent theory (see volume 1), and the Bohannans on the Tiv. This sacred trinity consecrated segmentary lineages, a segmentary vision that ruled well into the 80s and coloured every ethnography with the hue of segmentation. This was an extraordinary achievement, which was incredibly difficult to topple. After the failures of transactionalism and transcendental culturalism (see volume 1), not to mention post-modernism, only operationalism has been able to achieve it!

APPENDIX

An operational definition of marriage

We face a much bigger conceptual problem when it comes to reproduction. As with so many other concepts, the Abutia facts raised the question of its definition. Until the 1950s the Abutia celebrated a ceremony at the end of which two individuals considered themselves 'married'. This ceremony is no longer celebrated, and individuals mate and separate as they meet. We could conclude that the Abutia no longer marry, except that some of these couples have children and see themselves in a stable relationship. Whether we declare that Abutia marriages have disappeared or simply been transformed, we can only do so within the framework of coherent and rigorous definitions (all this analysis is already dated; see Verdon, 1981), and classical definitions do not allow us to make a decision. Once again, the ethnography calls for an operational definition.

In an operational perspective, marriage must be defined with reference to group formation, a task which requires first the identification of the activities in which 'married groups' are involved. The activity which has been almost universally acknowledged is the sexual one. In the performance of sexual activities, however, the group's criteria of membership are far from evident. There are many negative criteria which discriminate between those with whom sex is permitted, or even desirable, and those with whom it is forbidden. However, these criteria in themselves only delineate categories; they do not serve for the formation of any group. In fact, it seems that the only criterion which can be found in the performance of sexual activities is the performance of the activity itself (a somewhat cognate notion has already been derived by Harris 1969). Individuals form a group in the performance of sexual activities when the very performance of this activity is used to discriminate between members and non-members. I will call such a group a 'mating group'.

If the sexual involvement is not used as a discriminating criterion, the individuals concerned do not form a mating group (as with involvement with prostitutes, or collective sex, or generally promiscuous relations). It follows from this definition that the sexual involvement of one of the members of the mating group with someone outside the group blurs the discrimination between member and non-member and is likely to result in the disruption of the original group if this involvement is known to the other member (unless this outside involvement is with another spouse; as we shall see, conjugal relations are not purely sexual). Sex outside the mating group jeopardizes its existence since it contradicts its criterion of membership.

A second corollary of this approach is that mating groups can only be 'mating pairs'. Empirically, it is obvious that the original pair does not necessarily break up if one member forms another pair outside, but this situation would have to be accounted for in terms of personal and individual decisions (because money is involved, for instance); it does not affect the analytical postulate. The resulting 'triangle' would be analytically described as two mating groups overlapping in one of their members, and not as a mating group of three individuals. This overlap would be purely circumstantial, and would need to be explained.

A mating group, however, is not necessarily a conjugal group, and I do not believe that conjugal groups can be defined with reference to sexual activities only. There are good reasons, which have been reiterated many times in the literature, for wanting to separate sex and marriage analytically, since there are conjugal groups in which no sex is involved between the partners (ghost-marriage, woman-marriage, or simply sexless marriage) and there are mating groups which are manifestly not married (such as instances of Nigerian Plateau sigisbeism, or the lover-mistress institution of Western Europe), but there are no mating groups without any sex; that would be a contradiction in terms.

The conjugal group (as distinct from the mating group) seems indeed to be formed around two distinct sets of activities, namely sex and reproduction, with the emphasis on the latter. Reproduction, however, is a natural activity (an activity performed by nature, and not by people; only copulation is performed by people) which is also internal to women. Individuals cannot therefore form groups in the activity of reproduction itself (they can in copulation, in child care, or in the rituals surrounding pregnancy, but not in reproduction itself), because they are not agents in it (it is achieved without their direct intervention, only as a result of indirect action). There is nevertheless a universal connection between sexual activities and reproduction, whether based on spiritual or physical postulates. Genitors are indeed recognized universally (Scheffler 1974).

This connection between the two activities is associated with the woman only, since reproduction is internal to women. Conjugal groups thus seem to be formed around the sexual activities of women, insofar as sex is linked to reproduction, and 'marriage' would then be the criterion of membership of conjugal groups. I would therefore suggest the following operational definition of marriage. First of all, 'conjugal *units*' (and not groups because, by definition, a group presupposes an activity performed by intentional agents, and not by nature) are formed between one or many persons of any sex, on the one hand, and one woman, on the other (let us call her the 'reference woman'), around the sexual activities of that woman insofar as they are connected with reproduction. Second, the unit needs a criterion of membership. In fact, we find a conjugal unit when two conditions are met: (a) children born to the 'reference woman' will not intrinsically transform or disrupt the unit and, (b) these children will gain membership in the main religious and/or political groups of their mother, or of the person(s) (spouse) who has (have) formed a unit around the reproduction of that woman. Any fact or set of facts (such as a ceremony, night visitations made public, cohabitation, and so on (see Goodenough 1970)) which serve in the formation of units which meet these two conditions (i.e. conjugal units) thus constitute the conjugal unit's criteria of membership, and I define them as 'marriage'[76].

In many societies (such as the Abutia), the child is assured of membership in a political group (as well as all other groups) whether or not his mother is married to its genitor. Marriage, consequently, is not everywhere necessary to legitimate children or for social placement; nevertheless, where a woman's relationship to a man is not disrupted by the birth of a child, they form a conjugal unit only if the child can find social placement through its genitor or genitrix. Otherwise there is no marriage[77]. Furthermore, a child born to an 'unmarried pair' will trigger off a change in that pair. They may be requested to stop their involvement, or it may be terminated by itself, or the child may be killed, or the man may be asked to marry the girl, or they may be punished, and so on. If, after the birth of a child, a group organized around the sexual activities of the woman (whether it is mating or not) remains intrinsically unchanged and the child can trace political group membership through any member of that group, the group can be treated analytically as a conjugal unit, and the fact which gave it these two properties can be identified as marriage[78]. Operationally speaking, marriage is somehow defined like the notion of force in physics; it is not defined substantively, but through its effects. If the effects are

---

[76] This 'fact' equated with marriage may itself be a set of activities, such as a wedding or a marriage ceremony, in which special groups are formed.

[77] Among many populations of Sudan, Ethiopia, or the Nigerian plateau, for instance, a woman's first marriage (often established with the payment of bridewealth) can never be severed, although the women can leave their husbands and found stable relationships with other men, from whom they may have many children. According to my definition, such couples are not married, since their children cannot gain membership in the main political corporations or groups through either their genitor or genitrix, but only through the man who first paid bridewealth for the woman.

[78] Where marriage is the only way to have access to sex, the birth of children may lead to divorce for people who did not want children. This event, however, results from personal inclinations and is not built into the group's situation.

observed, we can then infer the existence of marriage and attempt to identify it.

By removing the notorious 'bundle of rights and duties' that Leach wrote about as defining marriage (see volume 1), this operational approach seems to have wider applicability. It easily extends to include woman-marriage, leviratic marriage, Caribbean marriage, Nayar marriage, and even marriage between two ghosts as practiced by the Singapore Chinese (Topley 1955, p. 35), with only one exception known to me, namely, homosexual unions. Where 'married' homosexuals are allowed to adopt children, there is a fiction of reproduction, and the resulting group could by extension be considered a conjugal one. Where 'married' homosexuals are barred from adopting, however, they do not form a conjugal unit and, whatever the actors say, their union is not to be treated analytically as a marriage[79].

I thus invert the classical (teleological) definition of marriage, rooted in the individual's reproductive aims and the way society sanctions them. I rather start from couples or units that have already been formed and study, not causes but effects, more specifically what the birth of a child entails for those responsible for it. If the birth transforms or disrupts the couple (for reasons extrinsic to the couple), I conclude that they were not married; if not, I infer that this unit had been forged around the woman's potential reproduction, and that the unit thus constituted was conjugal. I then posit that the elements that went into the formation of this unit (its membership criteria, in other words) have this effect of making the birth of a child normal within this unit; if the child

[79] This raises the interesting problem of the emic definition of marriage. Although homosexuals are ritually 'married' in some societies, this is far from meaning that their union should be treated analytically as marriage. Nuns may claim to be married to Jesus Christ, but no one would analyse a convent as a polygynous family! If a given people fancy claiming that their men are married to cows, this is not a sufficient ground to analyse the man-cow alliance as a conjugal group, even if sex is present... If a definition of marriage were based on the symbolic extensions that one finds in emic definitions, we would have to include the Kwakiutl case where, Boas informs us, chiefs could marry their leg!

affiliates with the main political and religious groups of his or her progenitor, I will presume that this element or these elements made up a 'marriage'. This is an attempt at a non-teleological definition of marriage.

What should be done about the 'marriages' of women past their reproductive age? From an ethnographic point of view, the problem is not as complicated as it may seem and the answer, of course, depends on the society in question. Some societies have preserved a ritual that clearly demarcates the moment of creation of a conjugal unit, allowing the observer to know automatically whether a couple is married or not. Elsewhere, couples form more or less at random, and when the reproductive period ends, we can hypothetically ask whether a couple would survive the birth of a child if the woman were still fertile.

Within the same population, different facts are sometimes used in the formation of conjugal groups (i.e. there are different types of marriages). These differences, moreover, appear to be associated with concomitant divergences in the women's (and children's) general social status. This stems from the fact that marriage (or, more accurately, membership in a conjugal unit) is itself a criterion of membership to other groups. Where different facts are used in the formation of conjugal units within the same society (i.e. where there are different types of marriages), one usually finds that they are used differentially in giving access to other groups or corporations. This is the operational equivalent of Leach's notion of bundle of rights. The manner in which different types of marriages influence a woman's membership in other groups in a society does not in any way affect the general operational definition of marriage.

If marriage is a membership criterion to conjugal units formed around women's sexual activities as linked to reproduction, what about the family? The family is made up of a conjugal unit and the children who belong to it by birth or adoption. As far as we know, there is no activity that intrinsically unites this group of individuals. Let us take the activities that have been associated with the family one by one. Sexual intercourse involves the parents only. Child care and socialization often involve the mother mostly, or the mother and individuals other than her conjugal partner. Members of the same family may occupy different residential groups and belong to different production, processing, distribution and consumption groups. If, in the final analysis, reproduction appears to be the activity performed by the family, we are once again mistaken. As I have already mentioned, reproduction is internal to the woman and stops at birth. After birth, we can speak of 'biological maintenance', child care and socialization, but not reproduction. The family thus groups a set of individuals around an activity that is internal to one of them, but in which no one participates as an intentional agent. From an analytical point of view, the family in fact performs no activity (Bender had already concluded that the family had no function – Bender, 1967) and, consequently, cannot constitute a group.

Consequently, the set of individuals circumscribed by the reproduction of a mating group will make up a 'biological unit' or 'reproductive unit' (for the same reasons that we speak of conjugal units and not conjugal groups), and we will call the set of individuals gathered around the reproduction of a conjugal unit a 'family'. It follows logically that the family has neither structure nor function since, on the one hand, its members do not engage collectively in any activity (the family therefore has no 'definitional function', see note 1) and, without activity, it cannot know of any division of labour; it has no structure! At the level of everyday experience, we perceive a family 'structure' because the family partially overlaps with other groups - residential groups, production groups, socialization groups, product distribution groups, food processing groups, consumption groups, and so on - which, for the most part, are structured. When we isolate the family analytically, on the other hand, it cannot logically be structured within the framework of my definitions.

BIBLIOGRAPHY

Abraham, R.C. (1940). *The Tiv People.* Nigeria, Crown Agents for the Colonies, 2nd edition.

Abrahams, R.G. (1967). *The Political Organization of the Unyamwezi.* Cambridge: Cambridge University Press.

Anglin, A. (1979). 'Analytical and folk models: the Tallensi case' in *Segmentary Lineages Reconsidered*, pp. 48–68, L. Holy, ed. Belfast: The Queen's University Papers in Social Anthropology, 4.

Augustin, G. (1989). *Comment se perpétuer?* Nanterre: Société d'ethnologie.

Barnes, John Arundel. (1954). *Marriage in a Changing Society.* Manchester: Manchester University Press.

Barnes, John Arundel. (1971). *Three Styles in the Study of Kinship.* London: Tavistock.

Barth, Fredrick. (1959). *Political Leadership among the Swat Pathans.* Bell, London.

Bohannan, Laura. (1952). 'A genealogical charter' *Africa* 22: 301–315.

Bohannan, Laura. (1958). 'Political aspects of Tiv social organization' in *Tribes Without Rulers*, Middleton, J. and D. Tait, eds, pp. 33–66, London: Routledge and Kegan Paul.

Bohannan, Paul. (1954). *Tiv Farm and Settlement*. London: Her Majesty's Stationery Office.

Bohannan, Paul. (1957). *Justice and Judgment among the Tiv*. Oxford: Oxford University Press.

Bohannan, Paul.(1963) *Social Organization.* New York: Holt, Rinehart and Winston.

Bohannan, Paul and Laura. (1953). *The Tiv of Central Nigeria*. London: International African Institute.

Bender, Donald R. (1967). 'A refinement of the concept of household: families, coresidence and domestic functions' *American Anthropologist* 69: 493–504.

Calhoun, C.J. (1975). *The Authority of Ancestors among the Tallensi.* M.A. Thesis, University of Manchester.

Calhoun, C.J. (1980). 'The authority of ancestors: a sociological reconsideration of Fortes' Tallensi in response to Fortes' critics', *Man* 15: 304–319.

Berndt, Roland M. (1955). 'Murngin (Wulamba) social organization', *American Anthropologist* 57: 86–106.

Berndt, Roland M. (1959). 'The concept of the 'tribe' in the western desert of Australia', *Oceania* 29: 82–107.

Berndt, Roland M. (1964). 'The Gove dispute: the question of Australian Aboriginal land and the preservation of sacred sites', *American Forum* 1: 258–295.

Berndt, Roland M. (1970). 'Comment on Birdsell', *Current Anthropology* 2: 132–133.

Berndt, Roland M. (1976). 'Territoriality and the problem of demarcating socio-cultural space', in *Tribes and Boundaries in Australia*, N. Peterson, ed., Canberra: Australian Institute for Aboriginal Studies.

Biernoff, David. (1978). 'Safe and dangerous places', in *Australian Aboriginal Concepts*. L.R. Hiatt, ed. Canberra: Australian Institute of Aboriginal Studies.

Birdsell, Joseph B. (1970). 'Local group composition among the Australian Aborigines: a critique of the evidence from fieldwork conducted since 1930', *Current Anthropology* II: 15–31.

Burridge, K. (1973). *Encountering Aborigines: Anthropology and the Australian Aboriginal*. New York: Pergamon.

Bohannan, Laura. (1952). 'A genealogical charter', *Africa* 22: 301–315.

Bohannan, Laura. (1958) 'Political aspect of Tiv social organization' in John Middleton and David Tait, eds., *Tribes without Rulers*, pp. 33–666. London: Routledge and Kegan Paul.

Bohannan, Paul. (1954). *Tiv Farm and Settlement*. London: Her Majesty's Stationery Office.

Bohannan, Paul. (1957). *Justice and Judgment among the Tiv*. London: Oxford University Press.

Bohannan, Paul. (1963). *Social Organization*. New York: Holt, Rinehart and Winston.

Bohannan, Paul and Laura (1953). *The Tiv of Central Nigeria*. London: International African Institute, Ethnographic Survey of Africa.

Burton, John W. (1978). 'Ghost marriage and the cattle trade among the Atuot of Southern Sudan', *Africa* 48: 398–405.

Clastres, Pierre. (1974). 'Échange et pouvoir: philosophie de la chefferie indienne', in Clastres, P., ed., *La société contre l'état*, pp. 25-42. Paris: Les Éditions de Minuit.

Colson, Elizabeth and Max Gluckman. (1951). *Seven Tribes of Central Africa*. Manchester: Manchester University Press.

Dixon, R.M.W. (1976). 'Tribes, languages and other boundaries in northeast Queensland', in *Tribes and Boundaries in Australia*, N. Peterson ed. Canberra: Australian Institute of Aboriginal Studies.

Doolan, J.K. (1979). 'Aboriginal concept of boundary: how do Aboriginals conceive 'easements' – how do they grand them?' *Oceania* 49: 161–168.

Dorward, D.C. (1974). 'Ethnography and administration: a study of Anglo-Tiv 'Working Misunderstanding', *The Journal of African History* 15: 457–477.

Downes, R.M. (1933). *The Tiv Tribe*. Kaduna: Government Printer.

Downes, R.M. (1971). *Tiv Religion*. Ibadan, Nigeria: Ibadan University Press.

East, Rupert. (1939). *Akiga's Story*. London: Oxford University Press.

Elkin, A.P. (1938). *The Australian Aborigines*. Sydney: Angus & Robertson.

Evans-Pritchard, E. E. (1933). 'The Nuer: tribe and clan', *Sudan Notes and Records* 16: 1–53.

Evans-Pritchard, E. E. (1934). 'The Nuer: tribe and clan', *Sudan Notes and Records* 17: 1–57.

Evans-Pritchard, E. E. (1935). 'The Nuer: tribe and clan', *Sudan Notes and Records* 18: 37–88.

Evans-Pritchard, E. E. (1937). 'Economic life of the Nuer: cattle', *Sudan Notes and Records* 20: 209–245.

Evans-Pritchard, E. E. (1938). 'Economic life of the Nuer: cattle', *Sudan Notes and Records* 21: 31–77.

Evans-Pritchard, E. E. (1940). a *The Nuer.* London: Oxford University Press.

Evans-Pritchard, E. E. (1940). b 'The Nuer of the Southern Sudan', in Fortes, M. and E.E. Evans-Pritchard, eds., *African Political Systems*, pp. 272–296, London: Oxford University Press.

Evans-Pritchard, E. E. (1945). 'Some aspects of marriage and the family among the Nuer', *Rhodes-Livingstone Papers*, No. 11

Evans-Pritchard, E. E. (1947). 'Bridewealth among the Nuer', *African Studies* 6: 181–188.

Evans-Pritchard, E. E. (1949). *The Sanusi of Cyrenaica.* Oxford: Oxford University Press.

Evans-Pritchard, E. E. (1950). a 'Kinship and the local community among the Nuer', in Radcliffe-Brown, A.R. and D. Forde, eds., *African Systems of Kinship and Marriage*, pp. 360–392, London: Oxford University Press.

Evans-Pritchard, E. E. (1950). b 'The Nuer family', *Sudan Notes and Records* 51: 21–42.

Evans-Pritchard, E. E. (1951). *Kinship and Marriage among the Nuer.* Oxford: Clarendon Press.

Evans-Pritchard, E. E. (1956). *Nuer Religion.* Oxford: Clarendon Press.

Fawcett, F.W. (1898). 'Notes on the customs and dialects of Wonnah-Ruah tribes', *Science of Man* I: 152–154, 180–181.

Firth, Raymond. (1951). 'Review of *The Web of Kinship among the Tallensi*', *Africa* 21: 155–159.

Fortes, Meyer. (1936). 'Kinship, incest and exogamy of the Northern Territories of the Gold Coast', in *Custom is King*, I.H. Dudley Buxton, ed. London: Hutchinson's.

Fortes, Meyer. (1940). 'The political system of the Tallensi of the Northern Territories of the Gold Coast, in *African Political Systems*, pp. 39–71, M. Fortes and E.E. Evans-Pritchard eds., London: Oxford University Press.

Fortes, Meyer. (1944). 'The significance of descent in Tale social structure', *Africa* 14: 362–385.

Fortes, Meyer. (1945). *The Dynamics of Clanship among the Tallensi.* London: Oxford University Press.

Fortes, Meyer. (1949). *The Web of Kinship among the Tallensi.* Oxford University Press, London.

Fortes, Meyer. (1953). 'The structure of unilineal descent groups', *American Anthropologist* 55: 17–41.

Fortes, Meyer. (1959). *Oedipus and Job in West African Religion.* Cambridge: Cambridge University Press.

Fortes, Meyer. (1970). 'Ritual festivals and social cohesion in the hinterland of the Gold Coast', pp. 147–163 in Fortes, M. *Time and Social Structure.* London: Athlone Press. Fortes, Meyer and E.E. Evans-Pritchard, eds.

Fortes, Meyer. (1940). *African Political Systems.* London: Oxford University Press.

Fried, Morton (1960). 'On the evolution of social stratification and the state, in Diamond, Stanley, ed., *Culture in History: Essays in Honor of Paul Radin*, pp. 713–731. New York: Columbia University Press.

Fried, Morton (1967). *The Evolution of Political Society*. New York: Random House.

Geist, V. (1978). *Life Strategies, Human Evolution, Environmental Design*. New York: Springer.

Glickman, Maurice. (1971). 'Kinship and credit among the Nuer', *Africa* 41: 306–319.

Glickman, Maurice. (1972). 'The Nuer and the Dinka: a further note', *Man* 7:586–594.

Goodenough, Ward H. (1970). *Description and Comparison in Cultural Anthropology*. Chicago: Aldine.

Goody, Jack (1976). *Production and Reproduction*. Cambridge: Cambridge University Press.

Gulliver, P.H. (1952 'The Karamajong cluster', *Africa* 22: 1–22.

Haight, Bruce (1972). 'A note on the Leopard-skin Chief', *American Anthropologist* 74: 1315–1318.

Harris, C.C. (1969). *The Family: an Introduction*. London: Allen & Unwin.

Hart, C.W.M. and A.R. Pilling (1960). *The Tiwi of North Australia*. New York: Holt, Rinehart & Winston.

Hart, Keith. (1972). *Cashing in on Kinship – a Modern Tallensi Case Study*. Unpublished ms., Cambridge: African Studies Library.

Hart, Keith. (1974). The Development of Patrilineal Institution in an Open Economy: Tallensi 1900–1970. Paper presented at the International Conference of Economic Anthropology, Florence.

Hiatt, L.R. (1962). 'Local organisation among the Australian Aborigines', in *Readings in Australian and Pacific Anthropology*, I. Hogbin and L.R. Hiatt, eds.

Hiatt, L.R. (1965). *Kinship and Conflict*. Canberra: Australian National University Press.

Hiatt, L.R. (1966). 'The lost horde', *Oceania* 37: 81–92.

Hiatt, L.R. (1968). 'Ownership and the use of land among the Australian Aborigines', in *Man the Hunter*, R.B. Lee and I. DeVore, eds. Chicago: Aldine.

Hiatt, L.R. (1970). 'Comment on Birdsell', *Current Anthropology* II: 124–135.

Holy, Ladislav. (1979). a 'The segmentary lineage and its existential status' in *Segmentary Lineage Systems Reconsidered.* L. Holy, ed., The Queen's University Papers in Social Anthropology, vol. 4, Belfast.

Holy, Ladislav. (1979). b 'Nuer politics', in *Segmentary Lineage Systems Reconsidered.* L. Holy, ed., Belfast: The Queen's University Papers in Social Anthropology, vol. 4.

Holy, Ladislav. (1979). c *Segmentary Lineage Systems Reconsidered.* Belfast: The Queen's University Papers in Social Anthropology, vol. 4.

Horton, Robin. (1971), 'Stateless societies in the history of West Africa', in *History of West Africa*, vol. 1, J.F.A. Alawi and Michael Crowder eds., pp. 78–120, London: Longmans.

Howell, P.P. (1954). *A Manual of Nuer Law.* London: Oxford University Press.

Howitt, A.W. (1891). 'The Dieri and other kindred tribes of Central Australia', *Journal of the Anthropological Institute* 20: 30–104.

Howitt, A.W. and L. Fison (1885). 'On the deme and the horde', *Journal of the Anthropological Institute* pp. 142–169.

Jackson, H.C. (1923). 'The Nuer of the Upper Nile Province', *Sudan Notes and Records* 6: 50–107, 123–189.

Johnson, Douglas. (1981). 'The fighting Nuer: primary sources and the origins of a stereotype', *Africa* 51: 508–527.

Jorion, Paul. (1977). 'Marks and rabbit furs: location and sharing of grounds in coastal fishing', *Peasant Studies* 7: 86–100

Jorion, Paul and Gisèle De Meur. (1982). 'La question murngin, un artéfact de la littérature anthropologique' *L'Homme* 20 (2): 39–70

Keesing, Roger M. (1970). 'Shrines, ancestors and cognatic descent: the Kwaio and the Tallensi', *American Anthropologist* 72: 755–775.

Kuper, Adam. (1982). *Wives for Cattle.* London: Routledge and Kegan Paul.

Lancaster, William. (1981). *The Rwala Bedouin Today.* Cambridge: Cambridge University Press.

Latreille, Martin. (2006). *Étude de la pauvreté en milieu rural tunisien, dans le contexte de la transmission foncière et du statut de la femme.* Ph.D. thesis, Département d'anthropologie, Université de Montréal.

Leach, Sir Edmund. (1954). *Political Systems of Highland Burma.* Harvard U.P., Cambridge, Mass.

Lienhardt, Godfrey. (1958). 'The Western Dinka' in Middleton, J. and D. Tait, eds., *Tribes Without Rulers*, pp. 97–135, London: Routledge and Kegan Paul.

Malinowski, Bronislaw. (1922). *Argonauts of the Western Pacific*. London, Routledge and Kegan Paul.

Malinowski, Bronislaw. (1926). *Crime and Custom in Savage* Society. Routledge and Kegan Paul, London.

Meggitt, M.J. (1962). *Desert People: a Study of the Walbiri Aborigines of Central Australia*. Sydney: Angus Robertson.

Middleton, John and David Tait. (1958). 'Introduction', *Tribes Without Rulers.* London: Routledge and Kegan Paul.

Mitchell, J.C. (1951). 'The Yao of Nyasaland', in E. Colson and M. Gluckman, eds., *Seven Tribes of British Central Africa*, pp.292–353, Manchester: Manchester University Press.

Mitchell, J.C. (1956). *The Yao Village*. Manchester: Manchester University Press.

Meyer, Iona. (1965). 'From kin ship to common descent: four-generations genealogies among the Gusii', *Africa* 51: 366–384.

Mountford, C.P. (1978). 'The rainbow-serpent myths of Australia', in *The rainbow serpent* in I. Buchler and K Maddock, eds. The Hague, Paris: Mouton.

Nukunya, G.K. (1969). *Kinship and Marriage among the Anlo Ewe*. LSE Monograph on Social Anthropology.

Paulin, Étienne. (2014). *Étude des migrations et de leurs effets sur la société tafraouti*. Ph.D. thesis, EHESS, Paris and Département d'anthropologie, Université de Montréal.

Peters, Emrys. (1960). 'The proliferation of segments in the lineage of the Bedouin of Cyrenaica', *Journal of the Royal Anthropological Institute 90*: 29–53.

Peters, Emrys. (1967). ' Some structural aspects of the feud among the camel-herding Bedouin of Cyrenaica', *Africa* 37: 261–282.

Peterson, Nicholas. (1976). a 'Introduction' in *Tribes and Boundaries in Australia*, N. Peterson, ed. Canberra: Australian Institute of Aboriginal Studies.

Peterson, Nicholas. (1976). b (ed.) *Tribes and Boundaries in Australia*. Canberra: Australian Institute of Aboriginal Studies.

Piddington, Ralph. (1971). 'A note on Karadjeri local organization', *Oceania* 41: 239–243.

Radcliffe-Brown, A.R. (1913). 'Three tribes of Western Australia', *Journal of the Royal Anthropological Institute* 43: 143–194.

Radcliffe-Brown, A.R. (1918). 'Notes on the social organization of Australian tribes', *Journal of the Royal Anthropological Institute* 48: 222–253.

Radcliffe-Brown, A.R. (1930). 'The social organization of Australian tribes', *Oceania* 1: 34–63.

Radcliffe-Brown, A.R. (1935). 'Patrilineal and matrilineal succession', *Iowa Law Review* 20: 286–303.

Radcliffe-Brown, A.R. (1951). 'Murngin social organization', *American Anthropologist* 53: 37–55.

Radcliffe-Brown, A.R. (1956). 'On Australian local organization', *American Anthropologist* 58: 363–367.

Rattray, R.S. (1932). *The Tribes of the Ashanti Hinterland,* 2 volumes. Oxford: Clarendon Press.

Ritter, M.L. (1980). 'The conditions favouring age-set organization', *Journal of Anthropological Research* 36: 87–104.

Rivers, W.H.R. (1924). *Social Organization.* London: Kegan Paul, Trench, Trubner & Co.

Sahlins, Marshall D. (1961).'The segmentary lineage: an organization of predatory expansion', *American Anthropologist* 63: 322–345.

Sahlins, Marshall D. (1965). 'On the ideology and composition of descent groups', *Man* 65: 104–107.

Sahlins, Marshall D. (1968). *Tribesmen.* Foundation of American Anthropology series. Englewood Cliffs, N.J. Prentice-Hall.

Salter, E. (1972). *Daisy Bates*. Sydney: Angus & Robertson.

Scheffler, H.W. (1966). 'Ancestor worship in anthropology: or observations on descent and descent groups', *Current Anthropology* 7: 541–551

Schneider, David. (1984). *A critique of the STUDY OF KINSHIP*. Ann Arbor, Michigan: The University of Michigan Press.

Service, Elman R. (1962). *Primitive Social Organization.* New York: Random House.

Shapiro, Warren. (1969). *Miwuyt marriage: Structural Aspects of the Bestowal of Females in northern Arnhem Land.* Ph.D. thesis, Australian University.

Shapiro, Warren. (1979). *Social Organization in Aboriginal Australia.* Canberra: Australian National University Press.

Shipton, Parker. (1984). 'Lineage and locality as antithetical principles in East African systems of land tenure', *Ethnology* 23: 114–132.

Spencer, B. and F. J Gillen. (1898). *The Native Tribes of Central Australia*. London: Macmillan.

Stanner, W.E.H. (1965) 'Aboriginal territorial organization: estate, range, domain and regime', *Oceania* 36: 1–26.

Strehlow, T.G.H. (1970). 'Geography and the totemic landscape in central Australia: a functional study', in *Australian Aboriginal Anthropology*, R.M Berndt ed. Nedlands: University of Western Australia Press.

Tindale, Norman B. (1974). *Aboriginal Tribes of Australia*. Berkeley: University of California Press.

Tindale, Norman B. (1976). 'Some ecological bases for Australian tribal boundaries', in *Tribes and Boundaries in Australia*, N. Peterson, ed. Canberra: Australian Institute of Aboriginal Studies.

Topley, Marjorie. (1955). 'Ghost marriages among the Singapore Chinese' *Man* 55: 35.

Turton, David, (1980). 'The economics of Mursi bridewealth: a comparative perspective' in J.L. Comaroff, ed., *The Meaning of Marriage Payments*, pp. 67–92, New York: Academic Press.

Verdon, Michel. (1980). a 'Descent : an operational view', *Man* 15: 129–150.

Verdon, Michel. (1980). b 'Shaking off the domestic yoke', *Comparative Studies in Society and History* 22: 109–132.

Verdon, Michel. (1980). c 'From the social to the symbolic equation: the progress of idealism in contemporary anthropological representations of kinship, marriage and the family', *The Canadian Review of Sociology and Anthropology* 17: 315–329.

Verdon, Michel. (1981). 'Kinship, marriage and the family: an operational approach', *American Journal of Sociology* 86: 796–818.

Verdon, Michel. (1982). a 'Where have all the lineages gone? Cattle and descent among the Nuer', *American Anthropologist* 84: 566–579.

Verdon, Michel. (1982). b 'The dynamics of *Dynamics*, or the Tallensi in time and numbers', *Journal of Anthropological Research* 38:154–178.

Verdon, Michel. (1983). a 'Segmentation among the Tiv: a re-appraisal', *American Ethnologist*.

Verdon, Michel. (1983). b *The Abutia Ewe of West Africa*. Berlin: Mouton.

Verdon, Michel. (1991). *Contre la culture. Fondements d'une anthropologie sociale opérationnelle.* Paris: Éditions des Archives Contemporaines.

Verdon, Michel. (1995). 'Les Yao: une chefferie matrilinéaire?', *Cahiers d'Études Africaines* 138-39: 477–511.

Verdon, Michel and Paul Jorion. (1981). 'The hordes of discord : Australian Aboriginal social organization reconsidered', *Man* (n.a.) 16: 90–107.

Wheeler, Gerald C. (1910). *The Tribe and Intertribal Relations in Australia.* London: John Murray.

Wrigley, E.A. (1978). 'Family strategy for the individual and the group', in Charles Tilly, ed., *Historical Studies of Changing Fertility*, pp. 134–154, Princeton: Princeton University Press.

Worsley, P.M. (1956). 'The kinship system of the Tallensi: a revaluation', *Journal of the Royal Anthropological Institute* 86: 37–75.

Yengoyan, Aran. (1968). 'Demographic and ecological influences on Aboriginal Australian marriage sections', in *Man the Hunter*, R.B. Lee and I. DeVore, eds. Chicago: Aldine.

www.ingramcontent.com/pod-product-compliance
Ingram Content Group UK Ltd.
Pitfield, Milton Keynes, MK11 3LW, UK
UKHW041914040325
4855UKWH00001B/54

9 781836 151159